D1525870

THE SECRET GOSPEL OF MARK

THE SECRET GOSPEL OF MARK

A Controversial Scholar, a Scandalous
Gospel of Jesus, and the Fierce
Debate over Its Authenticity

GEOFFREY S. SMITH
BRENT C. LANDAU

Yale

UNIVERSITY PRESS

New Haven and London

Copyright © 2023 by Geoffrey S. Smith and Brent C. Landau.
All rights reserved.

This book may not be reproduced, in whole or in part, including illustrations, in any form (beyond that copying permitted by Sections 107 and 108 of the U.S. Copyright Law and except by reviewers for the public press), without written permission from the publishers.

Yale University Press books may be purchased in quantity for educational, business, or promotional use. For information, please e-mail sales.press@yale.edu (U.S. office) or sales@yaleup.co.uk (U.K. office).

Set in Janson type by Newgen North America.
Printed in the United States of America.

Library of Congress Control Number: 2022938456

ISBN 978-0-300-25493-8 (hardcover : alk. paper)

A catalogue record for this book is available from the British Library.

This paper meets the requirements of ANSI/NISO z39.48-1992 (Permanence of Paper).

10 9 8 7 6 5 4 3 2 1

To François Bovon
Our mentor and friend
Who taught us always to begin
With the manuscript

Contents

Acknowledgments

ONE OF THE UNANTICIPATED delights of this book project was how essential the oral tradition was to our research—Papias would have been proud! We would therefore like to begin by acknowledging our deep gratitude to those colleagues, students, and friends of Morton Smith who took the time to share their recollections of him with us, oftentimes over Zoom. They include Tom Allwood, Levon Avdoyan, Shaye Cohen, Nina Garsoïan, Ralph Keen, Robert Kraft, James Sanders, Seth Schwartz, Robert Somerville, and Glen Thompson. Thomas Derr provided invaluable recollections about Quentin Quesnell's role in the Secret Gospel controversy. Special thanks must go to Allan Pantuck, who not only shared generously with us the personal papers and photographs of Morton Smith that he has curated, but who has also authored several of the most valuable recent studies on this subject.

A number of our colleagues in the field of religious studies provided valuable critiques, insights, and encouragement at different stages of the project. They include Harold Attridge, Scott Brown, Tony Burke, Stephen Carlson, Cavan Concannon, Ben Dunning, Bart Ehrman, Daniel Gullotta, Melissa Harl Sellew, Charles Hedrick, Elijah Hixson, Stephan Hüller, Jennifer Knust, Derek Krueger, Brenda Llewellyn Ihssen, Timo Paananen, Ariel Sabar, Katherine Shaner, Guy Stroumsa, Eric Vanden Eykel, Annewies van den Hoek, Adela Yarbro Collins, and Chris Zeichmann. We are also grateful to the anonymous readers who reviewed our book manuscript for Yale University Press. We are indebted to L. Michael White and

ix

to the Institute for the Study of Antiquity and Christian Origins at the University of Texas at Austin for supporting this project in a multitude of ways. Our current and recent department chairs at UT Austin—Azfar Moin, Steve Friesen, and Martha Newman—have all helped to create the conditions for a project such as this to flourish.

Special thanks go to Dr. David Kraemer, director of the library at Jewish Theological Seminary of America; Rabbi Jerry Schwarzbard, special collections librarian at the Jewish Theological Seminary of America; and members of their teams, including Samantha Bowser and Bérénice Sylverain. They were welcoming and generous during our on-site research in the Morton Smith Papers in 2019 and continued to be so for more than two years thereafter. Archivists and research librarians at Smith College and Columbia University also provided us with extensive documents that enriched our study. Christopher Hooker of the Society of Biblical Literature shared scans with us of the 1960 Annual Meeting program where Morton Smith first announced his discovery of the letter of Clement and the Secret Gospel.

This project began with our conviction that the only surviving manuscript of the Secret Gospel had not received nearly enough careful examination in the debate over this text. We were first introduced to the study of manuscripts by François Bovon and John Duffy at Harvard University. Sadly, François Bovon is no longer with us, though the dedication of this book to him demonstrates his formative influence on our research. However, John Duffy generously shared with us his own impressions of the handwriting and also provided a list of scholars specializing in Late Greek manuscripts for us to consult further. The scholars who took the time to correspond with us include Panagiotis Agapitos, Father Justin of St. Catherine's Monastery on Mount Sinai, Erich Lamberz, Zisis Melissakis, Inmaculada Pérez Martín, Agamemnon Tselikas, and Nigel Wilson.

We are indebted to the outstanding team at Yale University Press that has shepherded our book from the proposal stage through its long-awaited appearance in print. Jennifer Banks, our editor, greatly improved the effectiveness of our prose and presentation. Abigail Storch, her editorial assistant, provided invaluable support throughout the process of preparing the manuscript for publication.

Finally, we are indebted to our families for the deep reserves of patience they displayed as we attempted to write a book in the midst of a pandemic that brought a screeching halt to so many elements of normal life. Brent is grateful to Elizabeth, his wife, and to his children, Zachary and Charlotte. He also is indebted to his mother-in-law, Margaret Bangs, who read the entire manuscript of the book in its longer, unabridged form. Geoff benefited from the support and encouragement of Nic, James, Rhodes, and Miles, and is particularly grateful to Marina, who was an endless source of wise counsel at every stage of the project.

Prologue

THE WORLD FIRST LEARNED about the existence of a Secret Gospel of Mark in 1960 when Morton Smith, a brilliant yet controversial scholar, announced its discovery. Smith claimed to have found an unknown letter written by the Christian philosopher Clement of Alexandria in the ancient monastery of Mar Saba, located on the edge of the desert outside Jerusalem. In this letter, Clement reveals that a longer version of Mark's Gospel exists, a version that Mark himself created for the most spiritually advanced Christians. Clement quotes a portion of this Secret Gospel of Mark in which Jesus raises a young man from the dead. Readers learn that after being resurrected, the young man looks at Jesus, loves him, and begs Jesus to stay with him at his house, where they remain together for a week. On the seventh night, at Jesus's instruction, the youth comes to him, naked except for a linen sheet covering his body, and Jesus offers secret teachings to the young man. Clement also reports in his letter that a notoriously licentious band of heretics had gotten hold of this Secret Gospel and had added passages to the story to sexualize the relationship between Jesus and the young man. Clement, however, remains adamant that the true meaning of this shocking story is not carnal, but just as he is about to explain what the Secret Gospel really means, the letter breaks off.

In the years following Smith's announcement, some scholars have come to see the Secret Gospel as an earlier version of the New Testament Gospel according to Mark—a *proto*-Mark. Since Mark is thought to be the earliest of the four New Testament gospels, an early version of Mark could challenge our basic understanding of who Jesus was, how he interacted privately with his disciples, and whether he had a companion or even a love interest. Smith's discovery has the potential to rewrite the history of early Christianity.

Others have a very different understanding of the origins of the Secret Gospel. An outspoken group of scholars have alleged that no such Secret Gospel or letter of Clement existed in antiquity, and that the manuscript that Morton Smith "found" in the Mar Saba monastery was a modern forgery—likely created by Smith himself. After all, this ancient letter surfaced in a most unexpected place, copied into the endpages of a seventeenth-century printed book. And, for several decades after Smith announced its discovery, there was little to corroborate the existence of the manuscript except for Smith's personal photos of it. Furthermore, some scholars claimed to have found indications of forgery in the eighteenth-century Greek cursive handwriting of the manuscript, and others detected subtle clues in the text of Clement's letter that revealed Smith as its author. Several researchers also suggested that Smith was a gay man and his motive for inventing the Secret Gospel was to validate his own sexuality.

Many of these arguments that the Mar Saba manuscript was forged have been vigorously refuted by scholars who believe the document to be an authentic ancient letter of Clement. Even so, the allegations that Smith fabricated the letter were so numerous and intriguing that the text became enveloped in a cloud of suspicion, and many biblical scholars shied away from studying it. Thus, for all practical purposes, the "conventional wisdom" within biblical studies circles today is that the letter of Clement containing an excerpt of the Secret Gospel of Mark is a twentieth-century forgery crafted by Morton Smith.

As is often the case, however, this "conventional wisdom" is likely incorrect. In this book we offer a new theory about the origins and historical significance of the Secret Gospel of Mark.

But readers will soon become aware that the story of the Secret Gospel transcends the document itself, which incidentally is now lost. While the Secret Gospel of Mark can teach us something about Christianity's distant past, it also exposes the inner workings of a small cadre of biblical scholars tasked with reconstructing that past. In the end the Secret Gospel has less to say about the historical Jesus than it does about the preoccupations, politics, and rivalries of those who seek to uncover the truth about him.

CHAPTER ONE

The Announcement

O N THE EVENING OF December 29, 1960, in the Morn-
ingside Heights neighborhood of New York City, biblical scholars from across the United States and beyond
filed into the Horace Mann Auditorium at Columbia
University. They were in town for the annual meeting of the Society of Biblical Literature and Exegesis (SBLE; now known as the
SBL). The week's presentations had largely taken place in smaller
rooms at Union Theological Seminary, Columbia's neighbor to the
west. The auditorium—a six-hundred-seat theater with wraparound
balcony—was reserved for larger events, such as the presidential address of the Society earlier that day. But on this particular evening
the auditorium was reserved for a scholarly talk expected to draw a
crowd much larger than usual.

The attendees filed in and found their seats. This was not a simple presentation like the rest but a symposium: a paper followed
by a prepared response from another scholar, and then a time for
questions from the gallery to the presenter and respondent—all under the supervision of a moderator. The symposium was titled "A
Letter Attributed to Clement of Alexandria and Containing Quotations from a Secret Gospel Attributed to St. Mark," and its headliner
was Morton Smith of Columbia University.[1] Smith would debut an

4

astonishing new manuscript he discovered two years earlier while perusing the holdings of an ancient library outside Jerusalem.

Unbeknown to most in attendance, Smith also planned to announce his discovery to the world. In a coordinated media rollout, he invited members of the press to the talk.[2] He quietly sent his presentation to the Associated Press, United Press International, *Newsweek*, and *Time* magazine.[3] He even arranged to have a summary of his discovery appear in the *New York Times* the following morning. And it did . . . on the front page. Those reading about "Red China's" looming agricultural crisis, or a possible new trade deal between the "Two Germanys," would also learn of Smith's discovery of "A New Gospel Ascribed to Mark," should the mid-sized article on the bottom left of the page catch their eye.[4]

Smith entered the hall clutching his presentation, a typed script meticulously corrected by hand:

> . . . finding such a book ~~on~~ in a Greek monastery library . . .
> . . . Drs. Angelon~~u~~ and Dime~~a~~ras of the Greek National Foundation . . .
> . . . Undersecretary ~~of~~ in the Greek Dept. of Education . . .[5]

These are the annotations not of a scholar who prepared his presentation in haste, but of one with a dogged commitment to "getting it right," even if it meant refining the transcript until the eleventh hour.

At 7:45 p.m. Smith took the stage. At the time Smith was forty-five—still considered early to mid-career in a field that requires years of schooling before employment—but his nearly bald head gave the impression that he was a much older man. Though not particularly tall, he tended to tilt his head down when speaking to others, as if condescending from some lofty height. He read his opening remarks, beginning with a note of gratitude:

> Mr. Chairman, ladies and gentlemen:
> I must begin this report by expressing my thanks to His Beatitude Benedict, Patriarch of Jerusalem, who gave me permission to study the manuscripts at Mar Saba and publish

my findings. . . . I am [also] indebted to many scholars for assistance on many particular problems.

Then, onto the main event: a newly discovered letter written by one of the most fascinating but enigmatic early Christian writers, Clement of Alexandria. Smith set up the premise of the letter: A certain Theodore has written to Clement with questions about a secret version of the Gospel of Mark circulating among the heretics. Theodore wonders whether Clement knows about this text and whether it should be regarded as divinely inspired. Then Smith turned to Clement's reply: the *Letter to Theodore*. But Smith read aloud the letter only after issuing a stern warning to those gathered in the auditorium: "Before reading [Clement's reply], however, I must inform you that this text is copyrighted and is not to be quoted. It may be summarized and occasional phrases from it may be used in the summary, but any substantial direct quotation is strictly forbidden. The answer, then, reads as follows." Then Smith set down his transcript, pulled out a separate sheet, and from it read aloud the *Letter to Theodore* and the Secret Gospel of Mark.[6]

There is much to take in from this new document—a secret gospel hidden in Alexandria, heretics moved to action by demons, a previously unknown miracle performed by Jesus! In ordinary circumstances, this torrent of new historical information by itself would be enough to excite biblical scholars, who work with a limited set of well-studied ancient documents. But one detail from the letter overshadowed the rest: the Secret Gospel of Mark implies that Jesus had an intimate—perhaps even sexual—relationship with a young man.

While Smith did not spell this out in so many words, he certainly hinted at it in his presentation, even if only in jest. Robert Kraft, then a doctoral student at Harvard University, recalls Smith insinuating that Jesus instructed the young man under the bedsheets.[7] Helmut Koester, who would become a leading figure in biblical studies but was at the time attending only his second annual meeting of the SBL, recalled that during the presentation Smith quipped that any priest caught alone with a nearly nude young man "would certainly be in trouble with his bishop," an off-color joke that left Koester and others in attendance "shocked."[8] Members of the society were a hodgepodge of academics and devout preachers, with many finding themselves somewhere in between, so for most in attendance the implications were offensive, if not unthinkable. Even Kraft, one of the nonclerical members in the audience, recalls that Smith's unveiling of a "homosexual Jesus" was startling, nothing short of an "oh wow" moment.[9] Remember that this was 1960, long before the emergence of the counterculture later that decade, the sexual revolution, and the Stonewall uprising in 1969 that marked the beginning of the gay rights movement. When Morton Smith presented an ancient text that seemed to depict Jesus as a gay man, homosexuality was rarely mentioned in American public discourse.

Smith was quite capable of such rigorous and technical work, as became clear when he turned to the heart of his presentation, the question of the manuscript's authenticity. It's one thing to discover a text with Clement's name on it, but finding a genuine letter of Clement is another entirely. To make his case, Smith launched into a detailed analysis of the linguistic similarities between the *Letter to Theodore* and Clement's known writings—a semantic slog that would make even the most wonkish scholar squirm in his or her seat. The depth of Smith's research and breadth of his learning were on full display. Smith then concluded that Clement of Alexandria did in fact compose the *Letter to Theodore*, leaving open the possibility that the Secret Gospel is a previously unknown version of the Gospel of Mark composed by the evangelist himself.

His findings stunned many in the audience. Had Smith really chanced upon a new letter of Clement of Alexandria? Did Mark the Evangelist compose an alternative, secret gospel? And since Mark's Gospel is generally regarded as the earliest of the four in the New Testament, what implications would this discovery of a seemingly gay Jesus have for our understanding of Jesus's life and ministry? Smith's respondent, Pierson Parker from General Theological Seminary, was the first to raise objections, which he expressed not only in the auditorium that evening but also in a *New York Times* article that showcased his own perspective and appeared two days later: "Expert Disputes 'Secret Gospel.'"[10]

At the close of the symposium controversy over the Secret Gospel of Mark erupted. Despite the presence of media in the room, only a lone photograph from the session survives, and it captures well the mood: Labeled "pro- and antagonist," the photo depicts

Smith and an interlocutor standing face-to-face, the opponent armed with an arsenal of objections and questions about Smith's provocative new discovery, and Smith, mid-sentence, firing volleys in return.[11] All the while several scholars eagerly look on, as if deciding which side of the battle to join.

The controversy surrounding the significance of the Secret Gospel of Mark that emerged in the Horace Mann Auditorium and spilled out into the streets in late December 1960 continues today, more than sixty years later. One might assume that steady progress had been made over the years, and that fundamental questions about the discovery would now have decisive answers: Did Clement compose the *Letter to Theodore*, and did Mark write a secret version of his canonical gospel? If not, then who composed the *Letter to Theodore* and the Secret Gospel, when, and for what purpose? Yet after decades of work on the Letter and the Secret Gospel, it seems our understanding of precisely what Smith discovered all those years ago has become more uncertain. While Smith and Parker agreed that Clement likely composed the Letter, but disagreed over whether Mark the Evangelist or some other early Christian authored the Secret Gospel, some now suspect that Smith himself *forged* both the Letter and the Secret Gospel. Still others doggedly maintain that both the Letter and the Secret Gospel are ancient, and that the Secret Gospel could hail from the first or second century CE.

It is not often that experts disagree sharply about whether a text was composed within a generation or two of Jesus's death or in the twentieth century, but this is the bewildering state of affairs with the Letter and the Secret Gospel. This book is an attempt to move beyond the stalemate, to review the available evidence afresh and reinterpret it in light of recent advances in the field, especially methodological developments that have taken place largely within the past twenty years. We aim to bring clarity to the debate, to rule out unlikely if not implausible claims that have been made over the years about the Letter, the Secret Gospel, and even Morton Smith himself, and to make progress toward locating the Letter and the Secret Gospel in place and time.

We also aim to open up the scholarly conversation to new voices. As readers of this book will quickly become aware, the Secret Gospel of Mark tends to attract scholars of a particular demographic: white heteronormative males from elite private institutions, often having a special preoccupation with the New Testament. We ourselves must admit that we belong to this group: we both first learned about Secret Mark as graduate students at Harvard Divinity School while studying under Helmut Koester, who attended Smith's presentation in 1960 and who provocatively believed that the Secret Gospel of Mark was even older than the version of Mark's Gospel found in the New Testament. Yet over the course of our research we have not only broken with the views of Koester but have also become convinced that progress on Secret Mark will require problematizing the received wisdom on the topic and broadening the conversation to include underrepresented voices.

We strive in this book to revisit the evidence with open minds. The result is a new understanding of the Secret Gospel of Mark that departs from the views of Smith, Koester, and others who argue that the text hails from the first century, and of those who claim that Smith himself forged the manuscript in the twentieth century.

The truth, we argue, lies somewhere in between.

CHAPTER TWO

The Find

I N 1958, TWO YEARS BEFORE he stunned the world of biblical studies, Morton Smith left his cramped apartment in the
Upper East Side of New York City, where he taught in the Department of Classics at Columbia University, and jetted across
the Atlantic. Smith was a rising star in the field of biblical studies
and had developed a special expertise in manuscripts. A few years
earlier he won a prestigious Fulbright fellowship to travel to Greece
in search of manuscripts of Isidore of Pelusium, a fifth-century
Egyptian monk rumored to have composed more than ten thousand
letters.[1] Many of Isidore's writings had gone unnoticed for centuries
in the less frequented libraries throughout Greece, and Smith was
determined to locate as many as possible.[2] He found several interesting specimens and came home with some five thousand images.[3]
Perhaps Smith's greatest discovery on that trip was a love for leafing through dusty piles of books in search of some long-forgotten
treasure.[4]

It was this same drive that brought him back to the Mediterranean in 1958, this time to Jerusalem. Smith had recently settled
into his position at Columbia, having finally found stable work after
teaching at three universities in as many years.[5] He longed for a
change of pace—a working vacation—so he set his sights on Mar

Saba, an ancient monastery steeped in the tranquility of the desert, and traveled to Israel with the approval of the new patriarch of Jerusalem, His Beatitude Benedict.[6] A few years earlier Smith managed to curry the favor of the Orthodox Church in Israel when he traveled to Jerusalem as part of a nonprofit effort to raise money for the church as it struggled to accommodate a large influx of Palestinian refugees.[7] When in 1958 Smith asked His Beatitude Benedict for permission to travel to Mar Saba and catalogue its manuscripts, the patriarch was eager to return the favor and granted him access.[8] Although we do not know if the monastery's location in the Judean wilderness was a deciding factor in Smith's choosing to focus his energies there, it certainly could not have hurt. Mar Saba was, after all, not far away from the birthplace of Christianity, nor from the site of a spectacular manuscript discovery ten years earlier—the Dead Sea Scrolls.

Smith had quickly gained a reputation in the field of biblical studies for written work that was elegant and insightful, at times even playful. But Smith was also brutal in his evaluations of scholars he considered to be inferior, making him a great many enemies in the field. He'd routinely insult others in print, saying that a particular author "[writes] in a language I believe he believes to be English," or that a section of a book is "a soufflé of conjectures I cannot take seriously," or that one's prose "swarms with howlers and with solecisms."[9] He once bemoaned to his mentor, "Why is it that the study of religion attracts so many nitwits?"[10] Smith may have lamented the fact that he felt surrounded by idiots, but he found a fiendish pleasure in exposing them as such.

Despite his reputation as an outspoken and fearless truth-teller, Smith was guarded about his private life. A lifelong bachelor, he would later arrange to have most of his extensive personal correspondence destroyed. Smith's correspondence with his mentor Gershom Scholem survives only because Scholem kept copies. As Shaye Cohen—Smith's former student and literary executor of his estate—recalls, Smith "wanted to be remembered as a scholar, not as a source for academic gossip."[11] While the intimate details of Smith's private life lie buried in a landfill somewhere outside Manhattan—dumped in installments down the trash chute of his apartment following his death[12]—scholars continue to speculate about his private life, each bit of gossip furnishing more grist for the rumor mill.

Like many scholars of religion, Smith had a complicated personal relationship with his field of study. He was raised outside Philadelphia in an obscure branch of Christianity known as the New Church. This community was based on the teachings of Emanuel Swedenborg, an eighteenth-century mystic and scientist who claimed that the second coming of Christ had already taken place in the spirit world. Although faith claims such as these are no more (or less) incredible than better-known ones from the Christian tradition, we suspect that Smith—whose parents encouraged his love of books and critical thinking from the beginning—had probably started asking uncomfortable questions in Sunday school at a rather young age.

A Wartime Stranding

Smith's intellectual acumen took him to Harvard College, where he graduated in 1936 magna cum laude before beginning what he'd call his "serious work,"[13] a bachelor of sacred theology at the Harvard Divinity School. In 1940 he received a grant from Harvard to study abroad in Palestine. However, when travel to and from the Mediterranean halted because of the Second World War, Smith ended up stranded in Jerusalem for several years. He made the most of his time by enrolling in a doctoral program at the Hebrew University, where he wrote a dissertation—in Hebrew, no less—on the parallels between early rabbinic writings and the New Testament gospels. Upon the successful defense of his dissertation, Saul Lieberman, then dean of the Jewish Theological Seminary of America, sent a letter to Smith's parents congratulating them on their son's success and informing them that "as far as I know, he is the only non-Jewish scholar in the world who has such excellent first-hand access to ancient Hebrew and Aramaic sources." He added, "Since I do not like to flatter people to their face, it occurred to me that I write rather to you than your son, of whom you have every right to be very proud."[14] After the war he returned stateside and pursued a second doctorate, this time in Old Testament at Harvard University.

In the course of his training, Smith drifted away from his Swedenborgian roots and eventually joined the Episcopal Church, where he served as an ordained priest. In time, however, he would settle into a more academic—if not antagonistic—mode. He preferred to occupy the periphery of religion and throw stones at those in the center. A longtime colleague once likened Smith to "a little boy whose goal in life is to write curse words all over the altar in church, and then get caught."[15] Shaye Cohen, Smith's former student, would later recall that "the truth was always his most important goal and if it collided with sacred beliefs so much the better."[16]

Smith's propensity to provoke was already apparent in his dissertation at Harvard, where he set his sights on one of the core tenets of Judaism: monotheism. He broke with the scholarly orthodoxy of the day and argued that most ancient Israelites were actually polytheists, and that only later did a small but influential faction within Judaism come to believe in a single God.[17] Smith was not wrong—what was avant-garde in his day has become a standard scholarly view today—but the amusement he found in contradicting his colleagues and repudiating the deeply held beliefs of millions worldwide exposes the impulse to offend that occasionally got the best of Smith's otherwise evenhanded scholarly sensibilities.

As Smith prepared for his journey to Mar Saba in 1958, he couldn't have helped but recall his first visit to the monastery seventeen years earlier as a twenty-six-year-old student. Unable to leave the Mediterranean during the war, Smith settled into life in his temporary home abroad. He found lodging in a hostel near the Church of the Holy Sepulchre, the traditional site of Christ's crucifixion and burial. The hostel, a former monastery, was run by a certain Archimandrite Kyriakos Spyridonides, a high-ranking official within the Greek Orthodox Patriarchate of Jerusalem. Despite Kyriakos's lofty status in the church, Smith knew him chiefly as a fair landlord and generous host. As Smith would later recall, he "went out of his way to help me deal with the innumerable problems of life in a new and strange city."[18]

Father Kyriakos urged Smith to participate in the religious life of the city, initially by encouraging him to explore the Church of the Holy Sepulchre. The young American became enthralled with the complex, which was undergoing extensive repairs following an earthquake in 1927 that ravaged the region. Renovations were slow to start and were not completed until 1959 owing to disputes among the various Christian factions overseeing the site. The Church of the Holy Sepulchre struck Smith as a "tangle of struts and trestles, of mysterious shadows, tiny passageways, and unexpected enormous spaces, of bare wood and iron supports, of gilded carvings and mag-nificent marble."[19] He was captivated by the ways lived piety inter-acted with the ancient structure. Processions of priests and monks dressed in robes black and shimmering sinuated along the church's alleys and walkways, while the knell of church bells descended on the faithful. Smith found himself drawn to the church and even began attending Orthodox services there. "At the beginning of the mass," Smith recalls, "with the majestic opening of the great doors of the golden altar screen, the unspeakable solemnity of the procedure, I understood what the northern barbarians must have felt when they were permitted to enter Byzantium."[20]

Aware of Smith's growing interest in the Orthodox Church and its ancient holy sites, Father Kyriakos invited him to visit the mon-astery of Mar Saba, an offer that Smith was now primed to accept. One morning Kyriakos and Smith set out for the monastery, accom-panying an old man who brought food to the monks in the remote spiritual outpost weekly. Kyriakos rode ahead on horseback, while Smith and the old man traveled on donkeys at a much slower pace. The old man lagged on account of the provisions he carried, and Smith on account of his inexperience riding a donkey. For Smith this was not just a jaunt outside Jerusalem; it was a voyage back in time, "a journey into the middle ages," during which they passed a man covered in blood and sweat butchering a dead camel.[21]

Somewhere in the hill country halfway between Jerusalem and the Dead Sea—a liminal region at the edge of civilization, an "ever-present fringe," as it has been described[22]—one finds the mon-astery of Mar Saba (fig. 1). A region once inhabited by the prophet Elijah, John the Baptist, and Jesus, it is now home to a monastic for-tress.[23] The great tower, an unadorned rectangle in three dimensions, stands tall atop a mound and in the late-afternoon sun casts a length-ening shadow over the jumble of structures below. A lack of contrast between the monastery's rough-hewn stones and the surrounding landscape gives the impression of a structure not built up from the

*Figure 1. Morton Smith's photo of Mar Saba from his personal sketchbook.
Photo: T. Alwood.*

earth but carved out of it. As one scans the compound from a dis-
tance, from the hilltop tower to the buildings and cascading stair-
cases below, its precarious perch becomes evident, and it's hard not to
imagine the monastery clinging to a hill as it slides slowly off a cliff.

Established in 483 CE, Mar Saba is one of the oldest active
Christian monasteries. Its founder and namesake was a monk from
Syria born to well-to-do Christian parents. As a boy, Sabas found
himself living with an uncle after his father, a soldier, left their
hometown on deployment and elected to bring his mother along
with him.[24] Unable to get along with his aunt, Sabas fled to live with
another uncle. During his youth he traveled to Jerusalem, where he
attempted—unsuccessfully—to join a monastery. At the time prepubescent boys were often not allowed to live in communal monasteries because their fresh, beardless faces could arouse in the older
monks impure desires.[25] So the young Sabas was sent to live in a
cave with an older monk, who would prepare him for life in the
monastery. In time Sabas would mature and join a communal monastery. He would even establish several monastic communities of his
own—including Mar Saba.[26]

Yet Sabas's tenure was not without incident. He was nearly
ousted by a group of more erudite monks who accused him of being

a "rustic," or, in today's parlance, a hick. And rather than confront the problem head-on, he opted to flee to a remote spot and wait out the conflict. His struggle to deal with conflict notwithstanding, St. Sabas did gift Christendom with the monastery of Mar Saba, which has been continuously occupied for most of its nearly fifteen-hundred-year history. Over the centuries, many Christians have taken up residence in the monastery, including St. John of Damascus, who provides us with one of the earliest Christian evaluations of a new religion that emerged during his life—Islam. The monastery survived numerous incursions from the Persians and Arabs, but in the fourteenth century fell to the Serbs and Bulgars. However, the Greek Patriarchate regained control of Mar Saba in 1623, and it has remained in Greek hands ever since.[27]

And in 1942 Smith too beheld this ancient marvel. About twelve miles outside Jerusalem, Smith reports, the group he was traveling with "came over a rise and saw the monastery lying below us—a strong, medieval tower dominating two curtain walls that closed off a stretch of the wadi's rim and then plunged down it. The trail zigzagged past the tower and down to a narrow, fortified gate in the wall below."[28] Smith had arrived at Mar Saba, a place of "strange and venerable beauty" in the words of another twentieth-century pilgrim,[29] and Smith soon found himself within the walls of the monastery.

He decided to remain there after Kyriakos left for Jerusalem, completely cut off from the outside world, and he immersed himself in monastic life. Smith toured the complex and its surroundings, which included caves dug into the side of the hill once inhabited by hermits who preferred seclusion to communal life. Each day he would join the monks for a lengthy service that began at midnight and ended around six o'clock. Next came a snack: bread and coffee with the brothers. Lunch began promptly at noon, and the second service of the day began at one thirty and lasted approximately two hours. At five o'clock an hour of evening prayers began; by six it was bedtime. "Between the services," Smith recounts, "there was silence—the silence of the desert, no voices, no sounds of animals, not even wind in the trees."[30] Smith's daily routine of worship punctuated by periods of profound silence continued for the duration of his stay at Mar Saba.

Toward the end of his residency, however, a feeling of alienation befell Smith. Though he was living among the monks, he himself was no monk. The aesthetics of monastic life—its songs, metaphors, rituals—were intended to be acts of pious service to God, and this is how the residents of Mar Saba experienced them. But to Smith they were a form of hypnotism, "dazzling the mind and destroying its sense of reality."[31] Smith could consent to the overriding of his critical judgment for a time, but after two months at Mar Saba he'd had enough. He simply could not suspend his disbelief any longer, and he was ready to return to academic life. The next time Father Kyriakos visited Mar Saba, Smith returned to Jerusalem with him and resumed his work at Hebrew University.

Did Smith Return to Mar Saba in 1944?

The conventional wisdom is that Smith did not return to Mar Saba until 1958, when he discovered the Secret Gospel. But now there is reason to believe that Smith traveled to Mar Saba again in 1944. This newly discovered return trip would hardly be worth mentioning here were it not for the fact that all of Smith's activities connected with Mar Saba would eventually be scrutinized by those who suspected him of engineering an elaborate hoax. Readers who are less heavily invested in the minutiae of the forgery debate may prefer to skip ahead to the next section.

While interviewing one of Smith's last graduate students, we learned that Smith left him a sketchbook upon his death.[32] The sketchbook contains a series of black-and-white photos, notes made by Smith, and pencil sketches Smith made of Mar Saba and other sites of interest with accompanying dates. On pages 4 and 6 are Smith's own sketches of the sprawling monastery of Mar Saba; page 5, opposite page 6, is blank, but may once have included a photograph.[33] The first sketch looks up at the tower from the southeast, from the perspective of a location Smith labels "Pantalemon's house"[34] (fig. 2). Smith drew the second sketch from the perspective of the top of the tower; it looks down over the monastery in the opposite direction, as if meeting the line of sight of the first sketch (fig. 3). On the bottom of both sketches Smith wrote the same date: "Feb. 20, 1944."

Until now, Smith was not known to have returned to Mar Saba until 1958. He does not explicitly deny that he returned between 1942 and 1958, but readers of *The Secret Gospel*, Smith's popular account of his manuscript discovery, could easily get the impression that there was no intervening trip.[35] It is possible, but difficult, to argue that Smith visited Mar Saba only once during his wartime stranding. As Lent was approaching in 1944, Smith could have reflected back on his trip to Mar Saba two years prior and nostalgically sketched the monastery from two old photographs, one looking up at the tower and another looking down from it. He includes two photos of Mar Saba from similar perspectives in a 1960 article, photographs reprinted in *The Secret Gospel*.[36] Perhaps Smith originally included these photos in his sketchbook and sketched Mar Saba from the images.[37]

However, there are compelling reasons to conclude that Smith *did* return to Mar Saba in 1944, and that on this heretofore unknown trip he stood in front of the monk's house and atop the tower and sketched the monastery in person. First, though Smith published similar images of Mar Saba, they differ enough from the sketches to indicate that he did not sketch from these photographs, or indeed any photographs. The sketches include more lateral detail than a typical camera can capture, as though they were done in person with the benefit of peripheral vision or a field of view that is greater with eyesight than a camera lens. In other words, photos taken from these locations would lack the panoramic perspective the sketches have.[38]

Second, Smith's sketchbook does include additional sketches with no accompanying photographs: two sketches from Aegina, an island off the coast of Athens. One sketch looks out to the ocean from the Temple of Aphaia, and the other is of Ekklisia Isodia Theotokou from the adjacent coastal road. Both are dated April 23, 1952, when Smith was on a Fulbright and traveling around Greece and would have been able to make sketches of the temple and the church in person. While his sketch of Hagia Sophia does closely resemble the accompanying photograph, it is dated April 2, 1952, and could also have been done in person during his Fulbright year.

Finally, if during Smith's period of intense study at Hebrew University he ever had time to return to Mar Saba, it would have been in February of 1944. On May 13, 1944, Smith wrote a letter

Figure 2. Morton Smith's sketch of the tower at Mar Saba. Photo: T. Alwood.

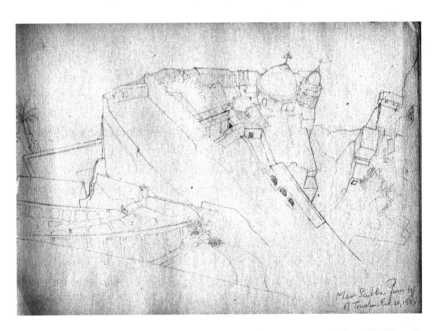

Figure 3. Morton Smith's sketch looking down from the tower. Photo: T. Alwood.

from Cairo to Harry Wolfson, his mentor back at Harvard. Smith had recently departed from Jerusalem and wanted to let his mentor know what he had been up to during the academic year. Smith tells Wolfson that though he'd been sick much of the year—and was even prescribed arsenic injections for a time!—he still managed to submit a complete draft of his dissertation during the "first week of February." By mid-February, while Smith was awaiting corrections from his readers, he would finally have had some downtime. Though Smith does tell Wolfson about some of his travels during the academic year—trips to northern Palestine and Syria—he does not mention a trip to Mar Saba. But there's no reason to expect Smith's account of his travels to Wolfson to have been comprehensive. The newly unearthed sketchbook makes it quite likely that Smith did return to Mar Saba in February of 1944, soon after submitting a full draft of his dissertation, possibly in search of some well-deserved rest and relaxation and the opportunity to sketch the ancient monastery that continued to captivate him even two years after his initial visit.

Some readers may be justifiably puzzled about why it matters so much whether Smith made a second visit to Mar Saba in 1944. The short answer is that those who have accused Smith of forging the manuscript that he claimed to have discovered at Mar Saba in 1958 have scrutinized virtually everything he said or did not say and everything he did or did not do, seeking to find hints of his fabrication (as we shall see in chapters 4, 5, and 6). As soon as we realized that we had compelling evidence of a previously unknown 1944 visit, we knew that this would become fodder for the forgery hypothesis. A proponent of this view might now propose that Smith forged the manuscript sometime between 1942 and 1944 (while being sure not to neglect his dissertation writing), and that it was during this second, concealed trip to Mar Saba that he deposited it in the tower library where he would "discover" it fourteen years later. Alternatively, perhaps Smith decided on this mysterious second visit to steal a book from the monastery and then, at a more relaxed pace, crafted his forgery and copied it into the book's endpages in the years that followed.

As intriguing as this newly discovered second visit to Mar Saba is, the simple fact remains that we have no evidence that Smith was interested in manuscripts at all during his wartime stranding. By all accounts, Smith began to focus on manuscripts after he returned to the United States from his stranding, when he began in earnest his second doctoral degree at Harvard and learned about manuscript studies under Professor Werner Jaeger.[39] The fact that he never mentioned this visit in print hardly indicates that he intentionally concealed it. Indeed, that his second visit took place shortly after he finished writing his dissertation arguably provides all the explanation we need for why he chose to return. He characterized his first visit to the monastery as "two months of absolute peace in a world of which the only concern was the daily round of work and worship,"[40] which—speaking from experience—sounds exactly like what someone who had just completed a dissertation might want and need.

"There Was Always the Chance That Something Had Been Missed"

When Smith returned once again to Mar Saba in 1958, he came not as a young man dabbling in religious tourism or as a spent graduate student with a sketchbook, but as a professor with a job to do. He had been shown the two libraries during his first visit but paid them little attention. But in 1958 he would spend nearly all of his time in the library housed in the tower, the same tower he'd sketched in 1944.

Throughout the centuries Mar Saba had been home to a treasure trove of ancient and medieval manuscripts. Cyril of Scythopolis (ca. 525–559), an acquaintance and biographer of St. Sabas, conducted research at several other Palestinian monasteries but completed his work at Mar Saba, taking advantage of the monastery's extensive holdings during his residency in what has been described as "the largest and most developed of those in all the monasteries in which [Cyril] was living."[41] Residents of Mar Saba also repaired old books in the collection so they could continue to be used by the monks,[42] and beginning in the eighth century, works from the collection were translated into Arabic and Georgian.[43] It should come as no surprise, then, that Mar Saba, with its large and diverse stacks, attracted authors from throughout the region.[44]

Some of Mar Saba's holdings occasionally ended up in the surrounding caves. A story is told of a monk and his assistant who, upon
receiving news of an impending raid on the monastery by local
Bedouins, relocated the monastery's most prized manuscripts to a
nearby cave. Unfortunately, the monk and his assistant died during
the attack and the manuscripts were never found.[45] Monks also reported finding fragments of manuscripts in caves, likely the remains
of books that hermits checked out from the monastery's library but
never returned—at least not completely.[46]

However, the monastery's holdings dwindled significantly beginning in the early eighteenth century, when a fire ripped through
the complex and destroyed numerous ancient volumes. In the 1860s
most of the writings that survived the blaze were transferred to
Jerusalem by order of the patriarch for safekeeping, leaving only
"scraps" and "printed books" for Smith to sort through and catalogue.[47] Well aware when he arrived that the collection had dimin-
ished over the past century, Smith didn't expect to find anything
revolutionary among the library's current holdings, now largely
stashed in the tower library. Nonetheless, he remained hopeful.
"There was always the chance that something had been missed," he
recalled years later, "or that other manuscripts had been brought in
by monks coming from other monasteries."[48] And so he began his
survey of the collection.

Smith got to work and soon settled into a routine. With a monk
by his side—chaperones are often required when looking at manuscripts at Greek Orthodox libraries—each morning except Sunday
Smith would ascend a series of stairs that led from his quarters to
the old tower. His escort would unlock the door, then wait patiently
as he sifted through stacks of books packed onto bookshelves and
strewn across the floor. Smith was not primarily looking for ancient
manuscripts—these had been destroyed or removed from the monastery years earlier. Instead, he spent most of his time leafing through
modern printed editions in search of "manuscript material"—that is,
notes, passages, or annotations written in margins and on flyleaves
by monks studying these volumes. When Smith found an inscribed
book, he would set it aside. After he had located three or four of
these, the monk would lock the door, they would descend the stairs,

and Smith would retreat to his quarters to examine the manuscripts he had found.

Smith located a surprising number of handwritten passages in printed books, particularly in books from the seventeenth through the nineteenth century, leading him to speculate that paper may not have been abundant at the monastery during that period.[49] In total, Smith was able to conduct a detailed inspection of approximately seventy manuscripts. Still, he did not have time to study an additional twenty manuscripts nor examine two large folders of fragments. Smith's notes on the collection were published, in modern Greek translation, in 1960.[50]

Most of Smith's discoveries were unsurprising. He reports finding "prayer books and hymns and sermons and lives of saints and anthologies from the Church fathers"—in other words, "the proper and predictable reading of a monastic community."[51] Occasionally he'd find bits and pieces of older manuscripts that had been recycled, used to stiffen the covers and bindings of newer books. But Smith chose not to investigate further, since his "permission to study the volumes did not include permission to take them apart."[52]

Yet one manuscript was unlike the rest—it was remarkable, perhaps even revolutionary. Near the end of his stay, Smith found himself again in his quarters examining the day's haul, when one manuscript caught his eye. The handwriting of the text was so inscrutable that he hadn't even attempted to read it in the tower. But now in the quiet of his room, he worked to decipher the challenging Greek script. As Smith squinted at the first few words of the difficult cursive hand, he became astonished at what he was seeing.

With some effort the opening lines became clear: "From the letters of the most holy Clement, the author of the Stromateis. To Theodore." Smith did not recognize the recipient of the letter (Theodore was a name as common in the ancient world as it is today), but as a scholar well versed in early Christian literature, he immediately identified Clement as Clement of Alexandria, a brilliant and prolific church father who composed, among other theological writings, the *Stromateis* or *Miscellanies*. But as the opening sentence made clear, this text was not from the *Stromateis*, nor from any of Clement's other surviving writings, but seemingly from a collection of his letters that had since vanished. A few words later, Smith recognized another name, the Carpocratians, an early Christian heretical group known for their adventurous sexual practices. What long lost treasure had he discovered?

Confident that he'd happened upon something of great significance, Smith photographed the manuscript (fig. 4–5)—"three times for good measure"[53]—and then set his sights on identifying the print book within which the *Letter to Theodore* was copied. As with many of the other manuscripts Smith catalogued, the *Letter to Theodore* was copied by hand onto blank pages at the end of a printed book. The title of the print volume was not immediately apparent since the book had lost its front cover and title page after years of use. But eventually Smith was able to identify the volume as Isaac Voss's seventeenth-century edition of the letters of Ignatius of Antioch, a Christian author and predecessor of Clement of Alexandria. Perhaps it's no surprise that a monk who pored over the letters of Igna-

Figure 4. *Morton Smith's photo of the last page of Voss's printed book and the first page of the* Letter to Theodore *manuscript. Morton Smith Papers, box 1/7, and Saul Liebermann Papers, box 1/11. Courtesy of The Library of the Jewish Theological Seminary.*

Figure 5. Morton Smith's photo of the second and third pages of the
Letter to Theodore *manuscript. The arrow in the bottom left was added*
by Smith to indicate the beginning of the quotation from the Secret Gospel of
Mark. *Morton Smith Papers, box 1/7, and Saul Liebermann Papers, box 1/11.*
Courtesy of The Library of the Jewish Theological Seminary.

tius would also have had an interest in a letter of Clement! By identifying the volume, Smith was able to secure a date after which—a
terminus post quem—the scribe copied the *Letter to Theodore* onto the
back pages of the volume: 1646.

Smith somehow resisted the urge to decipher more of the text,
opting instead to spend his time in residence hunting for more treasures among the library's holdings. He reasoned that "a library that
had yielded one such text might yield another."[54] So he returned
the book to the tower library, where he found it, and resumed his
inventory. In his remaining days at Mar Saba, Smith discovered an
interesting fifteenth-century manuscript attributed to Macarius of
Egypt—a well-known Coptic hermit—but nothing to rival Clement's *Letter to Theodore*. He set off for Jerusalem, where he told his
former mentor, Gershom Scholem, about the discovery. Smith then
entrusted his film to a skilled developer who could process the black-
and-white images he had taken.

Smith worried that if he made the discovery public before figuring out precisely what he had discovered, he could ruin his academic reputation. So he decided to keep it under wraps until he
could determine what he'd found, and for the time being he would
not discuss it with anyone beyond Scholem.

Despite his caution, the manuscript would soon ignite decades
of controversy in the scholarly world and beyond, and even threaten
to ruin his career and reputation.

CHAPTER THREE

The Vetting

Over the next few weeks, Smith finished his scheduled tour of the Mediterranean, traveling around Turkey and Greece exploring various ancient archaeological sites, but he couldn't stop thinking about the discovery. Smith finally arrived in Athens, where he was able to catch his breath and "sit down calmly and assess the situation."[1] He studied the prints he'd ordered in Jerusalem and managed to decipher much of the text of Clement's *Letter to Theodore*. What he found was even more intriguing and salacious than he initially thought when he first examined the letter in his cell at Mar Saba:

> From the letters of the most holy Clement (author) of the Stromateis, to Theodore. Rightly did you silence the unspeakable teachings of the Carpocratians. For they are the "wandering stars" that have been prophesied, those who wander from the narrow road of the commandments into the boundless abyss of fleshly and bodily sins. For having been puffed up in knowledge, as they say, about the depths of Satan, they are unaware that they are tossing themselves into the utter gloom of the darkness of lies. And even though they boast that they are free, they have become slaves to base

desires. These people, then, should be opposed on all sides and in all ways. For if they might say something true, one who loves the truth should not agree with them. For not all true things are truth, nor should the truth that merely seems to be true among people be preferred to the true truth that is in accordance with the faith.

Now concerning the chatter about the divinely inspired Gospel according to Mark, some are complete fabrications, and others, even if they contain some truth, are nonetheless not reported truly. For true things mixed with fictions are effaced, so that, as it is said, even salt loses its saltiness.

Now concerning Mark, during Peter's stay in Rome, he wrote about the Lord's deeds, not, however, disclosing all of them, nor intimating the mystical ones, but choosing what he thought most useful for increasing the faith of the initiates [catechumens]. But following the martyrdom of Peter, Mark came to Alexandria, bringing both his own notes and those of Peter, from which he transferred to his earlier book the things appropriate for making progress toward knowledge. He composed a more spiritual gospel for the benefit of those being made perfect. Nevertheless, he did not yet disclose the ineffable things, nor did he write out the esoteric teachings of the Lord, but to the things already written he added even more; further, he introduced certain sayings, the interpretation of which he knew would lead mystically the hearers into the innermost sanctuary of the truth that is veiled seven times. In this way, then, he prepared matters, neither grudgingly nor recklessly, to my mind, and after he died he left his book to the church in Alexandria, where it is still very well guarded, being read only by those being initiated into the great mysteries.

But since the defiled demons are continuously concocting ways to destroy the human race, Carpocrates, taught by them and making use of deceptive means, enslaved a certain presbyter from the church in Alexandria so that he might get from him a copy of the Secret Gospel, which he interpreted according to his blasphemous and carnal doctrine, and even defiled, mixing with the immaculate and sacred words lies most unabashed. From this merging is drawn off the teaching of the Carpocratians.

To these, then, as I said before, one must never yield, nor, when they propose their fabrications, concede that the Secret Gospel is from Mark, but even deny it with an oath. For not all true things are said to all people. Because of this the wisdom of God through Solomon commands, "Respond to the fool from his foolishness," teaching that the light of the truth should be concealed from the cognitively blind. Now it says, "From the one that does not have it will be taken," and "Let the fool walk in darkness." But we are children of light, since we have been illuminated by the dawning of the spirit of the Lord from the heights, and where the spirit of the Lord is, it says, there is freedom. For all things are pure to those that are pure.

Now, to you I will not hesitate to answer the questions you have asked, by refuting the lies with the very words from the gospel. For instance, after "They were on the road traveling up to Jerusalem" and what follows, until "After three days he will rise," it [the Secret Gospel] adds these very words:

And they came into Bethany, and a certain woman whose brother had died was there. And after coming she prostrated herself before Jesus and says to him: Son of David, have mercy upon me. But the disciples censured her. And Jesus, angered, went away with her into the garden where the tomb was. And immediately a loud cry was heard from the tomb. And Jesus approached and rolled away the stone from the door of the tomb. And entering immediately in to where the young man was, he extended his hand and raised him, grasping his hand. But the young man, looking at him, loved him, and he began to beg him to be with him. And leaving the tomb, they arrived at the young man's house—for he was wealthy. And after six days Jesus commanded him, and in the evening the young man comes to him wearing a linen cloth over his naked body. And he remained with him that night, because Jesus taught him the mystery of the kingdom of God. And from there he got up and returned to the other side of the Jordan.

And following these words is "And James and John came to him," and the rest of the passage. But "naked man with naked man," and the other things about which you wrote are not found.

And after the words "And he comes to Jericho," it [the Secret Gospel] only has:

and the sister of the young man whom Jesus loved and his mother and Salome were there, and Jesus did not receive them.

But many of the other things about which you write appear to be and are fabrications.

Now the true interpretation, also the one that agrees with the true philosophy . . .[2]

Too Good to Be True?

Now fully aware of what he'd discovered, Smith was overcome, though not with joy but with uncertainty. How could he have managed to find an authentic letter of Clement, let alone in the end-pages of a seventeenth-century book? Did Mark really compose an alternative, secret version of his gospel? Did the Carpocratians also possess a version of this gospel? Or, as Smith occasionally began to suspect, was the manuscript "a fake of some sort"?[3] At times he was flooded with elation at the prospect of a new letter from Clement and a secret version of Mark. But elation quickly gave way to doubt and despair as he considered again the possibility that the manuscript was a forgery. He entered into a period he would later characterize as the "dark night of the soul," borrowing the expression from the sixteenth-century mystic St. John of the Cross.

"A fake of some sort"—what did Smith mean by this expression? It is tempting, in light of more recent high-profile "forgeries," to think of a "forgery" or "fake" as the work of a modern con artist who conspires to deceive people by creating a falsified historical document, be it the private diaries of Hitler or a lost gospel in which Jesus mentions "my wife."[4] Yet Smith never seems to have seriously entertained the possibility that the *Letter to Theodore* might be a twentieth-century hoax. Even before Smith reached out to paleographers (specialists in older styles of handwriting), his hunch was that the style of handwriting used in the manuscript belonged to the eighteenth century. Thus, in his moments of deepest doubt, Smith questioned not why someone would have attempted to deceive unsuspecting readers by emulating an older style of writing, but why an eighteenth-century monk would have composed a text like this. "Who, *at that time*, could have made up such a thing? What monk knew anything about Carpocrates? What motive could there possibly have been for the invention of such a document?"[5]

For Smith there was an air of plausibility about the antiquity of the *Letter to Theodore* and the excerpts from the Secret Gospel of Mark. The language used in the letter sounded like Clement's, and key details about the Secret Gospel of Mark flagged it as believably ancient. For instance, a Christian writer from the early second century reported that Mark was the apostle Peter's assistant or interpreter, and that the gospel bearing his name was Mark's notes based on Peter's preaching.[6] If this information is correct, then the traditions in Mark would be venerable indeed, since Peter was one of Jesus's closest disciples and became a major figure in the early church. There are some reasons to be skeptical of this explanation for the origins of Mark's Gospel, but Peter's assistant is certainly a rather obscure figure to attribute a gospel to, so there may be some elements of truth in the claim.[7]

If there were a gospel that also existed in a secret, longer version, Mark would be a likely candidate. Mark's Gospel depicts Jesus as being furtive in his teachings, warning his followers not to divulge them to outsiders. There are also several passages in Mark that are so strange and difficult to understand that they may well have functioned as something like "inside jokes" for those in the know. The most perplexing of these is an incident that takes place at the moment of Jesus's nighttime arrest. All of Jesus's disciples flee, and then Mark reports that a young man was following Jesus's group, wearing nothing but a linen cloth. The authorities attempt to seize him, but he leaves the linen cloth and runs away naked (Mark 14:51–52).[8]

Nothing in this brief narrative explains the connection of the young man with Jesus, or why he is underdressed. The authors of Matthew's and Luke's Gospels, who each seem to have had a copy of Mark, evidently found the story confusing or embarrassing enough that both of them chose not to mention the episode. But the longer version found in the Secret Gospel of Mark apparently explains who this mysterious young man was. In an excerpt from the Secret Gospel that Clement quotes for Theodore, Jesus raises a young man from the dead. The young man loves Jesus and begs Jesus to stay with him in his house. Jesus remains there for a week, and at the end of his stay, he gives the young man a set of instructions. In response, the young man comes to Jesus at night, wearing only a linen cloth over his naked body. That night Jesus "taught him the mystery of the kingdom of God," as the Secret Gospel says.

Making Sense of a Newly Discovered Ancient Text in Four Easy Steps

So Smith set aside his doubts and plodded on, determined to figure out precisely what he'd found and, in time, to present his discovery to the world. He devised a game plan, a fourfold strategy for determining the authenticity and significance of the text. First, he would need to assess the handwriting. While he was relatively confident in assigning the hand to the eighteenth century, Smith contacted leading experts in dating Greek hands, especially late ones, since the handwriting was certainly later than the publication of Voss's 1646 edition of the Letters of Ignatius. Second, Smith needed to investigate the history of the text. While an eighteenth-century monk may have composed the text, he may also have copied it from an earlier—even ancient—manuscript. Could Smith locate a copy of or even a passing reference to this mysterious letter of Clement in the Patriarchal Library in Jerusalem, where many of Mar Saba's manuscripts had been relocated? Third, Smith had to answer the question of the authenticity of the text. Was this a genuine work of Clement, or was it the spurious work of some later author, ancient or medieval, who wrote under the pen name of Clement? Fourth and finally, he had to answer the question of the authenticity of the passage from the Secret Gospel of Mark. Did this letter in fact quote from an alternative version of the Second Gospel? If so, did the Secret Gospel predate the version of Mark that wound up in the New Testament? Or was this "secret" version based on the canonical version of Mark? Was it simply a retelling of the Gospel of Mark?

Progress was slow at first. On August 7, 1959, Smith updated his mentor on the manuscript he had told him about the prior year. "The material by Clement of Alexandria which I found at Mar Saba last year is turning out to be of great importance," Smith wrote to Gershom Scholem, "and as soon as I get all minor nuisances off my hands I must work hard at it."[9] While he was eager to make headway on the text, he was hindered by the slew of demands placed on a young professor with an ambitious research agenda. He was preparing an English translation of the Reshit HaKabbalah (Beginning of the Kabbalah), a medieval Jewish mystical text in Hebrew that he hoped to send to Scholem for comment. Smith was also contracted to write a short history of Greece to serve as a textbook at Cornell University.[10] Additional teaching commitments also slowed his progress on the Clement manuscript. He'd agreed to teach an extra course that academic year as a favor to Columbia's Department of Religion, and in the summer of 1959 his colleague Elias Bickerman left for Europe and asked Smith to cover his ancient history course, an opportunity that may have delayed his work on the Clement manuscript but helped him afford the rising cost of rent in Manhattan.[11]

Smith also had a large and expensive academic library to maintain and grow. By his own estimate, prior to 1960 he had spent approximately $23,520 on books, more than $200,000 today. He once confided in Hans Dieter Betz that he "was encouraged to buy books as a child," and that he now finds that "much of my life has gone into hunting, purchasing, shelving, moving, and taking care of books, not to mention reading them." Smith's library was so large that at one point he was forced to continue paying rent for his New York apartment *while* living abroad since "my apartment is so full of books that I can neither move out nor sublet."[12]

Smith's greatest "nuisance," however, may have been his upcoming promotion. In a couple of months, he would be considered for promotion to associate professor. With an open offer from Cornell University to join their faculty, Smith had a viable backup plan should he not receive tenure at Columbia. Nonetheless, he called on Scholem, the foremost expert in Jewish magic and mysticism, to broker the favor of the Divine: "I shall be considered for appointment with tenure this fall, so if you know any particularly powerful charms from practical Kabbalah, please put them to work."[13] Scholem was happy to oblige, assuring his former student that he'd be "working on some magical charms for your benefit."[14]

But no charm could help Smith understand Clement's *Letter to Theodore* and the Secret Gospel of Mark. He would need to clear his desk and focus on the manuscript. Smith wanted to make the discovery known to the scholarly world and beyond, so he prepared a preliminary report that he would eventually deliver at the annual meeting of the SBL, the largest gathering of biblical scholars in North America. It just so happened that in 1960 the society would convene at Union Theological Seminary in New York City, a stone's throw from Columbia. Smith planned only to present his initial thoughts, a "work in progress,"[15] but given the attention from scholars and media that the manuscript was sure to attract, he needed to have a good sense of what he'd found and why it was important.

Smith knew that even though he had many gifts as a scholar, he would require other types of expertise that he did not have in order to make sense of this puzzling text. So he needed to break his silence about the discovery and solicit feedback from friends and colleagues who could help him with their specialized skills. But sharing his preliminary work on Clement's *Letter to Theodore* was risky. "Circulation necessarily creates the possibility," Smith feared, "of some unauthorized, premature, and perhaps misrepresentative, publication."[16] So "to prevent any such untoward occurrence," he decided to file a preliminary transcription and translation of the text with the US Patent Office.

With this protection in place, Smith then began what we refer to today as crowdsourcing. From the public record and from his private correspondence, we know that Smith shared his discovery with an extensive network of his academic peers in the months leading up to the meeting of biblical scholars in New York. He drew on their diverse areas of expertise to shed light on any and all features of the letter of Clement and the Secret Gospel. In keeping with his four-pronged plan of attack (date of handwriting, date of composition, authenticity of the letter of Clement, and authenticity of Secret Gospel of Mark), he turned first to the issue of the handwriting.

The Date of the Handwriting

Before returning home from Greece, Smith consulted several experts in Greek handwriting from the National Foundation, the Department of Education, and the Academy of Athens. They all assigned the handwriting to sometime between the late seventeenth and early nineteenth century, with most preferring the eighteenth century. Smith's suspicion about the age of the hand seemed to be correct. One expert further suggested that the scribe was a monk, since the *Letter to Theodore* opens with the sign of the cross, a feature often found in monastic manuscripts. Smith was urged to consult Vanghelis Scouvaras, professor at the Gymnasium in Volos, since he was an expert on the many styles of handwriting from this period. Scouvaras offered a more precise date for the hand, and even suspected he knew where the scribe learned how to write! "It is an example," Smith recalls Scouvaras reporting, "of a type formed at the court of the Oecumenical Patriarch in Constantinople in the middle of the eighteenth century."[17]

Once stateside, Smith continued asking experts in ancient handwriting for their thoughts on the manuscript, reaching out to scholars both abroad, in Belgium and France, and in the States, at University of Cincinnati, Dumbarton Oaks Library, Princeton Theological Seminary, Harvard, and Yale. Smith writes that he received "substantially identical answers."[18] For him the dating of the handwriting was now settled: eighteenth century, give or take a few decades on either end. In other words, within a generation or two of the publication of Voss's edition of the Letters of Ignatius, someone, probably a monk, inscribed Clement's *Letter to Theodore* on its blank endpages.

Some might be skeptical of the idea that a text composed in antiquity would survive only in a single manuscript from the eighteenth century. And justifiably so, since in most cases a document preserved in, say, an eighteenth-century style of handwriting was also created in the eighteenth century. But this logic does not always hold, especially in the case of ancient religious writings. Prior to the invention of the printing press in the fifteenth century, the only way to ensure that a writing survived was to copy it by hand. For some of the most ancient Christian writings, like the Gospels or the letters

of the apostle Paul, we have at best copies of copies of copies of—
well, you get the idea—of the originals, and we are quite fortunate
when the copies we have were made within 150 years of when that
writing was first composed. But in the case of writings that were not
included in the New Testament (such as apocryphal writings), our
earliest known copies might hail from a thousand or more years after the writing's date of composition. All of this is to say that it is by
no means inconceivable that an early Christian writing, especially
one that purported to contain a rather shocking story from a longer
version of Mark's Gospel, would only have survived in a single, very
late manuscript. Presumably, the scribe who copied this letter in the
eighteenth century had access to a much earlier manuscript containing Clement's *Letter to Theodore*—but that earlier manuscript is now
either lost or destroyed.

The Date of the Letter

To help determine the date the letter of Clement was composed,
Smith had the benefit of being close friends with two prominent
scholars of religion. He first approached Erwin Goodenough, a
leading expert in ancient Judaism and Christianity and longtime
professor of the history of religion at Yale University. Upon hearing
Smith's summary of the letter, he exclaimed, "God alone knows what
you've got hold of," and then proceeded, like many senior scholars
who've occupied a prestigious position for decades, to incorporate
the new evidence seamlessly into his own, preexisting understanding of the early church. For Goodenough this was a church he knew
without a doubt to possess a secretive, even mystical element: "It
may not come from Clement, and of course the Gospel won't be
Mark. But I'm convinced that it's important. It fits. That's the essential. Wherever it came from, it gives you a glimpse of the esoteric
side of the religion, and that's what really matters. And what matters
most of all is to know that there *was* an esoteric side."[19]

Smith then approached Arthur Darby Nock, who since 1930
had been on the faculty of Classics at Harvard, where he became a
full professor at the age of twenty-eight, the youngest in the university's recent history. Nock, in Smith's words "a huge, fuzzy bear of a

man," had an imposing reputation. Nock's eccentric personality also inspired numerous stories about him, many apocryphal but with a kernel of truth.[20]

Well aware of Nock's brilliance, Smith decided to test him, opting not to brief Nock about the letter first, but to hand him the photographs of the Greek manuscript without comment. "I have a surprise for you," Smith teased as he handed Nock the photographs of the Greek scrawl.[21] Smith imaginatively recounts the reaction of the clever classicist, who was both deciphering the difficult cursive hand and considering in real time the historical significance of Smith's discovery:

> Ha, Clement! A fragment of a letter, no less. Congratulations! . . . The Carpocratians! I say, this may be important. (My God, this hand is cursive!) "Carnal and bodily sins" . . . "slaves of servile desires" . . . Yes, yes, that's what he'd say; that's the language. . . . This stuff on Mark is excellent. Just what Clement would say; of course he'd defend the Alexandrian position; look at Swete on Mark for that, still the best collection. . . . What's this, "a more spiritual gospel"? . . . "Hierophantic teaching of the Lord"? . . . Well . . . it does sound like Clement. . . . I suppose he would use the mystery language; they all borrowed it later. . . . "Foul demons" . . . "devising destruction" . . . "blasphemous and carnal doctrine," that rings true again. . . . Yes, now we get the quotations. . . . That's an odd text of Proverbs, you must look that up. . . . Good heavens, a gospel quotation! Oh no, this is too much! No, my dear boy, this can't be genuine. It must be something medieval; fourth or fifth century, perhaps. They made up all sorts of stuff in the fifth century. That's where this will come from; it's not an ancient *flosculum*. But, I say, it is exciting. You must do it up in an article for the *Review*.[22]

Nock passed the test, as Smith knew he would. Though an expert in ancient Greek, he was able to read the modern Greek cursive script almost effortlessly. He also recognized immediately in the letter words and expressions from Clement's genuine writings that could indicate that the letter was actually the work of Clement of Alexandria. Yet the quotation from Secret Mark gave Nock pause. He'd been in the field long enough to know that a new writing by Mark the Evangelist was unlikely to surface and to have gone unnoticed for so long. "No, my dear boy, this can't be genuine," he cautioned.

Nock was not suggesting that the manuscript might be a modern forgery, but that it likely was a copy of a text composed in the fourth or fifth century, when Christians produced apocryphal writings abundantly to fill in the gaps left in the earliest gospels and other writings (a comparison with modern "fan fiction" is not altogether inappropriate). Even though Nock thought it likely was not a genuine letter of Clement quoting a longer version of Mark written by the evangelist himself, he was still excited by the new text. He thought that Smith had chanced upon a fascinating apocryphal text from late antiquity, so he invited him to publish the manuscript in the *Harvard Theological Review*, a prestigious academic journal of which Nock was then lead editor.

Smith never took Nock up on his offer, perhaps because in time he would come to disagree with Nock's assessment of the Secret Gospel of Mark as a fourth- or fifth-century apocryphal writing, preferring instead to see the text as an excerpt from a much more ancient version of the Gospel of Mark. Yet Nock's assessment never fully faded from Smith's mind. When he debuted the manuscript in 1960 at the SBL meeting, he listed Nock among a small group of scholars who disagreed with his assessment. He would later write that among the dissenters, Nock's opinion was the most disquieting: "What troubled me . . . was that Nock persisted in denying the attribution to Clement, though in the face of the collected evidence he could give no reason for his denial save 'instinct.' That made me nervous and still does, not only because of Nock's immense knowledge of Greek and his remarkable feeling for Greek style, but also because, apart from his learning, he was a man of unusual intuition."[23] Perhaps Nock was too quick to discount the possibility that the Secret Gospel was an authentic work by Mark the Evangelist; then again, maybe Nock's gut feeling would eventually be proved right.

The Language of the Letter

With the date of the handwriting established and the impressions of two top scholars in mind, Smith turned to the language of the letter. Did the vocabulary of the letter—its words, phrases, idioms—resemble Clement's own style? Or was the letter written by someone else, a charlatan—be they a direct student of Clement, or an eighteenth-century monk, or anyone in between who falsely attributed his own thoughts to the great Alexandrian thinker? Only an exhaustive study of the style of Greek used in the letter could help Smith answer these questions. He began to compare the language of the letter "word for word and phrase by phrase" with Clement's authentic writings.[24] He recalls this painstaking and time-consuming process with vintage Smith sarcasm: it was a "simple matter . . . it took my spare time for two years."[25]

Nowadays powerful and comprehensive search engines facilitate such detailed word studies. Most notable is the *Thesaurus Linguae Graecae* (*TLG*), which allows scholars to search virtually all known ancient Greek literature for key words and phrases within seconds.[26] If, as occasionally happens, a fragmentary papyrus of a New Testament text is discovered, the *TLG* can help one confirm its identity in minutes or even seconds. But in the absence of powerful electronic tools like the *TLG*, Smith had little choice but to patiently leaf through printed books in search of parallels between the letter of Clement and Clement's known works—though he was somewhat lucky that a concordance to, or list of words used in, the writings of Clement had been published about twenty years earlier.[27] Smith was nevertheless aware that he was standing on the cusp of a technological revolution, and that the next generation of scholars would have much more powerful tools at their fingertips. Though still years away from creating a useful search engine for scholars like Smith, the *TLG* project team first met in 1972, a year before Smith published his findings on Secret Mark. The promise of powerful search tools for scholars of Greek literature was becoming apparent—at least to Smith. He wrote that with the aid of computers such an exhaustive search would not take two years but a mere two hours, and, with the incisiveness and sting of an Israelite prophet, he predicted that "the mechanization of learning promises to transfer much of it from the minds of scholars to the data banks of machines" and lamented the likelihood that "the scholar of the future may be one who knows how to consult reference devices, but does not know the primary material."[28]

Making use of the tools at his disposal, Smith was eventually able to complete the word study. What he found astounded him. The letter's words, expressions, tenses, citation conventions, worldview—all of these characteristics pointed to Clement as the author of the text! For Smith, even the occasional difference between the letter and Clement's own writings pointed to its authenticity: "Discrepancies in context between the letter and Clement's published works are to be expected if the letter is genuine, since it purports to tell secrets which the writer would not publicly admit."[29] Smith reasoned that the work was so close to Clement's style that it was either authentic or a careful forgery, and if it were a forgery, why would its author depart from Clement's style occasionally and risk ruining the ruse? Smith's willingness to marshal contravening evidence in support of his own argument demonstrates his intellectual acuity, but it may also suggest that he had become too convinced that he had discovered an authentic letter of Clement to consider seriously the alternative. Nevertheless, undeterred by any potential evidence to the contrary, Smith was ready to present his find to the world.

Making Headlines

By December 29, 1960, the time had come. Smith took the stage in Horace Mann Auditorium at 7:45 p.m. and, as we have already seen, shocked the small and rather stodgy world of biblical studies in more ways than one. By the close of the session, it was clear that the "wrangle" over the Secret Gospel had begun. Smith had already labored for two years over his strange discovery before he gave his presentation at the SBL annual meeting; but this was only the beginning of a long journey toward publication, a journey marked by controversy, breakthroughs, victories, and disappointments all mingled together.

The *New York Times'* announcement of Smith's discovery the day after his presentation was measured: "A copy," the piece began, "of an ancient letter in Greek that ascribes a secret gospel to Mark and that narrates a miracle absent from the present Gospel of Mark was made public last night."[30] The article went on to summarize Smith's assessment of the text and even included a photo of Mar Saba and a distinguished portrait of Smith himself. Smith "foresaw that if the letter received scholarly acceptance as having been written by Clement," the article continued, "the origin and character of the Gospels and the character and early history of the Christian church would have to be reconsidered."

Reactions to Smith's 1960 presentation from his fellow scholars were decidedly mixed. Some who attended the talk congratulated him for his careful handling of the new manuscript. The moderator of the session, James A. Sanders, professor of Old Testament and Second Temple Judaism at Colgate Rochester Divinity School, heralded Smith's talk in a private letter to him as successful, even exemplary: "Just a note to thank you personally for the splendid program your paper on the Mar Saba find afforded the SBLE. I should think that your paper could be an example of how such discoveries should be dealt with and reported. It was a model for scholarly communication. . . . Congratulations."[31]

Many, however, objected to Smith's handling of the new evidence, and they made their objections widely known. The first shot in what would become a decades-long battle over the meaning of the letter of Clement was fired the very next day, when the *New York Times* ran another article on the discovery bearing the headline "Expert Disputes 'Secret Gospel.'"[32] The expert in question was Pierson Parker from General Theological Seminary, New Testament professor and ordained priest in the Episcopal Church. Parker was the respondent at Smith's SBL presentation and had expressed skepticism about parts of Smith's argument that night. However, as soon as he went to the media, the controversy over the significance of the new discovery that had taken place at the SBL meeting spilled over into the public sphere.

Parker did not contest Smith's conclusion that Clement had in fact written the letter. Even if he had, his objection would likely not have made news. Disputes over authorship of texts attributed to early Christian writers like Clement take place all the time, but rarely—if ever—outside peer-reviewed journals and scholarly monographs. Instead, he anticipated a move many suspected would be Smith's next, a contention that was sure to captivate the general public: the claim that Mark the Evangelist actually composed the Secret Gospel. After all, if Clement did in fact compose the *Letter to Theodore*, then the text of the Secret Gospel would have hailed from the second century or earlier. And who better than Clement—an Alexandrian scholar with a large library that included several otherwise unknown apocryphal books—to possess an authentic secret writing of Mark the Evangelist?

Parker agreed that Clement likely authored the letter, but suspected that Mark the Evangelist was not the true author of the Secret Gospel. Clement, he concluded, was duped by a second-century apocryphal retelling of Mark. Parker argued that Secret Mark was an ancient forgery, the work of someone emulating imperfectly the style of Mark, and that Clement had been misled. He surmised that Secret Mark was "the work of a Jewish Christian of Alexandria, prior to Clement, who was acquainted with two or more of the canonical gospels."[33] And if Secret Mark was not, as Smith and others would eventually argue, a first-century source but rather a secondary elaboration on the canonical gospels, it was not likely to provide any new insight into the life and ministry of Jesus—or his sexuality.

What Parker did find exciting in Clement's letter is early evidence that Mark did indeed travel to Alexandria. This notion is foundational for many Christian communities, including the Coptic Orthodox Church; these Christians hold Mark to be the first bishop of Alexandria—the first Coptic pope—a belief that no other Christian writings mention until the fourth century. Parker believed that the *Letter to Theodore* provided a more ancient account of Mark the Evangelist's trip from Rome to Alexandria, one originating in the city of Alexandria itself and predating the earliest known account of Mark in Egypt by a century or more. The discovery of this new source had the potential to solve this long-standing mystery: it would strengthen considerably the possibility that Mark the Evangelist was in fact the first person to introduce Christianity to Egypt. Such early evidence confirming the authorship of Mark's Gospel would be especially invigorating for more conservative biblical scholars, since there was a widespread belief that anything later Christian sources told us about the authorship of the gospels was highly unreliable.

Though Parker presented his counterargument as a New Testament scholar, carefully comparing the language of Secret Mark to the language of canonical Mark and the other gospels, one wonders whether Parker the ordained Episcopal priest rejected the authenticity of the Secret Gospel for reasons other than linguistic. Had Mark really held back certain important details about the life and ministry of Jesus? Would he have passed down a secret document to those he regarded as spiritual elites? What else did the gospel writers hold back, and how might our understanding of Jesus change had they been forthright? These questions would be understandably uncomfortable to a person who had dedicated his life to the church and to its particular understanding of who Jesus is. Soon more responses rolled in, and by January of 1961, what began as a simmer became, as one reporter put it, a "boil" that would last "for years to come."[34]

The Secret Gospel of Mark and the Historical Jesus

With news of the discovery now public, and scholars beginning to weigh in on the meaning and significance of the text, Smith intended to publish a book on the manuscript swiftly. By January 30, 1961, he wrote to Gershom Scholem that while "there's so much to write about the Mar Saba manuscript," he was making good progress, with only "discussions of the allegedly Markan material, and the significance for church history and for New Testament criticism, still to write."[35] Smith hoped to send a draft of the book to a publisher by June. That didn't happen. What slowed his progress was exactly what Pierson Parker had feared: Smith was becoming increasingly convinced that the Secret Gospel quoted by Clement was actually composed by Mark the Evangelist or one of his close associates, and that it contained authentic, if until now secret, teachings about Jesus.

Scholars tend to have a (somewhat embarrassing) knack for making new discoveries fit very neatly into what they already believe to be true, and Smith was not immune to this temptation. He was arguably predisposed to find in the Secret Gospel authentic traditions about the historical Jesus, traditions that would present Jesus in a very unorthodox light. In Smith's letters to Scholem, it becomes clear that when in 1958 he discovered the Secret Gospel of Mark, he was nearing completion of another book about Jesus in the Gospel of Mark.[36] In a letter dated August 1, 1955, Smith tells Scholem that he had completed a "book on Mark" the previous summer; Smith's book sought to demonstrate that when composing his gospel, the evangelist made use of a collection of miracle stories much like those assembled by followers of the Greek healing god Asclepius, and that Jesus's early followers regarded him similarly. Ever eager for his teacher's feedback, Smith gave a draft to A. D. Nock for comment. Apparently, Nock did not believe that Greco-Roman healing cults could have influenced Galilean Jews such as those who would have assembled collections of Jesus's miracles. Undaunted and perhaps even provoked, Smith decided to move forward with the book and prove Nock wrong. "This goaded me to writing an additional chapter on Paganism in Jewish Palestine," he told Scholem, "and for this chapter . . . I now have about two hundred pages of notes."[37] Nearly three months later, Smith told Scholem that he was still gathering evidence to counter Nock: "I got involved in the study of Hellenistic influences in Palestine and am still at it, though now at last about to give it up and simply write an account of my results to date, which fill about 300 file cards."[38] By February 26, 1956, Smith reported that the book was nearly done, and promised that Scholem would be able to see a draft of it soon.[39] But the project dragged on, and Smith was still tinkering with it later that year when he mentioned it in a letter to Goodenough.[40]

This book, however, was never published. Smith apparently shelved the project in 1958 upon discovering the Secret Gospel of Mark. Some material from the abandoned study appeared in abbreviated form in a 1973 article,[41] and much of his research on the topic of pagan influence on the early Jesus movement likely laid the foundation for his *Jesus the Magician* (1978). For our present purposes, however, we should keep in mind that when Smith discovered the Secret Gospel of Mark, he was already years into investigating the influence of Greek thought on the early Jesus movement. While we don't know the exact details of Smith's argument from his unpublished book on Mark, we do know that his interpretation of the Secret Gospel was heavily influenced by this prior work.

In June of 1961 he wrote again to Scholem, not to boast of the completion of his manuscript, but to let his mentor know that he had been entertaining "the possibility that Jesus may actually have taught a libertine gospel."[42] In other words, Smith was beginning to think that the Secret Gospel of Mark was not some second-century apocryphal text written in Mark's name, but instead contained reliable information about the historical Jesus and his teachings. But when Smith tells Scholem that he suspects that Jesus taught a "libertine gospel," what does he mean? In its most basic sense, Smith uses "libertine" to indicate that Jesus taught that the arrival of the kingdom of God put an end to the literal observance of the law of Moses.[43] In the same letter to Scholem he points to Luke 16:16 as an example of Jesus speaking as a "libertine" who nullifies the law: "The law and the prophets were in effect until John came; since then the good news of the kingdom of God is proclaimed."[44]

Such an understanding of the historical Jesus, if correct, would be a discovery of enormous significance. This is because it is usually thought that Jesus and his closest followers were law-observant Jews, and that it was the apostle Paul who, despite also being a Jew, took the radical step of creating communities of Jesus-followers who did not observe the law of Moses.[45] Paul's letters, the earliest Christian writings we possess, demonstrate how hostile Jesus's closest disciples were to Paul's rejection of the law. Most scholars, therefore, consider it unimaginable that they would have bitterly opposed Paul's "libertine" position if their own teacher had also endorsed it.

Smith, of course, was not like most scholars. Ever the contrarian, he was, it seems, well on his way to uncovering a Jesus who rejected observance of the Jewish law in his abortive book on Mark. This vision of Jesus was so captivating for Smith that he seized on the narrative of the Secret Gospel as compelling new evidence of a "libertine" Jesus. What was the meaning of the climax of the Secret Gospel's narrative, where the young man comes to Jesus, at nighttime and nearly naked, to learn "the mystery of the kingdom of God"? According to Smith, it revealed that the historical Jesus initiated his followers into the kingdom of God through a mystical baptismal rite that also liberated them from the law of Moses. Even more subversive was that Smith was clearly aware of the sexual connotations that "libertine" has long possessed. Although he mostly used the term to refer to the rejection of the Jewish law, he nevertheless flirted with connecting it to Jesus's sexual practices. One of the most infamous and oft-quoted passages from *The Secret Gospel* is a rare instance when Smith brings together these two understandings of libertinism to describe the baptism ritual of the historical Jesus: "After that [i.e., disrobing], by unknown ceremonies, the disciple was possessed by Jesus' spirit and so united with Jesus. One with him, he participated by hallucination in Jesus' ascent into the heavens, he entered the kingdom of God, and was thereby set free from the laws ordained for and in the lower world. Freedom from the law may have resulted in completion of the spiritual union by physical union."[46]

Scholem was skeptical about parts of Smith's emerging suspicion that Jesus was a libertine, but Smith was undaunted and moved forward with the argument. By October 1962 he told Scholem that though progress on the book "creeps along by inches," he now had evidence to prove his hunch about Jesus and his teachings.[47] Smith would labor at his argument through summer of 1963, presenting his ideas to colleagues in person, over the phone, and in letters. After a brief break in 1963–1964 to pursue another research project, he finally managed to complete the book and send it off to the publisher. After nearly six years of work, Smith had finally figured out what he had discovered that fateful day at Mar Saba. His findings, if true, would send shockwaves through the scholarly community and beyond.

Smith had concluded that the story of Jesus and the young man quoted in the Secret Gospel of Mark was actually an archaic form of the famous story of the raising of Lazarus found in John's Gospel. Unlike Mark and John, which were written in Greek, however, Smith believed that the earlier story was composed in Aramaic. Why would the original language of the story be important? Because the earliest Christian communities in the villages of Galilee and elsewhere used Aramaic as their native language; it was only later, when Christianity spread to larger cities throughout the Roman Empire, that texts began to be composed in Greek. Therefore, if Smith was correct, the story contained in the Secret Gospel originated at an astonishingly early point in Christian history—though there are reasons to be cautious here, since we have never recovered any manuscripts containing Aramaic Christian texts from the first century. At any rate, Smith believed that this archaic story was translated from Aramaic into Greek by the authors of Mark (or perhaps a close associate) and John independently of each other. If Smith was right about the very ancient origins of the story in the Secret Gospel, then it could be a revelation of enormous significance for our understanding of who Jesus was, how he interacted privately with his disciples, and whether he had a companion or even a love interest. Smith's was, then, the rare academic discovery that had the potential to rewrite the history of Christianity.

There was one problem, however. Oxford University Press, the press Smith hoped would publish his book, didn't want it.

Finding a Publisher

After some deliberation, Oxford University Press passed on the manuscript and notified Smith in March of 1964. Smith was surprised by the news, especially since he had the support of Henry Chadwick, longtime professor of church history at Oxford University and prominent member of the editorial board at Oxford University Press. Already in August of 1961, Chadwick had expressed interest in the book, telling Smith that "we look forward to further news of your edition of Clement of Alexandria."[48] Yet Smith had his suspicions about why a book on a revolutionary discovery such as his might have been rejected. On March 31, 1964, he wrote to Erwin Goodenough, both to relay the "bad news" about the decision of the editorial board and to speculate about why the book was rejected. "Evidently there was quite a battle," Smith reported, "since it took them so long to reach a decision."

Apparently, Chadwick's support was not enough, since, as another member of the editorial board told Smith, "it was Daube who finally lowered the boom." David Daube, another Oxford professor, apparently found Smith's argument religiously objectionable and referred to him as "a scholar with no Christian affiliations whatsoever." "I am reasonably sure that what upset the apple cart," Smith surmised, "was the chapter on historical background, in which I related the gospel to the libertine tradition in early Christianity and suggested that the root of that tradition was in Jesus' practice of some ritual believed to enable his followers to enter the kingdom." This, it is important to note, is exactly the part of Smith's project that has continued to "upset the apple cart" and generate controversy up to the present day. To this bad news from Oxford, Goodenough replied with displeasure but not surprise. He found Daube's rationale objectionable and consoled Smith by saying that Daube had a reputation "on all sides" for being "a horse's arse," adding that Daube's remark about Smith's alleged impiety "certainly confirms such a judgment."

Whatever Daube's motives were in torpedoing the book contract, Smith would have to find a new publisher. He considered two other presses, Bollingen and Brill, but ultimately decided to ask Helmut Koester and Krister Stendahl, professors at Harvard Divinity School who had earlier expressed support for Smith's assessment of the *Letter to Theodore*, to recommend the book for publication with Harvard University Press.[49] Smith expressed "no great hope" in the prospect of publishing with Harvard, but conceded to Goodenough that "you never can tell." In the end Harvard did decide to move forward with the project and publish the book, but it would take an additional nine years for it to appear in print, in part because of the painstaking process of typesetting a monograph containing so much Greek, and in part because of Smith's host of competing commitments. Finally, in 1973, fifteen years after the discovery, Smith published his findings.

Though Smith had faced his fair share of critics in the years since his SBL presentation, nothing could have prepared him for the onslaught of fresh criticism he'd now face: charges that would range from misinterpreting the evidence to forging the very manuscript he spent years trying to understand.

CHAPTER FOUR

The Skeptic

I N 1973 MORTON SMITH's definitive study of his discovery at Mar Saba finally appeared in print, published with Harvard University Press under the title *Clement of Alexandria and a Secret Gospel of Mark*. Earlier that same year Smith released an account of his discovery and findings written for a general audience: *The Secret Gospel*, with the publishing giant Harper & Row. What had until then been discussed mostly in private—in Smith's personal correspondence with handpicked experts throughout the world, or in small groups of well-connected scholars close enough to New York City to attend the University Seminar in New Testament at Columbia—could now be studied and evaluated by anyone, be they specialists in biblical studies or curious laypersons.

In truth, though, access to the *Letter to Theodore* and the Secret Gospel remained limited in one crucial way: scholars still couldn't access the physical manuscript. And the alleged circumstances under which the text survived were rather strange, arguably even stranger than its content: it was not preserved in an ancient codex or a fragmentary papyrus but copied onto the endpages of a three-hundred-year-old book. While there are many instances of writings from antiquity surviving only in relatively late manuscripts, the *Letter to Theodore* remains an unusual case. Unfortunately, it was not possible to gain additional information about the physical manuscript—the details of its handwriting and ink, handwritten notes elsewhere in the book, and so forth—since the manuscript itself remained inaccessible, presumably still in the tower library at Mar Saba, where Smith had left it fifteen years earlier.

The remote physical location of the manuscript in the Judean desert was one problem, but it was by no means the most difficult one to overcome. As scholars who study ancient manuscripts are well aware, gaining access to many of the world's largest collections of rare books and manuscripts can be formidable, even with the right credentials. But such bureaucratic hurdles hardly compare to the challenges one would likely face when attempting to examine the private collection of a monastery, especially one of Christendom's most venerable sites. One does not simply walk into Mar Saba. Smith himself gained access to Mar Saba only after contributing extensively to efforts to resettle Orthodox Christian refugees from the Palestinian territories after the 1947 partitioning; he certainly did not get there by cold-calling the head of the monastery. Furthermore, once his visit had concluded, Smith did not expect to receive permission from the patriarchate to perform any additional, more invasive testing of the book or its handwritten endpages.[1]

Scholars could not easily access the physical manuscript, true; but they could still make use of several tools, even though they were an imperfect substitute for an autopsy (meaning, in this context, an in-person examination of a manuscript). There were, of course, the black-and-white photographs that Smith took of the manuscript, plates of which appeared in the Harvard volume.[2] One might suppose, as some critics did, that Smith should have taken color photos, and certainly color photography was increasingly popular and affordable by the late 1950s. Smith never seems to have defended his decision to take black-and-white rather than color photos; he may have found black and white preferable for manuscript photography because of the contrast it provided between the ink and the writing surface.[3] But there was some potential justification for questioning how Smith chose to photograph his sensational find. Nor did it help matters that Harvard University Press ended up cropping the photographs, apparently against Smith's wishes,[4] so that the edges of the book pages could not be seen.

Apart from the photographs of the manuscript and Smith's discussion of its paleographic features and probable dating in the first several pages of the Harvard volume, there was at least one other key resource for those who wanted to learn more about the manuscript and the other holdings in the tower library: the catalogue of the collection published by Smith, which contained brief descriptions of the manuscripts from the tower. But, perhaps because the Greek Orthodox Patriarchate of Jerusalem was doing Smith a favor by allowing him to nose about in the holdings of one of its most cherished monasteries, Smith's catalogue was published only in modern Greek translation in a somewhat obscure church periodical, ΝΕΑ ΣΙΩΝ ("New Zion").

Enter Quentin Quesnell

It was the obscurity of this manuscript catalogue that, ostensibly, led an up-and-coming professor of biblical studies and theology by the name of Quentin Quesnell to write Morton Smith. Quesnell was the first scholar to accuse Morton Smith of forging the manuscript that he claimed to have discovered. More recent scholars have crafted some new arguments in favor of the forgery hypothesis, but they have also heavily relied on the initial suspicions that Quesnell raised. He thus plays an enormously significant role in the fierce debate that emerged around the Secret Gospel.

The difficulties surrounding the catalogue of manuscripts were apparently the occasion for the first letter that Quentin Quesnell sent to Morton Smith. In this short letter, dated November 6, 1973, and sent from Southampton, Massachusetts, Quesnell makes a simple request: Where in the Greek manuscript catalogue does Smith discuss the Clement letter? Smith did not specify the relevant pages in his books, and ordering photocopies of the entire catalogue from the only library Quesnell knew to possess it would have been prohibitively expensive. Smith wrote back promptly—just three days later—and generously. He enclosed photocopies of the entry on the Clement manuscript from his own personal copy. Smith also apologized to Quesnell for his handwritten annotations on the pages in a comment that shows just how little input he had over the published form of the catalogue: "The corrections are due to the fact that I never saw even a copy of the Greek translation, let alone proofs, before the text was published."[5]

Quesnell politely told Smith that the information in the catalogue did not add much to what Smith had already written in his two books, and then asked Smith a series of questions about the manuscript. At face value, these questions read as neutral requests for clarification: he wonders what Smith knows about the current status of the manuscript, or whether Smith had attempted to arrange for any scientific tests that might provide more information about the handwriting and ink or about Voss's volume. But Quesnell's line of questioning was not as innocent as it appears. It has become clear in recent years that when Quesnell wrote to Smith, he had already decided that the Mar Saba manuscript was a forgery.

In his reply six days later (November 21, 1973), Smith answered Quesnell's questions with a series of variations on "no." No, Smith had not heard anything further from the patriarchate about the manuscript or whether other scholars had examined it after his visit: "So far as I know, the MS is still where I left it in 1958—in the top room of the tower library."[6] No, there has been no further scientific testing of the manuscript, because Mar Saba has no such equipment and would be very unlikely to hand it over to another institution. No, Smith did not seriously consider the possibility that the manuscript was a modern forgery, since the numerous paleographers that he consulted did not suspect this. And no, Smith did not have any plans to conduct a more thorough search for similar handwriting among the Mar Saba manuscripts that had been transferred to the Patriarchal Library in Jerusalem: he preferred to "leave that job to someone more skilled in modern Greek palaeography."[7] Despite this series of negative replies to Quesnell's questions, Smith remained cordial throughout the letter, presumably because Quesnell's letter gave him no reason to suspect that his correspondent might have been acting in bad faith.

There does not appear to have been any further exchange of letters between the two. The next time that Smith would hear from Quesnell, it would not be in a personal letter but in print, in a 1975 article for the prestigious academic journal *Catholic Biblical Quarterly*. The somewhat benign title of Quesnell's article, "The Mar

Saba Clementine: A Question of Evidence," concealed just how explosive its contents were: Quesnell alleged that Smith's discovery was in fact a twentieth-century forgery.

Quesnell's First Argument: Smith Failed to Document His Discovery Adequately

Quesnell makes two central arguments, the second building on the first. First, since Smith had the good fortune to make a discovery of potentially profound implications for the study of Christian origins, he also had a duty to ensure that the evidence for this discovery was kept safe and made readily available for other scholars to examine. In Quesnell's opinion, this was a duty that Smith neglected. Second, since Smith had failed to secure and document his find adequately, the possibility remains that the Mar Saba manuscript is a modern forgery. Quesnell speculated that it was most likely created by a scholar as an experiment to test whether specialists in the field of biblical studies would allow new data to change their preconceived notions about the early Jesus movement. Although Quesnell never explicitly calls Smith out as the probable forger and would later deny in his rejoinder to Smith that the intent of his article was to accuse him, Quesnell's profile of the forger is so specific that Smith is the only conceivable suspect. Let us begin with the evidence for Quesnell's first claim.

Quesnell grounds his critique of Smith's handling of the discovery by appealing to a work that he regards as something of a rulebook for detecting biblical forgeries: *Strange New Gospels*, published in 1931 by Edgar Goodspeed, a well-respected scholar who taught at the University of Chicago in the first half of the twentieth century. In it Goodspeed stresses that it is absolutely essential for scholars to be able to view the manuscript behind any sensational new textual discovery. Quesnell then claims that Smith has failed to fulfill Goodspeed's mandate. Yes, Smith did provide photographic evidence of his discovery, but Quesnell regards this evidence as inadequate in several respects: the photos should have been in color, not black and white; they were cropped carelessly in the Harvard monograph so that the edges of the pages are not visible; there are a number of discrepancies in lighting and texture between the photos of the first page of the manuscript in Smith's two books. Moreover, even if photographs might suffice when the actual manuscript is unavailable, Quesnell faults Smith for not arranging for his discovery to be corroborated "by the witness of some other competent observers who have checked them against the original and will verify them as true and satisfactory reproductions."[8]

In Quesnell's opinion, not only did Smith neglect his duty to document the manuscript by taking shoddy photographs, but he exercised poor judgment also by leaving the manuscript in a location where its safety and security could not be guaranteed, within the tower library at Mar Saba. Quesnell presents a number of alleged incidents, which he cites with page numbers from Smith's two books, that lead him to conclude that "the tower library is an insecure repository":[9] monks without scholarly expertise can enter the library simply by borrowing the key from their superior; books and manuscripts go missing from or are added to the collection without documentation; fires destroy parts of the collection; and older manuscripts are mutilated to strengthen the binding of timeworn books. Given such incidents, Quesnell argues that Smith should have at least informed the patriarchate of the text's importance. In his rejoinder to the response penned by Smith to his article a year later, Quesnell goes even farther in maligning the monastery's ability to safeguard its own cultural heritage. He likens Smith's discovery to a scholar going into the Judean desert, finding the Dead Sea Scrolls and taking pictures of them, and then leaving this historic find in the caves where he discovered it. Quesnell's implication, of course, is that leaving the manuscript in the care of the monastic community to whom it had belonged for centuries was the functional equivalent of abandoning it in the middle of nowhere.

Quesnell insists that his second argument, that the Mar Saba manuscript must be regarded as a potential forgery, can only be advanced once he has made a strong case for his first. It is, in his words, "the unavoidable next question." To his mind, "when adequate physical evidence for determining a document's age has not been provided, the scientific inquirer is forced to go on to ask about the possibilities of forgery."[10] Yet before we discuss Quesnell's arguments and suggested motives for forgery, let us pause to consider whether he has presented compelling evidence for his first set of claims. Namely, has Quesnell convincingly demonstrated that Smith failed to document his find according to the standards laid out by Goodspeed? And was Quesnell right to fault Smith for his decision to leave the manuscript in the "insecure repository" of Mar Saba's tower library?

Did Smith Fail to Document His Discovery?

We find Quesnell's claims about Smith's lack of documentation to be, for the most part, without merit. This critical assessment of Quesnell's arguments should not, however, be construed as a complete exoneration of Smith's handling of the Mar Saba manuscript, since Smith could have provided a more thorough account of his discovery. Still, most of Quesnell's criticisms are misleading or unrealistic.

Quesnell was correct to point out that the level of attention Smith gave to the physical characteristics of his specific find and its context among the other holdings in the tower library left something to be desired. For instance, Smith dedicates a scant three pages at the beginning of his Harvard study to a description of the handwriting style of the manuscript, and roughly the same amount of space near the end of the book on how his find fits into the history of manuscripts at the monastery. Doubling the length of these discussions would not have been difficult for Smith, particularly when one considers the number of paleographic experts in Late Greek hands that he consulted, as well as his familiarity with the scholarship on manuscript production at Mar Saba, much of which was published only in modern Greek. Moreover, it is difficult to understand why Smith did not also publish an English version of his Mar Saba manuscript catalogue, in which there would have been significant scholarly interest: after all, he did compose it in English before Archimandrite Michaelides of the Patriarchate of Jerusalem translated it into modern Greek.[11]

That said, there are several major flaws in the criticisms that Quesnell raises. First, Quesnell invoked Edgar Goodspeed's *Strange New Gospels* to fault Smith for not doing more to make his manuscript discovery accessible to scholars. But in appealing to Goodspeed's work as a "rulebook" for detecting biblical forgeries, he had to downplay two crucial facts: that Smith *did* take photographs of the manuscript, and that Goodspeed *did* recognize that good-quality photographs can and occasionally must suffice for manuscript discoveries where the original is difficult or impossible to consult.[12] Thus, given the fact that Smith documented his discovery with photographs, this is not the typical sort of instance on which Goodspeed's book focuses. In fact, Smith's discovery had virtually nothing in common with the examples discussed in *Strange New Gospels*.

Furthermore, Quesnell makes several attempts to cast aspersions on the photos taken by Smith; but the reality is that Smith's photos are quite good, especially considering the difficult lighting conditions one encounters in an ancient monastery, even after the introduction of electricity to Mar Saba. Contrary to Quesnell's assertion, photographing a manuscript in color is not unquestionably superior to black and white in every case; if one must choose between the two, black and white is arguably the safer option, since it will often make the ink more legible because of the contrast between light and dark. In addition, while it is true that the cropping of the photos in the Harvard volume was less than ideal, it hardly seems reasonable to fault Smith for the publisher's shortcomings.

In connection with these criticisms of Smith's photographs, it is important to mention that although Quesnell desired an analysis of the manuscript under microscope, one that might reveal potential evidence of forgery in the mechanics of the handwriting, he did not point out any places in the manuscript that he regarded as suspicious in this respect. Although we can only guess at why Quesnell did not allege signs of forgery in the handwriting, two possible (and not mutually exclusive) reasons might have been (1) that he simply did not see any clear indications of a "forger's tremor" (more about this in chapter 6) or other handwriting anomalies; or (2) that he did not expect to be able to find any evidence of forgery in the handwriting unless it were possible to view the manuscript under magnification. As we shall see, Quesnell eventually did have the opportunity to examine the manuscript in person and was actually the last person known to have seen it—though this information was almost unknown until quite recently. And, try as he might, Quesnell was forced to admit that his own autopsy of the manuscript failed to turn up any obvious signs of forgery.

Apart from this misrepresentation of Goodspeed's own position on the adequacy of photographic evidence, there is a far more egregious act of deception involved in the way Quesnell invokes *Strange New Gospels*. Quesnell describes Goodspeed's book only as a "classic work,"[13] and then plucks a series of quotations from it about the sorts of criteria required to detect a biblical forgery. This is, however, a rather narrow description of Goodspeed's project in this book. If one takes the time to read even just a few chapters from his study, it very quickly becomes clear that these "strange new gospels" bear little resemblance to the text discovered by Smith. Goodspeed's "gospels" include such writings as *The Life of Saint Issa*, published in 1894 by the Russian journalist Nicholas Notovich and claimed as evidence that Jesus traveled to India during his "lost years." Other such writings are a transcript of Jesus's trial and the deathbed confession of Pontius Pilate, both of which were also alleged to have come to light in the late nineteenth century. In short, Goodspeed's book focused on a group of writings where neither the physical manuscripts nor any photographic reproductions of the writings were known to exist, even after their "discoverers" were pressed to provide them. By appealing to the rules set forth by Goodspeed in *Strange New Gospels*, Quesnell therefore implicitly associates Smith's Mar Saba manuscript with the sorts of crude nineteenth-century biblical forgeries that would not have fooled *any* competent biblical scholar, Goodspeed or otherwise.

Quesnell's use of Goodspeed's *Strange New Gospels* to criticize Smith is therefore highly misleading. Other criticisms are problematic because they are not only misleading but also unrealistic, particularly his faulting of Smith for failing to perform an exhaustive range of tests on and studies of this manuscript and others during his time at Mar Saba. It was this list of desiderata Quesnell raised in his letter to Smith, to which Smith responded with explanations as to why the action in question would have been difficult or impossible to perform. Evidently Quesnell was either not satisfied with or not interested in Smith's explanations, since he raised them anew in his *Catholic Biblical Quarterly* article and omitted most of Smith's answers.[14]

In this long litany of "things a responsible scholar should have done," Quesnell ignores two crucial and intertwined extenuating circumstances: Smith's stated timeline for when he was able to transcribe and translate the Clement manuscript, and the capabilities (or lack thereof) of a desert monastery like Mar Saba to perform rigorous and specialized scientific tests on its manuscripts. Regarding Smith's timeline, he makes it clear in *Secret Gospel* that he only had enough time to read the first few lines of the manuscript while he was at Mar Saba, identifying the document as a letter of Clement of Alexandria to a certain Theodore concerning a dispute with the Carpocratians. As intriguing as this was, it would have been irresponsible of Smith to abandon his project of cataloguing the remaining manuscripts at Mar Saba, and not because of some abstract sense of duty to finish the task he had started. No, if Smith focused exclusively on the Clementine manuscript in his limited amount of time left in the tower library, he would run the risk of missing out on an even more spectacular discovery.

Moreover, even if Smith had been given permission to stay at Mar Saba indefinitely and had possessed the resources of time and money to be able to do so (which he did not), the monastery lacked the scientific equipment needed to conduct the tests and analyses that Quesnell faulted Smith for not performing. Nor would it have been an option to take the manuscript to Jerusalem for testing: Smith knew that the monks at Mar Saba were unlikely to permit their cultural heritage to be removed from the monastery, and making such a request might have potentially damaged his relationship with the patriarchate. To complicate matters further, Mar Saba and East Jerusalem were under Jordanian control in 1958, and any scientific testing would most likely have required bringing the manuscript into Israeli-controlled West Jerusalem. It would only be after Smith had crossed over into Israel, in West Jerusalem, that he was able to have his photographs of the Clementine manuscript and others from Mar Saba developed and printed so that he could then transcribe and translate the text in its entirety.

Thus, Smith did not in any clear sense "know what he had" until he had already departed from Mar Saba and the Jordanian-controlled West Bank. By then, the political realities combined with the availability of scientific equipment created a very real catch-22 whereby it was impossible to bring the science to the manuscript or the manuscript to the science. That situation had improved somewhat by the time Quesnell and Smith exchanged letters in 1973, since the Six-Day War in 1967 had redrawn Israel's borders to include Mar Saba and the rest of the West Bank. Smith therefore expressed to Quesnell some optimism that further scientific study was now possible: "Now that Israel has de facto control over the territory, the trained personnel and equipment could, I suppose, easily be got out to Mar Saba, even if the monks would not consent to have the MS removed."

Nevertheless, some of the scientific tests that Quesnell called for were still not easily performed in the mid-1970s. We know this because a group of scholars connected with Hebrew University in Jerusalem visited Mar Saba in 1976, found the Clement manuscript in the tower library where Smith had left it, and then relocated it to the Patriarchal Library in Jerusalem with the assistance of Archimandrite Meliton. Given the controversy over the authenticity of the manuscript that had been raised by Quesnell's article one year earlier, these scholars hoped that a scientific analysis of the ink used by the scribe could be performed. They learned that the only institution in Jerusalem with that capability was the police headquarters, and Archimandrite Meliton steadfastly refused to hand the manuscript over to the Israeli police.[15]

Did Quesnell Believe That Smith Forged the Manuscript?

We will turn momentarily to the specific pieces of evidence that suggested to Quesnell that the manuscript Smith discovered was a modern forgery. To make this discussion more efficient, however, we need to begin by addressing a question: Did Quesnell believe that Smith himself was the one who forged the manuscript? Quesnell seems to deny in his article that he is accusing Smith, but newly unearthed documents make it certain that he believed that Smith was the culprit.

In his reply to the article, Smith states, "Quesnell insinuates that I forged the MS."[16] Then, in the rejoinder that immediately follows, Quesnell begins by suggesting that Smith has seriously misunderstood the piece he wrote: "Dr. Smith feels the point of my article was to prove that he forged the Clement text. If that had been my point, I would have stated it clearly. He would not have had to compose his reply in terms like 'insinuates . . . suggests . . . insinuation . . . suspicion . . . etc.'"[17] Instead, Quesnell insists that his article was about a basic principle that had been "formerly taken for granted by scholars" like Goodspeed but dispensed with by Smith: "that a person who introduces an exciting new manuscript find to the world has the basic responsibility to make the manuscript available for scientific examination." The point of his article, according to Quesnell, was not to accuse Smith of forgery but instead "to challenge the violation of this principle by Dr. Smith."[18]

How can we be so certain that Quesnell believed Smith to be the forger, despite his apparent protestations against this accusation? In the first place, Quesnell repeatedly named Smith as the culprit in statements to a number of people throughout his lifetime. Two examples will suffice. First, as part of the research that Scott Brown did for his detailed study of the Secret Mark controversy that was published in 2005, Brown interviewed Quesnell in a series of letters. In the course of the interview, Brown pointedly asked Quesnell whether he thought that Smith forged the manuscript. Quesnell's reply: "Did I personally think Smith (in collaboration with 'the one who knows') had forged the document? Of course I did. But that was not the point of the article. Why did I not make it the point of the article? Because it was a conclusion based on negative evidence. All that followed from the evidence made available was that the document could have been produced anywhere between 1936 and 1958."[19] In this letter to Brown, then, Quesnell continues to insist that accusing Smith of forgery was not the point of his article, since he could demonstrate only that the manuscript was likely created during a twenty-two-year period between 1936 (the reason for this specific year will be explained below) and Smith's visit to Mar Saba in 1958. Regardless of how convincing one finds Quesnell's argument, in this exchange he declares plainly his fundamental conviction that Smith fabricated the Mar Saba manuscript.

Alongside this evidence from written correspondence, we also have the recollections of Tom Derr, one of Quesnell's last surviving colleagues from Smith College, about conversations where

Quesnell laid bare his conviction that the manuscript was a forgery. Derr stated in no uncertain terms, "As for Morton Smith, Quentin was caustic in private and was convinced the Secret Gospel 'does not exist,' i.e. is a fake."[20] He also shared with us what he remembered of Quesnell's suspicions about why Smith would create such a forgery; these hypothesized motives, as we will see shortly, were far more malevolent than the ones that Quesnell suggested in print.

In addition to these written and oral exchanges with colleagues that reveal Quesnell's deeply held belief that Smith forged the manuscript, there is new evidence that is even more damning. Recall that Quesnell sent Smith a letter with a series of questions about Smith's interactions with the manuscript and his communications with the patriarchate regarding the importance of his discovery. This series of questions seems, on the surface, to be a straightforward and earnest attempt to learn more about the circumstances surrounding Smith's remarkable find. Yet it turns out that this letter that Quesnell sent Smith was a second, thoroughly revised draft; the first draft of the letter, found among Quesnell's papers in the special collections of Smith College, is significantly longer and contains allegations that he excised from the second draft.

What Quesnell removed from the second draft was a lengthy section where he laid all his cards on the table and presented—to the alleged forger himself—his working hypothesis that Smith forged the manuscript. In the revised version that he sent Smith, he concludes his series of questions, and the letter as a whole, with the following two sentences: "I realize I am in the area of what you call 'foreseeable stupidities' (287), but I have to take that risk. As a bit of a peace-offering, I'm enclosing a list of typographical errors I've run into so far, in case you may have missed any of them." As it reads here, it appears that what Quesnell calls "foreseeable stupidities"[21] are the questions he posed to Smith, perhaps especially the seventh and final question where he raises the possibility that examining the manuscript under a microscope might reveal evidence of forgery in the handwriting.

However, in the initial draft between these two sentences, Quesnell included several paragraphs laying out his suspicion that Smith forged the manuscript. Producing a full transcription of Quesnell's three-page draft presents difficulties. His handwritten annotations are often challenging to decipher; but the more significant problem is that one cannot simply combine the typescript and the handwritten annotations to produce one single version of Quesnell's first draft of his letter. Instead, Quesnell created several possible phrasings for key sections of this draft by hand and by typing, crossing out and moving around phrases as he decided how best to present his thesis. This reveals, among other things, how calculated and deliberate Quesnell was in his initial, but abandoned, attempt to broach the question of forgery with Smith. The quotation from Quesnell's first draft that follows, then, is not a straightforward transcription but rather our own combination of several potential renderings of this drafted material. In our combination, we have attempted to convey the central ideas put forth by Quesnell here in what we consider to be the most lucid prose.

Here then is an approximation of what Quesnell apparently wrote to Smith initially, but ended up deleting:

> I realize that I am in the area of "foreseeable stupidities" (287), but I have to risk it. To me there would be nothing implausible in a modern scholar's creating something like this letter and confronting the exegetical world with analysis of it such as yours, simply as a controlled experiment in exegetical and historical method and in the current state of the discipline. Of course he would have to have the intention of revealing what he had done after letting scholars kick the thing around for a couple of years. He would probably want at that point to be able to show that his original presentation of the material contained enough hints of a hoax that scholars should have been able to detect it on their own if only they read carefully enough.
>
> Now, having once conceived this possibility (originally on the grounds, I believe, of your two dedications), I seem to be running into such hints and indications everywhere. (If this is all just my imagination, you must by now either be angry or be laughing very hard.) Anyway, a problem results. If this hypothesis is correct, I have no right to expect you to reveal yourself by admitting it to me now. Nor, if my possible explanation is wrong, can I fairly ask you to save me

from myself by pointing out the obvious absurdities in the hypothesis.

If I broach the possibility in public (I haven't yet), I have to be willing to take the consequences, including the probability of a devastating Smith counterattack.

So, if I can't reasonably expect you to comment either way, why am I telling you this? I suppose just because it is the truth about where my analysis is at the present moment. And because it explains why I am so interested in the prior questions raised in the body of my letter.

As a peace offering . . . [Here follows Quesnell's list of errata from Smith's book.]

Two intertwined features of this remarkable palimpsest are immediately noticeable. First, we see that the forgery hypothesis that Quesnell would later advance in his article for *Catholic Biblical Quarterly* is already present and fully formed in the first draft of his letter to Smith, even before he received answers from Smith to the series of questions he posed. Second, there is a deep hesitation that Quesnell appears to have about sharing his forgery hypothesis with Smith, which recurs throughout the draft. His reticence seems to have less to do with fear about how Smith will react to his idea (though he does mention "the probability of a devastating Smith counterattack") and more to do with the risk that his idea is completely wrong. Quesnell even raises the possibility that his imagination may simply have gotten the best of him, and that he has erroneously read into Smith's analysis of the manuscript a whole host of clues and hints that were not actually there. He also expresses concern that Smith might not yet be ready to reveal his "controlled experiment" and instead prefers to let "scholars kick the thing around for a couple of years," which would leave Quesnell with no confirmation about whether his theory is correct. Despite these reservations, Quesnell chooses to confide in Smith, not knowing what else to do.

Yet Quesnell never sends this first draft to Smith. He instead mails him a thoroughly sanitized version that contains only the series of questions and says almost nothing about the forgery hypothesis that he has already developed, save his final question about examining the handwriting under a microscope and the quotation of the phrase "foreseeable stupidities" that Smith used to refer to any forthcoming allegations that the document was forged. Given Quesnell's trepidation about his bold theory, one can understand why he ultimately chose not to share it with Smith. Why then did he take the far more consequential step of publishing it in a leading biblical studies journal? We suspect that Quesnell was not as unsure of his theory's correctness as he let on in the first version of his letter. At any rate, in the version of the letter that he did send, he was not inquiring about the circumstances of the manuscript's discovery simply to satisfy his own curiosity. The available evidence makes clear that Quesnell had already made up his mind and had worked out his forgery hypothesis—or at least one version of it—in some detail.

Once more, the interviews Brown conducted with Quesnell prove valuable here. Thanks to these interviews, we know that just before Quesnell wrote Smith, he had completed a review of Smith's *Secret Gospel* for the *National Catholic Reporter* (more about this brief but curious review shortly). Reviewing the book had raised many questions about the veracity of Smith's discovery, as well as one obvious answer, which Quesnell shared with Brown: "Everything seemed so familiar. All the characteristics of a hoax were present; all the classic mistakes that popular summaries like Goodspeed's warn against were being made. I listed them and drew the scientific conclusion that had to be drawn—until further and better evidence appears, this has to be judged a forgery."[22] Since Quesnell had already arrived at this conclusion prior to writing Smith, what we seem to be witnessing in the multiple drafts of his letter to Smith and even in the published article itself is Quesnell's deliberation between several distinct strategies in his quest to reveal—or, better, to persuade Smith himself to reveal—the Secret Gospel as a forgery.

Quesnell attempted to bait Smith in various ways to come clean about the truth of the Mar Saba manuscript. In the first draft of his letter, he wore his heart on his sleeve: presenting himself as having stumbled on a shocking insight about Smith's manuscript, and wondering out loud to Smith whether he was about to make a terrible mistake for his career and reputation by alleging the discovery to be a forgery. Yet Quesnell eventually decided against this option. Possibly he felt it was too risky to share so much of his theory with Smith, despite his hope that the pathos he deployed in this letter might have moved Smith to confess. In the second draft of his letter, Quesnell took a far more conservative approach, choosing only to ask Smith a series of questions about his examinations of the manuscript and interactions with the patriarchate. As we noted, these seven questions culminated in a final query about using a microscope to detect signs of forgery in the handwriting. Quesnell thus raised the specter of forgery near the end of the letter, and then followed it up in the very next sentence with a quote from deep in Smith's book about "foreseeable stupidities," which Smith would immediately recognize as coming from his preemptive attack against those who might suspect the manuscript to be a modern forgery.

So Quesnell sent this version of the letter, perhaps hoping that his series of questions and the subtle hints about forgery might be enough to procure from Smith a confession. Unfortunately for him, Smith did not take the bait: he responded to Quesnell's questions directly and briefly, focusing on the infeasibility of the scientific tests his correspondent desired. Quesnell may have decided in retrospect that this approach was too conservative, since he had not laid out enough of the evidence and motive for the forgery that he sought to uncover. He would have to be bolder in his next move, though deciding on the most effective course of action would be difficult. Presenting his hypothesis directly to Smith in another letter would presumably have little chance of success, since Smith in his reply did not seem at all inclined to give serious considerations to the possibility of the manuscript being a modern forgery. He could go the route of publication and hope that calling attention to those elements of Smith's discovery that he regarded as suspicious in a high-profile venue might impel Smith to confess his forgery. But Quesnell would have to be careful, since directly accusing Smith in print of forgery could have adverse consequences, especially if Smith continued to refuse to admit what he had done.

The best option, Quesnell apparently decided, would be to make his case for forgery in print, but only to go as far as faulting Smith for not providing adequate evidence for the veracity of his discovery. To be sure, most of the failures of which Quesnell would accuse Smith were unrealistic in light of the constraints that Smith was working under when he made his discovery. But Quesnell's goal in raising them was presumably not to advance legitimate criticisms; instead, he hoped to sow enough doubt about the security of Mar Saba as a repository for manuscripts and about the thoroughness of Smith's documentation of his find to open the door to the possibility that the manuscript was a modern forgery.

As we saw in the unsent fragment from the first draft of Quesnell's letter to Smith, when he laid out his forgery hypothesis and the motives that he theorized for the forger, he very rarely addressed Smith-as-forger in the second person, preferring instead to speak even there of the theoretical forger in the third person. This (deliberate?) rhetoric carried through from Quesnell's first draft all the way to his published article. So it may be that Quesnell considered it more likely that Smith would confess if the profile of the forger was presented in hypothetical terms. We might speculate that Quesnell hoped that Smith would begin his response to the article something like this: "Quesnell has correctly pointed out a number of puzzling features in my publications discussing my discovery at Mar Saba. In doing so, he has proven himself to be more adept than many of his more famous colleagues, who were not nearly cautious enough about the manuscript of Clement and the Secret Gospel. Now that the game is up, it is incumbent upon me to reveal that I, Robert Morton Smith, am the true author of this document."

If this was what Quesnell waited expectantly for, he must have been sorely disappointed when he received Smith's reply: the sort of "devastating Smith counterattack" that Quesnell had worried might come in response to the first draft of his letter. It must have been now painfully clear to him that Smith was never going to admit to his forgery. To make matters worse, even if Quesnell had not directly accused Smith of forgery, most of his colleagues had little doubt about the subtext of Quesnell's article. Those in Smith's corner were predictably indignant about Quesnell's insinuation. There were, of course, many other scholars who disliked Smith and were pleased that someone had at least attempted to embarrass him. But there was no rush to get on Quesnell's forgery bandwagon; a few scholars would cite his article favorably,[23] but no more than that. In fact, it would be another fifteen years before anyone else would argue publicly that Smith had forged the manuscript. Quesnell remained largely a voice crying in the wilderness.

Quesnell's Second Argument: Indications of Forgery

Now we come to the second argument raised by Quesnell in his article. This argument is two-pronged, consisting of suspicious features that might indicate forgery and an inventorying of what a modern forger would have needed in order to pull off such a deception. As for what specifically Quesnell considers suspicious, he points to some features of the manuscript and the text it contained, and also to some remarks from Smith's writings—though he is careful not to make his accusation of Smith too explicit. He may have thought that the choice of the book into which the manuscript was copied was an intentional clue that it was a forgery, though his comments about Isaac Voss's volume are so brief that it is difficult to be certain. Recall that the book was Isaac Voss's edition of the letters of the second-century Christian writer Ignatius of Antioch, and Voss's study was of great significance because he was the first to recognize that some of the letters attributed to Ignatius were actually medieval forgeries.[24]

Quesnell also regards the production of a forgery such as this not to be exceptionally difficult to engineer. Yes, the handwriting used in the manuscript seemed to be a cursive Greek hand of the eighteenth century, but Quesnell surmises that with a sufficient degree of practice it could be imitated. This would be even easier if the forger were working with an accomplice, particularly a native Greek speaker.[25] Recall that Quesnell also suspected evidence of forgery could be observed using a microscope to look for indications like a "forger's tremor," though in his initial article he himself does not claim to have examined Smith's photographs under magnification. He also complains about, but does not enumerate, some differences between the photos of the manuscript found in the two volumes. Overall, however, Quesnell does not base much of his case for forgery on the physical characteristics of the manuscript.

Quesnell does address a few features of the text itself that he believes heighten the likelihood that it is a forgery. As with his assessment of the manuscript, Quesnell does not appeal to evidence from the text itself in his case for forgery as extensively as we might expect. The main point he raises about the text contained in the manuscript is that it would be difficult to create a forged letter from a gifted ancient rhetorician such as Clement of Alexandria, but that

the challenge became a great deal easier after 1936. This was because that year Otto Stählin had completed his fourth and final volume of Clement's writings, which included a tool known as a concordance: a list of all Greek terms Clement used, how frequently he
used them, and references to passages where they appear. Therefore,
Quesnell concludes in his article that the manuscript must have
been forged sometime between 1936 and 1958, between the publication of Stählin's concordance and Smith's visit to Mar Saba.[26] Let
us simply note here that this drastically narrows down the number
of possible suspects for the forgery, especially since the forger would
presumably have to know the manuscript would soon be discovered
by a prominent biblical scholar, despite depositing it in a remote
monastery with limited visitors.

Quesnell more than makes up for the lack of evidence for forgery within the manuscript itself and the text contained therein with
evidence he gleans from Smith's published works about the discovery. That Smith's own words constitute the largest repository of
Quesnell's evidence for forgery is striking, given the fact that he
refrains from accusing Smith directly. This is best understood as yet
another indication—on top of those we have already examined—
that, despite protestations to the contrary, Quesnell had no doubt
that Smith was the culprit.

Perhaps chief among this evidence is Smith's dedication of the
Harvard volume to Arthur Darby Nock, since Quesnell refers to it
in the first draft of his letter to Smith as the clue that initially spurred
his investigation. The significance of this dedication, Quesnell believed, can only be appreciated when one also takes into account
Smith's mysterious dedication in *Secret Gospel*, combined with Nock's
own assessment of the authenticity of the document Smith discovered. The dedication in *Secret Gospel* reads, quite cryptically and all
in capitals, "FOR THE ONE WHO KNOWS." Such a dedication,
naturally, prompts a reader to ask: Who is this one, and what does he
or she know? (We ourselves have a hunch, which we will present in
chapter 5.) Quesnell suggests that it is connected to Nock, because
the other book is dedicated to him,[27] and he also makes much of the
fact that Nock was one of the few scholars who were not convinced
that Clement authored the letter. In fact, Quesnell uses a statement
Nock made in one of the last letters he sent Smith before his death,

that a writer after Clement's time produced the text as "mystification for the sake of mystification," as his own starting point for a profile of the hypothetical forger.[28]

Quesnell singles out other instances of Smith's prose that he finds suspicious. Two examples will suffice. In a passage near the beginning of his article, Quesnell subjects Smith's statements about the location of the manuscript to thorough, perhaps excessive, parsing: "Smith describes his 1958 visit to the monastery of Mar Saba and states that the Clement letter was 'among the items examined' during that visit (CA, p. ix). The presumption of course is that what he describes is still there in the tiny library in the old tower. But Smith does not exactly say so. Nor does he state whether or how access to the manuscript is possible for 'other investigators who may be interested to verify [his] discovery.'"[29] Here Quesnell asserts that Smith has been deliberately vague in his wording about where the manuscript came from and its current location, such that readers might incorrectly assume that Smith discovered the manuscript in the tower library at Mar Saba and left it there, when in fact, Quesnell implies, Smith actually planted it there. But that is the most straightforward and obvious interpretation of Smith's quite ordinary remarks; to read what he says as concealing some sort of nefarious purpose requires an extraordinary leap of logic.

A second example of Quesnell's hunt for suspicious details hidden within Smith's prose is when he calls attention to a passage from *Secret Gospel* in which Smith describes the reactions of two leading scholars upon learning about his discovery. Quesnell characterizes this as an instance when "Smith tells a story on himself";[30] that is to say, Smith casts suspicion on himself (intentionally?) by telling it. In this passage, Smith relates the differing reactions of Erwin Goodenough and Arthur Darby Nock when he presented them with photographs of the manuscript for the first time. Both scholars, Smith observes, were able to make the data from Clement's letter fit into their preconceived understandings of how Christianity developed. Smith used this as a textbook example of the inability of even the greatest thinkers to interpret new data *as it really is*, instead of forcing it to fit within their preexisting paradigms.

Smith's purpose in relating this anecdote—and here Quesnell is good enough to quote Smith at length so that readers can see his point for themselves—is to express hesitation about whether he himself can get at the true significance and meaning of Clement's letter any better than these brilliant minds could: "If scholars of the caliber of Goodenough and Nock could react in this way, how far can I trust myself? Not far, I fear, but at least I'm aware of the problem. That is why I look forward to the scholarly discussion that will follow the publication of the text."[31] It is one of many instances in *Secret Gospel* of the remarkable transparency that Smith displays to his readers about his own perceived limitations and doubts. Such candor is unusual for any book written by a biblical scholar for a general audience, and it is all the more striking when we consider that Smith was otherwise known to be confident, even stubborn in his beliefs.

What Did Quesnell Think Smith's Motive for Forgery Was?

For Quesnell, however, this was a slip by Smith, a place where he revealed too much about what he was up to with his discovery. Taking this instance of Smith "telling on himself" as a clue, Quesnell suggests that the forgery may have been created by a scholar who was "fascinated with the question of how scholarly conclusions relate to evidence" and "found himself moved to concoct some 'evidence' in order to set up a controlled experiment."[32] In other words, Quesnell hypothesizes in his article that the letter of Clement was created by a biblical scholar to test how other biblical scholars would react to a sensational new discovery, and how they would allow (or, presumably, not allow) this new discovery to impact their overall understanding of the development of early Christianity. According to Quesnell, "many others besides Smith" must have shared his lifelong interest in how scholars force new data to fit into their preconceived notions. Recall that this idea of a "controlled experiment" was also present in the first draft of the letter that Quesnell never sent Smith.

Quesnell's proposal that Smith created the letter of Clement as a thought experiment to test scholars is certainly imaginative, but it stands in sharp contrast to the kinds of motives that later scholars would allege. As we shall see, later writers often focus on the homoerotic overtones of the Secret Gospel fragment, using this aspect of the text to suggest that Smith forged it to justify his identity as a gay man, or to outrage conservative scholars, or both. In comparison, Quesnell seems to show no interest at all in his article in the homoeroticism of the Secret Gospel and instead advances the far less salacious motive of "controlled experiment" for the forgery. But did the fact that this text appeared to depict Jesus and a young man as lovers really have absolutely nothing to do with Quesnell's suspicions that it was a forgery? Morton Smith, for one, did not buy it, and stated in his reply to Quesnell, "He challenges the text solely because of its content. The other texts from the library go unquestioned. But one should not suppose a text spurious simply because one dislikes what it says."[33] In his rejoinder, Quesnell denied that his theory of forgery was at all based on what the text said: "As for the content, I find it quite harmless and in no way implausible for the period in question."[34]

Despite Quesnell's protestations, it appears that the ostensible homoeroticism of the text was far more troubling to him than he admits in the article or his rejoinder. First of all, we have Tom Derr's recollections of his conversations with Quesnell about the motives that Smith may have had in creating this forgery. The motives about which Quesnell speculated with Derr are very different than the "controlled experiment" hypothesis that he presented in his *Catholic Biblical Quarterly* article: "I really don't think Quentin put much stock in the idea that Smith was just testing how far he could push deception, just to pull off a scholarly trick. At least Quentin never mentioned that to me. His comments to me about Smith's motives were along the line that Smith was trying to plant a critical seed that would seriously harm Christianity, and that the homoerotic hint would do the trick."[35]

Even more revealing of Quesnell's true concerns was his first publication on Morton Smith's discovery—which was not, in fact, the article for *Catholic Biblical Quarterly* in 1975. It was his short review of Smith's *Secret Gospel* for the November 30, 1973, issue of the *National Catholic Reporter*. Since the correspondence between Quesnell and Smith begins on November 6 and ends on November 21 of the same year, we may surmise that Quesnell's review of *Secret Gospel* was most likely written shortly before he began corresponding with Smith, or perhaps even during their correspondence.

In his *National Catholic Reporter* review, what Quesnell finds problematic about the text that Smith discovered has practically nothing in common with the issues of method and presentation of evidence that he dwells on in his *Catholic Biblical Quarterly* article. Quesnell appears particularly animated about the intimation of homosexual sex, and it is revealing to quote the first few sentences: "The young man who ran naked from Gethsemane (Mark 14, 51)— What was he doing there? Taking a midnight swim? Walking in his sleep? Was he a camper? A lover? An exhibitionist? Morton Smith suggests the youth might have been caught short at his own baptism. Perhaps Jesus practiced all-night initiation rites over naked young men, while the disciples stood guard against Peeping Toms."[36]

This little-known review from a Catholic newspaper may tell us what was truly of concern to Quentin Quesnell about Morton Smith's discovery. He accuses Smith of playing a game in which one finds a new or overlooked text and then crafts an interpretation of it "involving the greatest possible reconstruction of history, the more bizarre and scandalous the better."[37] And what could be more "bizarre and scandalous" than a text suggesting that the historical Jesus engaged in a homosexual act? If this reading of Quesnell's review is correct, then it may be that the motive he theorized for Smith's forgery of the manuscript—as a "controlled experiment" to test scholarly presuppositions—was not what he actually believed Smith was up to. The "controlled experiment" hypothesis, which Quesnell nearly presented to Smith himself in a letter, would then be simply a snare, a dignified motive that Quesnell invented solely for the purpose of getting Smith to admit his forgery—for which, Quesnell knew, Smith had more nefarious motives.

The Aftermath

In the next chapter, we will fast-forward to the early 2000s, when Quesnell's accusations of forgery started to gain more prominent and outspoken adherents. This is not to say, however, that nothing of importance took place in the Secret Gospel saga in the intervening period. On the contrary, several scholars around the same time as Quesnell developed intriguing hypotheses that the Mar

Saba Clementine was indeed a forgery—but an early modern one from the seventeenth or eighteenth century, not from the twentieth century nor from the hand of Morton Smith. There would also be accusations of forgery against Smith that emerged shortly after his death in 1991, raised by one of Smith's most famous and prolific protégés. Despite the significance of these developments, space does not permit a full discussion of them in our study. We will therefore briefly summarize the essentials here, though we will revisit one of the hypotheses of an early modern forgery in the next chapter.

Herbert Musurillo, professor of patristics and church history at Fordham University, was actually the first scholar to suggest in print that the manuscript was a forgery.[38] His article appeared in 1974, one year before Quesnell's, though his assessment of Smith's find was published in Fordham's relatively obscure (and now defunct) in-house periodical. For this reason, Musurillo's thoughts on the letter of Clement and the Secret Gospel of Mark have not received the attention they deserve. His skepticism about Clement's authorship is based on the fact that many figures throughout Christian history could have known Clement's style well enough to imitate him. Musurillo also notes that, from antiquity down to the present time, the genre of writing that has most frequently been used for forgeries of seminal figures is the letter. Though he does not rule out the possibility that the letter is an ancient forgery, he seems more taken with the idea that it was forged—though for uncertain purposes—by Voss himself or one of a number of gifted scholars active throughout Europe in the seventeenth and early eighteenth centuries.

In contrast, the arguments of Charles Murgia, a classicist at the University of California, Berkeley, have had a much more noticeable impact on the ongoing debate over the Secret Gospel, and we will discuss them further in the following chapter.[39] Murgia made his case for forgery at a 1975 colloquium on Smith's discovery organized by the Center for Hermeneutical Studies in Hellenistic and Modern Culture (which operated under the auspices of the Graduate Theological Union in Berkeley). His central argument was that many elements of the letter appear to function as a "seal" guaranteeing its authenticity—in other words, the letter is trying very hard to make readers believe that it is what it claims to be.

But the observation of Murgia that later proponents of the forgery hypothesis seized on was that the letter appeared to lack any serious copying errors. For Murgia, it was inconceivable that a second-century document could survive into the eighteenth century without some scribal mistakes creeping in. This led him to conclude that whoever copied the letter into the back of the Voss volume was also the one who composed it. Although this is obviously a valuable argument for those who believe Smith forged the manuscript, the minutes of the colloquium make it clear both that Murgia thought it was forged in the eighteenth century and that he regarded Smith's Greek as not nearly strong enough to create such a document. These points from the minutes tend not to be mentioned by proponents of the forgery hypothesis.[40]

Finally, a major turning point in the Secret Gospel saga occurred in the early 1990s. The first event was Smith's death in the summer of 1991. Up to this point, only Quesnell had been bold enough to suggest in print that Smith had forged the Mar Saba Clementine, and even he refrained from a direct accusation. But in 1994 a very influential scholar of religion confidently characterized Smith's discovery as "what must now be declared the forgery of the century."[41] He went on to lambaste Smith's publications on the Secret Gospel as a "disgrace," "slovenly," "grotesque," and "a personal vendetta of a lapsed clergyman."[42]

Smith's accuser was Jacob Neusner, an extremely prolific scholar of ancient Judaism who reportedly authored over eight hundred books during his lifetime. He was also a protégé of Smith's who wrote an endorsement for his mentor's *The Secret Gospel* and edited a four-volume collection of essays in honor of Smith's sixtieth birthday. Neusner's accusations of forgery appear not to have stemmed from any privileged knowledge or new findings, but rather from a very ugly falling out that teacher and disciple had in the late 1970s and early 1980s. In Smith's opinion, Neusner's scholarship had become so careless and error-laden that he had no choice but to disavow him. Smith did so on two very public occasions, including a panel honoring Neusner at the 1984 Society of Biblical Literature Annual Meeting, during which Smith distributed copies of an absolutely scathing review of Neusner's latest book by a recently deceased expert in rabbinic Judaism. It is difficult to excuse Smith's attempts to humiliate Neusner, which undoubtedly played a major role in Neusner's decision to turn against Smith after his death. Despite the fact that Neusner's accusations were not based on new evidence of forgery, the fact that such a prominent scholar had now voiced his suspicions about Smith's discovery almost certainly emboldened others to join the fray.

The Popularizer

I N 2003 BART EHRMAN WAS not the most well-known and bestselling biblical scholar of all time. Not yet. But he was not far off. By 2005 Ehrman's *Misquoting Jesus: The Story behind Who Changed the Bible and Why* would be on the *New York Times* bestsellers' list in nonfiction, and he would be making appearances on *The Daily Show* and *The Colbert Report*, venues typically reserved for well-known actors, musicians, and other celebrities. The rare heights of fame that Ehrman would attain, highly unusual for a religious studies professor, were still several years away. In the early 2000s, Ehrman was an increasingly prominent and occasionally provocative biblical scholar who was beginning to gain some traction outside the field, thanks to his New Testament textbook and a handful of other semipopular tomes that he published with Oxford University Press.

What did Ehrman write about that would eventually catch the attention of the general public? He was trained in New Testament textual criticism, a field that at the time had a reputation as a dusty and arcane corner of biblical studies. Such a negative reputation is surprising once one knows what the goal of textual criticism actually is: to determine the original, or at least the earliest recoverable, words of the New Testament. For example, when the author who we conventionally call "Mark" wrote the gospel bearing his name, what exactly did he write, word by word? How did he begin the story of Jesus? Where did he end the story? And how much of what "Mark" actually wrote did scribes change over the centuries? Is the version of Mark's Gospel that appears in translations of the New Testament today quite close to what its author wrote, or has it been tampered with so much over the centuries that it now differs drastically from what the original looked like?

With the promise of answers to questions like this, one may wonder why anyone would consider text criticism to be a dry endeavor. But until one has someone like Bart Ehrman to explain what textual criticism is and why it matters, there is a very steep learning curve even to read and understand academic writing in this subfield. In a few short paragraphs of a textual criticism article, one might well encounter enough cryptic symbols in close proximity to one another—perhaps $\mathfrak{P}$, $\aleph$, Θ, $\mathfrak{M}$, f^{13}—to wonder whether they are instead reading a paper on theoretical physics.

But if one can sidestep such necessary but imposing features of the discipline and focus on the big picture, New Testament textual criticism offers some stunning takeaways. First, even though thousands of New Testament manuscripts exist, only a precious handful of witnesses preserve what might be the original wording of the earliest Christian writings. Second, there is no one manuscript that always contains the most accurate readings; instead, scholars have to weigh carefully the wordings of a number of manuscripts to arrive at the most ancient form of the text. Third, scholars largely have to be content with recovering the earliest attainable form of the New Testament writings—that is, as they looked about one hundred years after they were first composed. This is because we do not have any autographs, only copies removed several times over from the originals, and we cannot be sure how much the Gospels and other writings were altered in the first century after they were written. Fourth, and perhaps most shocking, it was not only the "heretics" who corrupted the original versions of the New Testament writings, but also well-meaning "orthodox" scribes, those holding what eventually was regarded as the right kind of Christian beliefs. They would "correct" readings in manuscripts that they were sure must be mistakes, since these readings disagreed with what they believed about Jesus or God; but their corrections very often ended up corrupting what the writings originally said.

Ehrman had documented this phenomenon in his second scholarly book, appropriately titled *The Orthodox Corruption of Scripture*, which appeared in the mid-1990s and put him on the map as a fresh thinker in the field of New Testament textual criticism. But Ehrman had his sights set on a much broader audience, and he published the first edition of his widely used New Testament textbook in 1996 (the seventh edition was issued in 2019). *Misquoting Jesus* was the first book that Ehrman wrote for a major trade press: HarperCollins, descendent of Harper & Row, with whom Morton Smith himself published *The Secret Gospel* and then *Jesus the Magician*. After this impressive debut came his 2010 follow-up with Harper, *Jesus, Interrupted: Revealing the Hidden Contradictions in the Bible (And Why We Don't Know about Them)*.

With book titles that implied that Jesus had been "misquoted," or that the Bible had "hidden contradictions," and a life story that saw him transform from a fundamentalist Christian into a skeptic, Ehrman drew the ire of his former evangelical coreligionists—but garnered a huge following among liberal Christians and the non-religious. He also demonstrated a keen interest in apocryphal gospels, taking the unusual step of devoting a chapter to them in his introductory New Testament textbook. With this intellectual profile, one might expect Ehrman to have been of the same mind about the importance of the Secret Gospel of Mark as was Morton Smith or other prominent scholars influenced by Smith's work.

But if one pores over Ehrman's early publications seeking to discover his thoughts on the Secret Gospel, one will come away surprisingly empty-handed. Ehrman says nothing in his textbook about the writing discovered by Smith, despite its obvious shock value. Nor, in his works on textual criticism, does Ehrman show any interest in examining the possibility that the passages from the Secret Gospel mentioned in Clement's letter might have belonged to an early version of Mark's Gospel that was excised from the later, "official" version of Mark by prudish scribes—an especially salient case of the "orthodox corruption of scripture." Why, then, does Ehrman seem to write as if Secret Mark never existed—or as if it had been long ago dismissed as a forgery by overwhelming scholarly consensus? Ehrman would eventually break his silence on Morton Smith's Secret Gospel in 2003, and in so doing he would open the floodgates for a torrent of new allegations (along with quite a few reiterations of old ones) that the Mar Saba Clementine was a forgery and that Smith was the mastermind who created it. But first, it will be helpful to know more about Ehrman's formative influences as a scholar, since they may provide a partial explanation for the unexpectedly skeptical stance he takes toward Secret Mark.

Ehrman's Inheritance: Bruce Metzger's Reminiscences and the Secret Gospel

As noted, Ehrman grew up as an evangelical Christian, and his choices for college and graduate school reflect this orientation. He first attended Moody Bible Institute for a certificate program, then completed his undergraduate degree at Wheaton College (Illinois), and finally went to Princeton Theological Seminary for his master's and doctorate. To be sure, Princeton Theological Seminary is far less conservative than either Moody or Wheaton (it is affiliated with the Presbyterian Church [USA], a mainline Protestant denomination), but it has had a reputation going back to the late nineteenth century as a stronghold of opposition to more liberal and radical forms of theology. The scholar from whom Ehrman learned textual criticism at Princeton Theological Seminary, Bruce Metzger, was quite comfortable in this more conservative venue.[1] And, as we shall see, Metzger is known to have had long-standing doubts about the authenticity of Secret Mark, seemingly based in large part on the content of the writing. It is therefore reasonable to consider the possibility that Metzger's position on Secret Mark had a significant influence on Ehrman, even if Ehrman would eventually leave behind his evangelical past.

Metzger's discomfort with the content of the Secret Gospel is multiply attested. One piece of testimony comes from our personal communication with James Sanders, an emeritus professor who knew Morton Smith well—and who sadly passed away shortly after we corresponded with him. It was Sanders who moderated the 1960 SBL session in which Smith debuted the manuscript. In the 1960s and 1970s, Sanders also regularly attended the Columbia University Seminar on New Testament, which brought together scholars in proximity to New York City for the presentation of new research several times a year. Sanders vividly recalled the meeting of the seminar where Smith presented his preliminary research on the Clement manuscript from Mar Saba. His recollection is striking, not only for the way in which he remembers Smith framing his discovery, but also for his mention of one particular attendee of the seminar whom he implied was especially scandalized by Smith's interpretation:

> [Smith] had shared it with me in advance and delighted in noting that only a few members of the seminar could read it during the session. He told me later that he was tempted to ask the members to translate the text in seminary manner, his assuming they couldn't. Those of us who knew him personally were not at all surprised at the implication that Smith drew about the youth who fled naked being homosexual. One felt that the immediate response was that of Smith's being glad that Jesus too was gay, at least that seemed the implication of the presentation. You can imagine Bruce Metzger's utter silence through the whole session (Metzger, as you know, was a dedicated Presbyterian Elder and a regular member of the Seminar).[2]

Two aspects of this recollection are striking. First, Sanders is quite confident that Smith emphasized the homoerotic elements of the Secret Gospel, and this accords with statements by other scholars who attended presentations by Smith on his findings.[3] Smith rarely discusses in print the homoeroticism in the Secret Gospel, but he seems to have emphasized it much more frequently in his public presentations. Although it is difficult to know with certainty why there is this difference between Smith's oral and written presentations of his discovery, there are several possible explanations that are not mutually exclusive. On the one hand, it may have been that Smith regarded the implication that the historical Jesus had a homosexual encounter to have been the most important feature of the text by far, but was reticent to focus on this feature too much in his published writings—perhaps because of the general homophobic climate of the time. On the other hand, Smith was a provocateur who clearly enjoyed scandalizing conservative biblical scholars, and he may have preferred to emphasize the homoeroticism of the Secret Gospel particularly in his public presentations for the shock value, where he could see their visible discomfort.

The second striking feature of Sanders's recollection is that he singled out Bruce Metzger as the scholar particularly upset by Smith's insinuation that Jesus had a homosexual encounter. It was certainly not the case that Metzger was the only attendee of the seminar who was more traditional in his religious commitments, since rarely does a gathering of biblical scholars lack a sizeable contingent of religiously conservative men. Indeed, Smith's idea to ask participants to translate the letter on the spot was likely a dig directed at those more pious attendees, whom Smith regularly regarded as his intellectual inferiors. Nevertheless, for reasons that we now cannot know, Sanders chose to mention Metzger alone, presumably as a paradigmatic example of the sort of scholar that Smith took great pleasure in offending.

A second, very extensive collection of evidence for Metzger's negative assessment of Smith's discovery is his own words in his memoirs, *Reminiscences of an Octogenarian*. They occur in a chapter titled "Literary Forgeries," in which Metzger recounts a number of definite and possible forgeries that he studied or even had firsthand acquaintance with during his career. After he relates the circumstances of Smith's find at Mar Saba, Metzger summarizes the content of the Secret Gospel fragments—not by providing a full translation or a neutral paraphrase, but instead by salaciously recasting it: "Jesus was a magician who practiced a secret nocturnal initiation of individual disciples, involving baptism and an ecstatic experience of ascent into the heavens—the whole thing with homosexual overtones. This, according to Smith, was what was 'going on' at Gethsemane when Jesus was arrested."[4]

Now, in fairness to Metzger, this very provocative framing is not far removed from how Smith tends to use the Secret Gospel to reconstruct the historical Jesus and his ministry. The main difference is that Metzger explicitly characterizes the fragment from Secret Mark as homoerotic, whereas Smith almost always tends to be more circumspect about any sexual dimensions to the narrative in his published writings. It is significant, however, that Metzger presents Smith as claiming that Jesus was performing this erotic initiation ritual in Gethsemane the very night that he was arrested. While it is true that there are some instances in Smith's works where he seems to connect the Secret Gospel's narrative with this very specific time and place in Jesus's life, he also often treats it as a typical example of a baptismal ritual that he believes Jesus performed on numerous occasions throughout his career.[5]

Metzger may have in mind published discussions in Smith's writings when he characterizes the content of the Secret Gospel in this way, but we wish to propose a different source for this salacious framing: Smith himself, but in oral form, not written. Multiple independent sources indicate that Smith frequently included in his public presentations on the Secret Gospel a faux newspaper headline that described the incident in the following terms: "Cops Arrest Rabbi in Park with Naked Teenager."[6] The wording alone is quite sexually suggestive, but if we recall that Smith was making this quip in lectures in the 1960s and 1970s in New York City and elsewhere, it would certainly conjure up for those who heard it associations with incidents of gay men being arrested in public places for attempting to engage in clandestine sexual activity. Our guess is that this "headline" was part of Smith's presentation at the Columbia Seminar, and that his quip about Jesus being apprehended in the midst of an indecent public act shocked Metzger so much that he could still vividly reminisce about it in his eighties.

Metzger clearly found the homoerotic features of the Secret Gospel unsettling. His treatment of Smith's discovery in his memoirs also shows a strong inclination to regard the Mar Saba Clementine as a forgery. First, there is the general context in which Metzger discusses this document. As noted above, his comments on the Secret Gospel appear in the chapter of his book titled "Literary Forgeries." From this chapter title alone, readers would presumably expect to find few, if any, ancient texts written by their purported authors. In the first part of the chapter, Metzger discusses the earlier history of biblical forgeries, but just before he commences his discussion of the Secret Gospel, he includes the following transitional sentence: "In addition to my reading about literary forgeries produced in previous centuries, it has been my lot to be acquainted with several persons who either may have perpetrated a literary fabrication or were the victims of such a hoax."[7] After the section on the Secret Gospel, Metzger treats two other possible forgeries: the "Partridge Manuscript" and the "Amusing Agraphon." These two other manuscripts discussed by Metzger are both obvious forgeries: in the case of the former a professor fell victim to one, and in the case of the latter a professor produced one. By locating his discussion of the Secret Gospel alongside these two cases, Metzger makes it clear that he regards the Secret Gospel as a forgery, and that Smith either forged the manuscript or was duped by someone who did.

Metzger's treatment of the Secret Gospel spans only a few pages, and most of what he says is the sort of common knowledge one would find in any brief overview. There are, however, several instances in which Metzger reveals his strong preference for understanding the Secret Gospel as a modern forgery, even if he stops short of ever making the claim outright. First, there is an odd paragraph where Metzger's ostensible purpose is to describe how Smith went about attempting to authenticate the manuscript and its text after he discovered it; its strangeness lies in the fact that Metzger cannot even cover this basic information without interjecting statements of doubt, leading to a rather disjointed reading experience. He states in the opening sentence of the paragraph that Smith shared his Greek transcription of the letter of Clement with colleagues after he returned from overseas. Then, in a second sentence whose relationship to the first is not at all clear, Metzger declares, "I could never make up my mind whether the text was a forgery—ancient or modern."[8] Does Metzger interject this here because he was one of those with whom Smith shared his transcription? This seems unlikely, since there is no evidence of Smith having a close relationship with Metzger. The phrasing of Metzger's sentence is also ambiguous: Should it be taken to mean that he was certain that it was a forgery, but unsure whether it was an ancient or modern one? Or that he could never decide whether it was a forgery or an authentic text? Then the third sentence of the paragraph notes that Smith had shown his photographs of the manuscript to several paleographers, who had all agreed in dating the manuscript to sometime between the late seventeenth and early nineteenth century. Yet Metzger apparently cannot let this paleographic judgment stand uncontested:

he is compelled to mention at this point Charles Murgia's observation that the manuscript appears not to have suffered any major
scribal errors in its copying, a feature that Murgia believed might
reveal the manuscript as a forgery (though a forgery created in the
eighteenth or nineteenth century in Murgia's opinion, a key point
that Metzger fails to mention).

Several paragraphs later, Metzger provides the summary of the
text that we already noted for its salacious quality and speculated that
Metzger's main source for this summary might have been Smith's
own oral presentation of his discovery at the Columbia Seminar.
Then, immediately after presenting this summary, the next paragraph begins as follows: "The whole account does credit to Smith's
ability to enter into the spirit of the Carpocratians, who did indeed
make use of the Christian gospels in order to convey an impression
of libertinism of this kind."[9] Metzger's statement that Smith's work
embodies the mindset of the Carpocratian sect is yet another ambiguous sentence in his treatment of the Secret Gospel. It could be
taken to suggest that Smith has crafted the Secret Gospel in such
a way that an ancient libertine heresy might have done—in other
words, that Smith forged it. But then Metzger goes on in the rest of
the paragraph to point out parts of Smith's interpretation that strike
him as quite tendentious, such as Smith's belief that the tradition
contained in the Secret Gospel is very ancient or his willingness to
engage in conjectural emendation (that is, suggesting the original
text had a different reading when no evidence of this reading appears in manuscript copies) in order to make the text better fit his
theories. Perhaps Metzger's point in this paragraph is not to imply
that Smith forged the manuscript, but instead to claim that Smith
played fast and loose with the New Testament gospels with the same
sort of ideological bent that the Carpocratians did. Regardless of
what Metzger's aim is in this paragraph, a reader could easily come
away with the belief that Metzger was making a subtle accusation
of forgery.

Metzger then spends several paragraphs favorably mentioning the work of scholars who have raised questions about whether
the Secret Gospel is a forgery, such as Quentin Quesnell and Jacob
Neusner, before declaring, "This is not the place to debate further
the authenticity of the secret gospel."[10] But before he goes on to

treat the case of the Partridge Manuscript, an undeniable forgery, Metzger bemoans the lack of scientific testing on the Mar Saba manuscript and concludes that it is not at all surprising that "legitimate doubts continue to persist concerning the authenticity of the document edited by Smith."[11] Thus, while Metzger does not state unequivocally that he believes Smith forged the manuscript, the overriding tone of his discussion of the Secret Gospel leans heavily toward forgery.

What Ehrman Stepped Into

When Bart Ehrman, Metzger's most famous protégé, finally chose to enter into the Secret Gospel controversy in 2003, he did so at a time when several important new pieces of evidence were coming to light. First, three years earlier, Charles Hedrick had published a previously unknown set of photographs of the Mar Saba manuscript, photos not taken by Morton Smith. These had been given to him by Kallistos Dourvas, who was then head of the Greek Orthodox Patriarchal Library in Jerusalem, and unlike Smith's 1958 photos, these were in color. Not only were they taken after Smith's visit, and after the Voss volume and its inscribed pages had been transferred from Mar Saba to Jerusalem in 1976, but they also revealed that the manuscript material had been separated from the rest of the book in shockingly rough fashion—especially since Dourvas claimed that separating the pages with handwriting would allow the library to conserve them better. The circumstances under which these color photographs were taken were not specified to Hedrick (though they would eventually be disclosed in a rather stunning development in 2017), but the upshot of their publication was that they revealed that someone other than Morton Smith had also seen the manuscript.

The second key piece of evidence about the manuscript came to light during a cocktail party in the fall of 2002 that Ehrman himself attended, at the home of the eminent professor of ancient Christianity at Duke University, Elizabeth Clark. The guest of honor at this party was Guy Stroumsa, a professor at Hebrew University in Jerusalem who was visiting Duke because his daughter was beginning a doctorate in classics there. Ehrman was in the final stages of writing a pair of volumes for Oxford University Press that explored heretical forms of ancient Christianity and the scriptural texts that they produced—titled *Lost Christianities* and *Lost Scriptures*, respectively. Since Stroumsa had given a public lecture earlier that day on Clement of Alexandria and Ehrman had not met him previously, he mentioned to Stroumsa that he had just completed a draft of a chapter on the Secret Gospel of Mark for *Lost Christianities*. In a remarkable instance of one-upmanship, Stroumsa replied that he had actually seen the manuscript himself. In 1976, intrigued by the firestorm of controversy that had erupted around Smith's discovery and publications, Stroumsa and several other scholars from Jerusalem drove down to Mar Saba to see if the manuscript could indeed be located. They found it in the tower library on a shelf, right where Smith stated he had left it. Since they were accompanied by an official from the Greek Orthodox Patriarchate, they succeeded in having the manuscript transferred to Jerusalem for safekeeping—over the protestations of the head abbot of Mar Saba.

As Stroumsa unwound this astonishing story, Ehrman recalls, "I immediately stopped drinking and started listening."[12] It also happened that the host of the gathering, Elizabeth Clark, was one of the chief editors of the *Journal of Early Christian Studies* and had recently received a submission from Hedrick on the "stalemate" that had come to exist between the two camps of scholars who studied the Secret Gospel. Clark wisely recognized that this was an opportunity for the journal to showcase a major update on one of the most contentious of all ancient Christian writings with a trifecta of articles. It would begin with Hedrick's assessment of the lamentable impasse in the scholarly conversation about the Secret Gospel and his hope that new pieces of evidence, including his recently published color photographs of the manuscript and Stroumsa's account, would finally put an end to the accusations that Smith forged the text.[13] The second article would be Stroumsa's first-person description of his encounter with the manuscript; as Clark framed its significance in her editor's note at the beginning of the volume, "Guy Stroumsa revealed in conversation that he is one of the last living Western scholars to have seen the contested manuscript pages that Morton Smith made famous."[14] In his report Stroumsa would also announce the existence of a large collection of letters between Smith and Gershom

Scholem (from which we have quoted on several occasions) that Stroumsa considered to be valuable evidence that Smith's thinking about the Mar Saba Clementine continued to develop and change in the years after he discovered it.[15] Third and finally, Bart Ehrman would offer a response to the articles of Hedrick and Stroumsa that was informed by his recent research on the Secret Gospel for his *Lost Christianities* book.[16] Ehrman's arguments in the journal article and book chapter would prove to be his most substantial engagement with Morton Smith's discovery. They also, we believe, helped open the floodgates for a surge of publications by other scholars who claimed to have discovered compelling evidence that Morton Smith forged the Mar Saba manuscript.

In his journal article, Ehrman begins by characterizing the main thrust of Charles Hedrick's article in this way: "I take the burden of his discussion to be that . . . we should accept the Clementine letter as authentic and leave off discussing it as a possible (modern) forgery, for example, by Smith himself."[17] This certainly does appear to be the outcome favored by Hedrick, even if Hedrick does not ever say so in such explicit terms. But by accepting these as the only options in the debate, Ehrman regrettably missed a valuable opportunity to consider other possibilities for the origins of the Secret Gospel. Given how interested he had been and would continue to be in the problem of literary pseudepigraphy, it is strange that he did not even raise the question of whether the entire letter of Clement was yet another instance of a category of literature he knew very well: a pseudepigraphic (or "forged," Ehrman's preferred term) text composed in late antiquity and falsely attributed to a much more famous figure. Rather, as has almost always been the case in this scholarly debate, he could not get past the false choice of it being *either* an authentic letter of Clement of Alexandria *or* a twentieth-century forgery most likely created by its discoverer.

Hard Not to Find Amusing: Ehrman's Case for Forgery

Ehrman organizes most of his article around three sets of features of the text, the manuscript, and Smith's publications on it that he regards as suspicious. Although he emphatically asserts that he is not accusing Smith of forging the manuscript,[18] his designations for these categories leave little doubt as to where he stands regarding the authenticity of the document: "hard to understand," "hard to explain," and "hard not to find amusing" (an example of the catchy formulations that have contributed to Ehrman's success in reaching a general readership).[19] Although there is some overlap between these groupings, the first category, "hard to understand," refers to Smith's reaction to the forgery allegations. For Ehrman, it seems inconceivable that someone with Smith's expertise would have neglected to return to Mar Saba and perform additional tests on the manuscript—unless, as Ehrman's framing implies, he knew something about the manuscript that others did not. "But why," asks Ehrman, "would he spend fifteen years of his life reading and analyzing the words in the photographs knowing full well that the clues to forgery could not be found in the photographs but only in the physical specimen?"[20]

Was Ehrman correct in supposing that Smith's lack of interest in returning to Mar Saba was evidence of nefarious behavior? It is true that many scholars (including we ourselves) would want to examine a manuscript as significant and puzzling as this one on multiple occasions and with as many tools and resources as we might be permitted, especially if there were any reason to doubt its authenticity. While this is not what Smith did, we believe that his behavior is neither "hard to understand" nor in any way an indication of his guilt—provided that one knows enough about how Morton Smith interacted with scholars whom he regarded as his intellectual inferiors. It is exceptionally well documented in both his published and private writings that if Smith believed that a scholar disagreed with his arguments about the Secret Gospel (or anything else, for that matter) because of their own religious presuppositions, then he would not hesitate to attack not only their arguments but also them as human beings. This is, of course, what is known as *ad hominem* argumentation and the world would be a much nicer place if no one ever deployed rhetoric of this sort. But Smith did resort to it frequently; one might even say that he wielded this ugly rhetorical technique as elegantly as any scholar ever did.

Knowing that this was how Smith reacted to (most) scholars who argued against him is of immense importance for understanding why he never returned to Mar Saba to study the manuscript further or arranged for scientific testing of it. He found the suggestions that he had forged the manuscript to be absolutely preposterous, and worthy only of his ridicule and scorn, not of any serious consideration or engagement. For this reason, even if he did desire to return to Mar Saba and Jerusalem to hunt for additional evidence pertaining to the letter of Clement (and we have no evidence that he did), we believe that he would never have done so. In his mind, any further onsite research on this manuscript would imply that those who considered it possible that he had forged it were justified in their suspicions. This, for us, is why Smith appears to have had very little desire to "clear his name" from the allegations of forgery: in his way of thinking, the only people who would have seriously considered the Mar Saba Clementine to have been forged by him must be both stupid and pious. He had nothing but disdain for opponents of this sort, and if they imagined him to be so talented and dastardly to have produced a forgery this complex, so much the better.

Before going on to discuss the rest of Ehrman's suspicions, there are two points that we should make clear about the previous paragraph. First, we must stress that it is *Morton Smith* who would write off proponents of the forgery hypothesis as "stupid and pious." We ourselves, in contrast, absolutely reject this characterization: it is inaccurate, inflammatory, and does nothing to move the scholarly conversation about this text in a more productive direction. Nevertheless, we believe that Smith's unbridled contempt for those who suspected him to be capable of forging an eighteenth-century manuscript provides more than enough of a reason for him to refuse to participate in any further in-person research at Mar Saba or in Jerusalem.

Second, for the purposes of answering Ehrman's question about Smith's failure to do additional study of the manuscript, we have provided an explanation that we believe makes the most sense in terms of what is known about Smith's personality and temperament. An alternative explanation for Smith's lack of interest in further study would, of course, propose that Smith forged it and knew that additional testing would reveal his guilt. But this explanation requires compelling evidence in the manuscript and in the text itself that it was a twentieth-century forgery and that Smith was its creator.

The existence of such evidence has been mostly argued for by other scholars writing after Ehrman's contribution, so we will address it more thoroughly in the next chapter. As we shall see momentarily, however, it was Ehrman himself who opened the door to the use of this particular kind of evidence.

The second category of Ehrman's suspicions, "hard to explain," refers to three features of the letter of Clement and to the manuscript itself that he considers difficult to square with Smith's contention that he discovered an eighteenth-century copy of an authentic composition of Clement of Alexandria. Two of these are aspects of the letter's content that Ehrman believes raise significant doubts about whether Clement was really its author. First, Ehrman notes that several scholars have pointed out apparent discrepancies between Clement's teachings in the letter and in his undisputed works. These include the absence of any references by Clement outside the letter to the use of hidden, secret texts for the instruction of more advanced Christians, as well as the urging Clement gives in the letter for Theodore to deny the existence of the Secret Gospel under oath, since Clement elsewhere exhorts Christians never to lie.[21] Second, Ehrman calls attention to the finding in an earlier issue of the same journal showing that the letter has an odd propensity to use words that appear only once in Clement's other writings, while refraining from words found nowhere else in Clement's works. It is, in Ehrman's interpretation, "as if someone knew Clement's rare words (easily done since Stählin's 1936 list of Clementine vocabulary) and wanted to use a number of them to show the Clementine distinctive vocabulary (but overdoing it), while fearing to use words occurring nowhere else lest one suspect a non-Clementine style."[22] To be sure, these features do raise important questions about whether the *Letter to Theodore* was actually written by Clement. But all this means is that there is a strong possibility that the letter is a pseudepigraphic composition by someone who knew Clement's style well. Such a person could certainly have been active in late antiquity; yet Ehrman's first parenthetical remark reveals that Smith is still his prime suspect, since he implies that the forger would have used Stählin's 1936 concordance of Clement of Alexandria.

The third and final feature that Ehrman categorizes as "hard to explain" is Charles Murgia's observation that there appear to be virtually no serious copying errors in the Mar Saba Clementine manuscript, despite being a very late copy of an early Christian writing—a fact that led Murgia to conclude that the document was a forgery. We briefly mentioned Murgia's argument at the end of the previous chapter, and since Ehrman emphasizes its importance so strongly in his own case for forgery, we will address Murgia's observation about a lack of scribal errors here.

Ehrman is certainly correct that Murgia's case for forgery remained one of the most formidable counterarguments to Smith's position. Yet there are two problems with Ehrman's appeal to Murgia, though Ehrman can only fairly be faulted for the second one. The first of these is that Smith did offer a rejoinder to Murgia's argument about the absence of scribal errors with several counterpoints. Although Smith's rebuttals were cogent, he only made them in two writings that never saw the light of day: a private letter to the organizer of the colloquium at which Murgia presented,[23] and an article on the Secret Gospel for a reference series that Smith never completed.[24] Smith's counterarguments included noting a few places in the letter where he detected minor scribal corruptions, as well as pointing out that Greek prose works by Clement and other patristic Christian writers were much less susceptible to significant copying mistakes than the very difficult Latin poetic texts with which Murgia had expertise. That Smith only discussed the formidable arguments by Murgia about the lack of textual errors in the manuscript in private correspondence and unpublished writings is regrettable. Smith seems to have been so certain that the letter was an authentic composition of Clement of Alexandria that he did not consider the refutation of arguments that the manuscript was a much later forgery to be a high priority.[25]

While Ehrman cannot be blamed in any way for not including Smith's unpublished rejoinders to Murgia, his failure to mention Murgia's overall conclusion about the identity of the forgery is a serious and misleading omission. Although Murgia regarded the letter as a forgery, he believed that it originated in the seventeenth or eighteenth century; he adamantly rejected the hypothesis that Smith himself forged it, in part because he thought that Smith's Greek was not good enough to compose such sophisticated prose.[26] While it is true that Murgia's position that the letter was an early modern forgery remained somewhat ambiguous in his paper and became completely apparent only in the minutes of the 1975 colloquium discussion, a careful reading of the proceedings of the colloquium in its entirety makes Murgia's argument very clear. It is therefore curious that Ehrman flags Murgia's article as "much overlooked" in the debate over the authenticity of the Secret Gospel but shows no awareness of Murgia's broader conclusion, in which he exonerates Smith.

Following the Breadcrumbs

Ehrman's final category of features that he regards as problematic is termed "hard not to find amusing." These consist of elements of the text and Smith's publications on it that he finds so humorous that they must have a deeper, hidden meaning. In the first two categories, Ehrman was largely content to reiterate the arguments made by earlier scholars and signal his agreement with them. In contrast, although some of the "hard not to find amusing" material had already been pointed out by Quesnell, it is here that Ehrman finds several new indications that the Mar Saba Clementine is an elaborate practical joke.

The first case of something "hard not to find amusing" that Ehrman cites is the abrupt ending of the letter at what he regards as the most tantalizing point in Clement's disclosures to Theodore about the Secret Gospel: what this story about Jesus and the young man actually means. In Ehrman's words: "Anyone inclined toward thinking that the Clementine letter is a forgery has to appreciate how it ends. Just as the author has gotten rid of the nefarious views of those lascivious Carpocratians, he indicates that now finally he will provide 'the true explanation and that which accords with the true philosophy. . . .' And that's where the text breaks off."[27] On the one hand, Ehrman is correct that the text has broken off at a pivotal moment; it has probably reminded more than a few readers of the frequent practice of ending a riveting television show on a cliffhanger, making viewers wait until the next episode to see how it is resolved. Yet Ehrman's opening remark that this abrupt ending could be appreciated only by those who view the letter as a forgery implies that this feature must be a practical joke on the part of the text's creator.

There are, however, other plausible explanations for why the letter breaks off at this crucial point. Two analogous instances from other ancient texts will suffice. In some cases, a text really does break off at an inopportune time; consider, for example, this passage from the apocryphal Gospel of Philip: "[As for Mary] Magdalene, the [Savior loved her] more than [all] the disciples. [He would] kiss her on her [. . .] often."[28] We would very much like to know where on Mary Magdalene's body Jesus would kiss her, but the brittle piece of the papyrus containing the missing word has gone missing because of the ravages of time, or perhaps the appetite of a hungry book-worm. Of course, many texts in the Nag Hammadi codices are damaged in this way, whereas the manuscript from Mar Saba seems to present the letter of Clement as fully preserved with the exception of the ending. Nevertheless, there are numerous examples of ancient manuscripts where the ending or the beginning of a text has been lost: as anyone who has heavily used a spiral-bound notebook can attest, it is the first or last pages that are most likely to go missing.

Though it cannot be ruled out that the Mar Saba Clementine has lost its ending because its exemplar (that is, the earlier manuscript from which the eighteenth-century copy was made) had suffered damage, Ehrman is probably right that the letter of Clement breaks off where it does intentionally: that is, because whoever composed the letter chose to end it in this way, at precisely this point. But even in this case, one should not assume that the only reason an author might end a text so abruptly would be for the purpose of having a laugh at the reader's expense. One of the most famous abrupt endings in all of biblical literature is found in the Gospel of Mark: several of Jesus's female followers go to his tomb early on Sunday morning and find it empty, an angel tells them that Jesus has been raised and that they must proclaim this to the twelve disciples, but they flee from the tomb in terror and say nothing to anyone, the end (Mark 16:8). Although interpreters speculated for centuries that the original ending of Mark's Gospel had been lost or that the evangelist had died suddenly, most scholars now agree that this abrupt ending was in fact the conclusion to the gospel that its author intended to write (though explaining why would take us too far afield). Might the author of the letter of Clement have similarly chosen to end the work abruptly, but exactly where he or she decided it needed to end?

True, it is hard to imagine Clement of Alexandria himself intentionally breaking off in midsentence, but one could certainly conceive of numerous reasons that an ancient pseudepigraphic writer might have chosen to do so. Imagine, for example, if the social situation or controversy that gave rise to this pseudepigraphic letter was so closely tied to the content of the letter and the Secret Gospel that the relevance of it would have been immediately clear for the document's intended audience. In this case, its author might have considered it to have greater rhetorical force if "Clement" *did not* spell out the proper interpretation of the Secret Gospel.

The second instance that Ehrman regards as "hard not to find amusing" comes not from the text of the letter itself but rather from Smith's publications on it. If Ehrman did not directly implicate Smith in calling attention to the abrupt ending of the letter, he comes much closer to doing so by casting suspicion on the dedications of Smith's two books on the Secret Gospel. The dedication of Smith's Harvard monograph reads as follows: "This book was written for Arthur Darby Nock and is dedicated to his memory." Why did Smith dedicate this book to Nock? Two obvious answers are: Nock was Smith's most influential mentor and one of the very first scholars with whom he shared his discovery, and Nock's untimely death in 1963 at the age of sixty prevented him from seeing the fruits of Smith's labors on the letter of Clement and the Secret Gospel. Yet Ehrman is fixated, as was Quesnell, on the fact that Nock was one of a very small number of scholars who rejected Clementine authorship for the document Smith discovered: "Arthur Darby Nock, Smith's own teacher, never did accept the letter's authenticity, but came to think that it was a 'mystification for the sake of mystification'—that is, a forgery made by someone to see if he could get away with it. He stayed true to that view until the day he died."[29]

But this description of Nock's viewpoint misleadingly implies that he considered the text to be a very late, modern forgery, when Nock believed no such thing. In every instance where Smith quotes or paraphrases Nock's interpretation of the Mar Saba Clementine, it is quite clear that Nock's hunch was that the document was composed in the fourth or fifth century.[30] Nock's description of the text as "mystification for the sake of mystification"[31] has often been understood by advocates of the forgery hypothesis in the way that

Ehrman glosses it here: "a forgery made by someone to see if he could get away with it." But if one reads the broader context in which this quotation is embedded, Nock does not mean that the text is a practical joke or is meant to deceive others for substantial personal gain. He instead has in mind cases where ancient authors ascribed texts to famous individuals so they would have a venerable name attached to them. Nock cites as one example a magical incantation that an ancient Christian writer, Julius Africanus, claimed was originally included in Homer's *Odyssey* but fell out, though this claim is almost certainly false.[32] Whether or not Africanus was aware that he was perpetuating a falsehood, the fact is that it was not an elaborate attempt at deception but rather an embellishment with no sinister motive behind it. So Nock understands the (ancient) pseudepigraphic letter of Clement as a relatively benign ploy by an unknown author to attract greater interest in the text; he certainly did not see it as a "controlled experiment" conducted on modern biblical scholars by one of their own, or anything else nearly as elaborate.

Ehrman then juxtaposes the dedication in the Harvard volume to Arthur Darby Nock with the dedication from Smith's popular account of his discovery published with Harper & Row. The dedication in *The Secret Gospel* is much less straightforward by comparison: it reads, as we have noted, "FOR THE ONE WHO KNOWS." Quesnell had already latched onto this as a secret code that, if unraveled, would perhaps explain everything about the mysterious Mar Saba Clementine; he points it out at the very end of his 1975 article and poses two questions: "Who is 'the one who knows'? What does he know?"[33] Quesnell apparently thought that the pair of dedications had some sort of deep connection, though he does not disclose what the link might be. Other commentators have speculated that perhaps it meant that Nock was somehow complicit in the forgery, or at least aware of it.[34] Since Ehrman essentially reproduces this speculation by Quesnell in slightly different wording, we can only assume that he too believes that the two dedications are interrelated and have a hidden significance—despite including a caveat so as not to yoke himself too tightly to Quesnell: "Intriguing if nothing else."[35]

Ehrman may have found Quesnell's theory that Nock was involved "intriguing"; but to us it is implausible if not preposterous.

It is one thing to suspect that Morton Smith forged the Mar Saba Clementine, as incredibly difficult a task as this would have been for him working alone; but to imagine that Arthur Darby Nock conspired with him to do this sounds, well, like a conspiracy theory. In one case where a scholar attempted to publish a forged saying of Jesus, Nock (who was at the time the editor of *Harvard Theological Review*) was suspicious enough about the veracity of this article to contact Bruce Metzger and then to refuse to publish the article without compelling evidence that the manuscript containing this saying of Jesus actually existed.[36] We would then have to suppose that he was willing to *participate* in the creation of a forgery—or at least to keep silent about Smith's creation of it. And it will not do to say that he would only do such a thing for someone as close to him as Morton Smith. Although Smith had great respect for his mentor, there were also periods of acrimony between them, particularly in the years just before Smith's discovery when Nock was critical of some of the arguments Smith made in his abandoned book on the Gospel of Mark. Are we then to imagine that the letters from this period in the 1950s that reveal the tension between Nock and Smith over the latter's proposed research trajectory are an elaborate ruse to disguise their plot to forge a manuscript discovery?

Yes, it's true that the identity of "THE ONE WHO KNOWS" is not entirely certain. We have spoken to many of Smith's former colleagues and students, including the student who typed the manuscript of *The Secret Gospel* in its entirety from Smith's handwritten draft of the book: none of them have any certainty about who this mysterious dedicatee might be. To our mind, however, there is a likely candidate: Clement of Alexandria. "The one who knows" is an English translation of the Greek *ho gnōstikos* and can also be rendered "the gnostic." It just so happens that Smith's decision in 1973 to dedicate his Harper volume to "the one who knows" came on the heels of a review he'd written in 1970 of a book about Gnosticism, ambitiously titled *The Origins of Gnosticism*.[37] This volume grew out of a 1966 conference in Messina, a coastal town on the island of Sicily, where leading scholars attempted once and for all to define "Gnosticism," a squirrely notion that is notoriously difficult to pin down.[38] One of the shortcomings of the Messina definition, according to Smith, was the lack of attention paid to self-definition. Surely,

Smith reasoned, any definition of Gnosticism should start with a survey of those who in antiquity thought of themselves as gnostics.

Unfortunately, the committee did not take this route. In his review, Smith laments the fact that "not one of the writers who attempted to define 'gnosticism' ever thought of asking just which ancient groups did call themselves 'gnostics,' or just which were called so by their neighbors."[39] Smith then adds the following parenthetical remark: "Had these questions been asked, someone might have noticed that the most insistently self-styled 'gnostic' whose works have come down to us is Clement of Alexandria." Smith is correct: in their attempt to come up with a definition of Gnosticism, the committee had neglected to take seriously the evidence from Clement of Alexandria.[40] Among early Christians, no one claims to be a gnostic—"one who knows"—as frequently and with as much ardor as Clement of Alexandria. Smith would continue to insist that any definition of Gnosticism take seriously Clement's repeated claims to be "the one who knows," even as other scholars dismissed Clement's use of the self-designation "gnostic" as irrelevant or an attempt to co-opt the term from the *real* gnostics. When Smith revisited the issue in 1981 in a now famous article titled "The History of the Term Gnostikos" (a prime example of Smith's ability to level a field in a single pass), he repeatedly insists that scholars take seriously Clement of Alexandria's claims to be "the one who knows."[41]

Between the publication of these two articles that feature Clement of Alexandria—"the one who knows"—Smith published *The Secret Gospel*, which he wrote "FOR THE ONE WHO KNOWS," with the entire text of the dedication in capital letters. We suspect that Smith was probably emulating the ancient Greek practice of writing all letters as uncials, or capitals. So even if some find it intriguing to speculate that "the one who knows" is a cypher for A. D. Nock, who had known all along that Smith forged the Secret Gospel, and may even have had a hand in the ruse, we find it far more likely that Smith dedicated the book to Clement of Alexandria. We also suspect—and this point is pure speculation—that Smith would have found it endlessly amusing that readers could miss the obvious reference and would have found a perverse delight in watching them spin off into desperate flights of fancy in search of "the one who knows."

Ehrman's decision to co-sponsor Quesnell's speculation about the dedications of the two books having a hidden significance means that we have now entered into a group of arguments about Smith's forgery of the manuscript from Mar Saba that need to be recognized for their common set of characteristics. We have termed these "breadcrumbs": they consist primarily of alleged features, clues, codes, and so on that Morton Smith embedded in the manuscript he studied and others from Mar Saba, in the letter of Clement and the excerpts of the Secret Gospel, and in his own publications. All of them, individually but especially in the aggregate, are thought to point to Smith as the true author and creator of this forgery. Understanding this is of paramount importance: the most substantial arguments for forgery in the last two decades have relied very heavily on detecting such breadcrumbs to make their case. Biblical scholars now are more likely than not to believe that Morton Smith forged the Mar Saba Clementine because recent researchers have amassed a pile of what they argue are clues and hints that Smith himself concealed.

Despite the precariousness of this approach for demonstrating that the Mar Saba Clementine is a modern forgery, Ehrman nevertheless doubled down on it for the third and final of his "hard not to find amusing" observations. This was a new breadcrumb that had never been noticed prior to Ehrman, but his discovery of it may have prompted other scholars to look even harder for such hints. What Ehrman regarded as significant was the specific placement of the letter of Clement in Voss's edition of the letters of Ignatius of Antioch. Throughout the Middle Ages, discoveries of additional letters by Ignatius multiplied, such that this second-century church leader even apparently corresponded with the Virgin Mary. But Voss, in a crucial development, recognized that a sizable portion of the Ignatian letters were very late forgeries, and one of the central purposes of his 1646 volume was to publish an edition of only the authentic letters. Smith recognized that a manuscript copied into the endpages of a seventeenth-century printed book was not a common occurrence, but he took this as an indication that paper was in scarce supply at the monastery at this point in its history. In support of his argument, he was able to produce several other examples from Mar Saba of very ancient texts that survived only in late, repurposed materials. Therefore Smith did not regard the content of the Voss volume as determinative for where the letter of Clement was copied. Both the book and the manuscript dealt with epistolary texts written by early Christians, but this was at best a superficial similarity. The most important requirement that the Voss volume possessed was blank endpages.

Ehrman, in contrast, considers the Voss volume to be a conscious choice of enormous significance. Moreover, if one reads his discussion of this point in his popular book instead of in the academic article, Ehrman elaborates there in more detail about what he regards as suspicious. The first way in which the choice of Voss's edition is significant relates to the fact that he helped to distinguish the authentic letters of Ignatius from the spurious ones. "And what," asks Ehrman, "is the newly discovered text of Clement? A letter that describes forged documents and interpolations made into Mark's text by theologically motivated scribes. And it is a letter that itself may have been forged! Is this a craftily placed fingerprint or an intriguing coincidence?"[42] Ehrman here floats the possibility that the forger has deliberately planted a fabricated letter of Clement in a book whose author's primary contribution was to distinguish between authentic and forged letters of another early Christian.

Second, Ehrman sees an even more specific and insidious connection between the content of the final printed page in the Voss volume and the handwritten letter of Clement, which begins on the facing page. On this final page of his tome, Voss drew a comparison between the forgeries of Ignatius that he had identified and some additional, spurious passages that a scribe had copied into a manuscript of another very early Christian text, the Epistle of Barnabas. Voss concluded his discussion by shaming the scribe responsible for these embellishments: "That very impudent fellow filled more pages with these trifles."[43] What does any of this have to do with the presence of the letter of Clement, which begins on the very next page—and necessarily so, since it was the first of the blank endpages? Ehrman believes that the individual who copied the letter of Clement was fully cognizant of and delighted in the fact that Voss had just wagged his finger at naughty scribes who add forged material: "Was there an 'impudent fellow' involved in these interpolations as well, either in ancient or modern times?"[44]

Ehrman finds one further twist in the forger's use of the Voss edition. And since it pertains to Smith's choice of where to include (or not include) a photograph of the last printed page of the book and the first page of the manuscript of the letter of Clement, it is hard to see how Ehrman cannot intend to implicate Smith with this particular breadcrumb. Ehrman suggests that Smith has buried Voss's reference to that "impudent fellow" in a place where scholars would be less likely to find it—in the popular volume that Smith wrote: "Surprisingly, scholars have not taken any notice of what is on the facing page, the final printed page of Voss's volume. Possibly they haven't noticed because the facing page is not found in the photographs of Smith's scholarly edition, the one that scholars engage with, but only in the popular edition, where the intended readers obviously cannot make heads or tails of it, since it is a commentary written in Latin about texts written in Greek."[45]

For Ehrman, then, Smith would not only have selected the end of Voss's volume to copy his forged text into so that the "impudent fellow" Voss referred to would actually be Smith. He also would have managed to turn the disdain that some scholars have for their colleagues who "popularize" against them—by hiding a photograph of the relevant portion of Voss's text in his popular book. It is a remarkable, even ingenious hypothesis. It also is so intricate and relies so much on barely perceptible minutiae that we regard it as highly improbable.

What Ehrman Wrought

This third and final piece of "hard not to find amusing" material presented by Ehrman serves as an excellent segue to the two most recent scholars who have claimed that the Mar Saba Clementine was a forgery created by Morton Smith. For when we come, in the next chapter, to examine the arguments of Stephen Carlson and Peter Jeffery, this pile of breadcrumbs will multiply precipitously. It is possible, however, that the distinctive approach of Carlson and Jeffery would have emerged if Bart Ehrman had never chosen to weigh in on the authenticity of the Secret Gospel. After all, the notion that Smith's publications on his discovery were potentially filled with breadcrumbs goes back to the very first critic to suggest in print that the document was a forgery—Quentin Quesnell. Quesnell's hyper-suspicious interpretations of perfectly mundane remarks in Smith's writing, combined with his raising the question of whether the dedications of Smith's two books had some sort of hidden, interconnected meaning, showed well enough how willing he was to make his case—at least partially—through the discovery of breadcrumbs.

But even if this fascination with finding subtle evidence of Smith's forgery long predated Ehrman's involvement, his influence on the direction of subsequent scholarship on the Secret Gospel must not be underestimated. First, we have to take into account Ehrman's increasing visibility in the field in the early 2000s, a visibility that would mushroom into something approaching celebrity status (at least by the standards of religious studies professors) by 2005, when he published *Misquoting Jesus* with HarperCollins. If Ehrman was able to succeed in making New Testament textual criticism appealing to both scholars and laypeople alike, then what he said about one of the most controversial manuscript discoveries of the twentieth century was certainly going to make people pay attention.

Second, Ehrman not only considered it fair game to speculate about whether Morton Smith might have forged the Secret Gospel, but also legitimized a particular way of making the case that Smith did so. Prior to Ehrman, scholars who suspected forgery primarily stressed that Smith had not taken the necessary steps either to subject the manuscript to rigorous scientific testing or to ensure that other scholars could have unrestricted access to study the manuscript. The insinuation was that since Smith took the photographs himself, scholars could not be certain that the manuscript had ever been seen by anyone else, or even that it was really in the tower at Mar Saba and not tucked away in his cramped New York City apartment. But then Charles Hedrick succeeded in procuring more recent, color photographs of the manuscript from the Jerusalem Patriarchate's head librarian. And then Guy Stroumsa testified that he and a team of scholars had successfully located the manuscript in the tower library of Mar Saba and had it transferred to Jerusalem for safekeeping.

After these new facts had come to light, it became impossible to argue that Smith was the only person known to have actually seen the document in person. Scholars who continued to suspect Smith of forgery would instead need to focus on demonstrating this with other types of evidence. Thus, writing after Hedrick and Stroumsa (*literally* right after, in the pages of the *Journal of Early Christian Studies*), Ehrman chose to revive and galvanize a type of argument for forgery that was first used—but only sparingly—by Quesnell: the notion that Smith had embedded subtle clues in his publications on the Secret Gospel pointing toward his creation of this most impressive forgery. Ehrman took Quesnell's hermeneutic of hyper-suspicion and also applied it to the physical form of the manuscript itself with his remarks about the connection between the last page of Voss's edition and the handwritten letter of Clement.

As a final indication of how open Ehrman is to considering the possibility that Smith forged the manuscript, he closes his chapter in *Lost Christianities* by suggesting that we should perhaps even assume that the manuscript is a modern forgery until and unless it can be demonstrated otherwise; an exact mirror image of Hedrick's plea that scholars simply accept the text as an authentic letter of Clement, a plea that Ehrman rightly rejects. He first speculates in general about what a forger might have required to create this artifact and what might have been the motivations for doing so. Then Ehrman argues that Smith cannot be ruled out as a potential suspect, sounding rather like a prosecuting attorney making his closing argument to the jury: "But maybe Smith forged it. Few others in the late twentieth century had the skill to pull it off. Few others had enough disdain of other scholars to want to bamboozle them. Few others would have enjoyed so immensely the sheer pleasure of having pulled the wool over the eyes of so many 'experts,' demonstrating once and for all one's own superiority. Maybe Smith did it."[46]

CHAPTER SIX

The Conspiracy

O THERS WOULD COME AFTER Ehrman to continue this hunt for breadcrumbs, both in Smith's writings on the Secret Gospel and in the Mar Saba manuscript itself. It is high time we meet them, since they have had "the last word" on Morton Smith's discovery until now. Although a number of scholars have marshaled this type of evidence in the last two decades,[1] we will restrict our discussion to the two who have published book-length arguments in favor of the forgery hypothesis. Even then, we will not attempt to assess each and every breadcrumb that these two authors have presented, but will instead treat just those arguments that have been considered the most damning indications that Smith forged the text.

To be sure, our approach—covering only two of the most recent authors and addressing but a selection of the arguments they present—might be perceived by some observers as not engaging with the full body of evidence for Smith's guilt. Our response to this anticipated criticism is twofold. First, we can assure readers that we will hardly be cherry-picking the weakest or most inconsequential arguments, and will instead confront those pieces of evidence that the authors themselves and their supporters hold up as the ones most in need of explanation. Second and more importantly, it is our conviction that the category of "breadcrumbs" that these authors rely heavily on is so speculative, impressionistic, and subjective that it fails to offer a realistic explanation for how Smith forged the manuscript and embedded clues indicating his responsibility. If all or even most of the arguments of these authors were somehow proven to be correct, they would necessarily transform Morton Smith from a very gifted but also arrogant, stubborn, and cantankerous scholar into the sort of evil super-genius that exists only in fictional thrillers. Given these intrinsic qualities of the breadcrumbs that scholars present, there are good reasons to offer readers a sampling of the arguments that have been acknowledged as the strongest, rather than attempting to be comprehensive. We suspect that, by the end of our survey of this material, readers will have seen enough to make their own judgment about whether this line of argumentation is persuasive.

Although both of the authors we will examine are religious studies scholars, only one, Stephen Carlson, specializes in the field of early Christianity. Yet when Carlson published his 2005 book, *The Gospel Hoax: Morton Smith's Invention of Secret Mark*, he did not yet have any formal training in the academic study of religion. He was a lawyer at a firm in Virginia, specializing in patent law and having received his JD from George Mason School of Law (now known, since 2016, as the Antonin Scalia Law School, in memory of the late US Supreme Court justice). Soon after publishing *The Gospel Hoax*, Carlson began doctoral studies in early Christianity at Duke University, where his dissertation was co-chaired by Bart Ehrman (who teaches at nearby University of North Carolina, Chapel Hill). Carlson is now a senior research fellow at Australian Catholic University and has since published a number of well-regarded articles and two books on the New Testament and early Christian writings.

Despite the fact that Carlson wrote *Gospel Hoax* as an outsider to the field of biblical studies, his arguments for forgery have to be taken with the utmost seriousness for at least three reasons. First of all, he was already quite well informed about the academic study of early Christianity when he wrote his book despite not yet receiving formal training, and his subsequent academic career shows an impressive research dossier. Second, Carlson succeeded in demonstrating that a different biblical manuscript (unrelated to the Mar Saba manuscript) was a nineteenth-century forgery, despite previously being regarded as genuine by an array of adept scholars.[2] Since he also claims to have detected evidence of forgery in the handwriting of the manuscript that Smith discovered, his arguments cannot be dismissed out of hand. Third and finally, Carlson's book is still cited as the most compelling case for Morton Smith's forgery of the Mar Saba letter and thus remains highly influential, even if Carlson himself appears to have left his study of this text in the past.

The other book-length study of the Secret Gospel controversy that we will consider is Peter Jeffery's *The Secret Gospel of Mark Unveiled: Imagined Rituals of Sex, Death, and Madness in a Biblical Forgery*, published by Yale University Press in 2007. Jeffery's academic specialty is not biblical studies but the history of Christian liturgy—in which he is a highly accomplished scholar, having received a prestigious "Genius Grant" from the MacArthur Foundation in 1987. He received the MacArthur while at the University of Delaware and went on to positions at Princeton and Notre Dame. It was Jeffery's expertise in liturgical history that apparently first drew him to the Secret Gospel controversy: another prominent liturgical specialist, Thomas Talley, had argued in 1981 that the Secret Gospel might explain some peculiar features of the Christian period of Lent as it was practiced in Egypt.[3] It is important to note that although Carlson's book was published in 2005, two years before Jeffery's book appeared, Jeffery had already completed the manuscript of his book by the time he was able to read Carlson's. Therefore, these two books represent independent efforts to demonstrate that Morton Smith forged the Mar Saba manuscript.

Anomalies in the Handwriting of the Mar Saba Manuscript?

Let us examine Carlson's observations about the handwriting of the manuscript first. Strictly speaking, this would not be an example of a "breadcrumb," since we use this term to refer to the belief that Smith *intentionally* deposited a series of clues, jokes, and the like in the forged text and his writings on it to identify himself as the creator. In this case, what Carlson believes he saw in the handwriting characteristics of the manuscript were indications that someone was not writing naturally, which inadvertently exposed the fabricated nature of this writing. If you have ever been in the uncomfortable position of needing to write in someone else's style of handwriting (don't worry, you need not tell us why), then you know how difficult that task can be. The imitation of another's handwriting leads one, if not practiced at it, to retrace the letters in order to get the shape right; to lift the pen in the middle of writing to consult an example of the handwriting that is being imitated; to write with exaggerated flourishes in order to make it look effortless; or to produce tiny disturbances in the formation of letters as a byproduct of imitation, a phenomenon appropriately termed "forger's tremor."

It is precisely these types of features that Carlson believes appear in the Mar Saba manuscript. Relying on the photographs of the manuscript that Smith included in his Harvard volume, Carlson, in *The Gospel Hoax*, provides numerous examples of what might appear to be indications of unnatural handwriting behaviors with accompanying details from the photographs. In the debate over Morton Smith's enigmatic discovery, Carlson's careful attention to the characteristics of the handwriting in the manuscript seemed to mark a major new development. No previous scholars who had studied the Secret Gospel—whether they considered it authentic or a forgery—had examined the handwriting so closely; even Smith himself dedicated only a few pages out of more than 450 in his Harvard volume on the paleography of the manuscript. Quesnell had suspected that evidence of forgery might be present in the handwriting if the manuscript could be examined more closely, but even he did not provide any specific examples.[4]

After Carlson published his book, a majority of reviewers concluded that he had made a compelling case that the Mar Saba manuscript was a modern forgery. Although his thesis was based on a range of arguments, it was the focus on the handwriting anomalies that reviewers far and away considered to be the most persuasive.[5] The foreword to Carlson's book was written by Larry Hurtado, an accomplished textual critic with a deep knowledge of ancient manuscripts, who singled out this part of Carlson's approach as especially innovative: "His analysis of the properties of the handwriting of the text opens up a whole new line of discussion."[6] Despite this praise, some aspects of Carlson's analysis of the handwriting remained un-clear. Carlson stated that he had used Smith's photographs of the manuscript; but did he consult the original photos, or did he use only the reproductions from the Harvard volume—and did it matter which he used? Furthermore, what role did the more recent color photographs published by Hedrick play in Carlson's analysis? He refers to these photos at several points in his discussion, but all the details he includes come from Smith's black-and-white published photos.

While these questions about what type of representation of Smith's photographs Carlson was using may at first seem trifling, they in fact determine what Carlson saw in the handwriting—or, better, what he wished to see. For Carlson did not use Smith's actual photographs (which are housed with his papers in the archives of the Jewish Theological Seminary of America), nor the color pho-tographs procured by Hedrick, nor high-resolution digital scans (for instance, at 1200 dpi, or dots per inch) of either set of pho-tos. Instead, he relied on the reproductions of Smith's photographs from the Harvard volume, which were of far lower quality. Already in 2006 Scott Brown suspected that using these reproductions for forensic analysis might be problematic, though he admitted that his own level of familiarity with this field of study was quite rudimen-tary. Nevertheless, after examining studies of document analysis in such periodicals as *FBI Law Enforcement Bulletin*, Brown had serious doubts: "Carlson's decision to use the 100 dpi halftone reproduc-tions of the black-and-white photographs in Morton Smith's book . . . rather than high-resolution scans or prints made directly from the colour photographs makes no sense to me."[7]

Several years later, scholars with more expertise in the various methods of reproducing visual images would follow up on Brown's hunches and in the process deal a devastating blow to Carlson's as-sessment of the handwriting. Thanks to the fact that many of us carry around extremely powerful cameras built into our smartphones and like to share photos we have taken with friends and family, a sizeable percentage of readers will already know intuitively that a 1200 dpi image offers a far more detailed and accurate representation of an object than a 100 dpi image. But in their 2013 article "Distortion of the Scribal Hand in the Images of Clement's Letter to Theodore," the Scandinavian scholars Roger Viklund and Timo Paananen explain *why* this is the case.

Though their discussion is necessarily technical, the problem boils down to the fact that photographs are "continuous tone images" (composed of various shades of gray in the case of black-and-white photos) whose richness requires a special type of paper and equipment to be represented satisfactorily. But in books and other print media, "halftone images" are instead used to reproduce photographs: such images are made up of many tiny dots, of either a single color or a small group of colors.[8] Part of the issue involves economic considerations: as the number of dots per inch increases, the printed reproduction becomes a more accurate representation of the original photograph, but also becomes more expensive (whether measured in ink or bytes). Therefore, 100 dpi reproductions of black-and-white photographs—such as those taken by Smith at Mar Saba—might be a satisfactory and cost-effective tradeoff for a press: readers will be able to view an approximation of what the manuscript in question looks like, and the press will avoid making a book that already had significant production costs (due, in part, to typesetting the multiplicity of alphabets and languages used by Smith) even more expensive.

But the key word here is "approximation": when Carlson attempts to use these photographic reproductions under magnification to detect evidence of forgery in the handwriting characteristics, their relatively low resolution of 100 dpi becomes visually misleading. The halftone photographic reproductions that appear in books and other printed media rely on tricking one's eye into viewing a large swarm of dots as a coherent image. But under magnification the dots become more apparent, especially if the resolution is fairly low. As Viklund and Paananen note, this becomes especially problematic when one examines something as fluid and dynamic as human handwriting: "When these halftone images are magnified to the degree necessary for forensic document examination, lines that are not both perfectly straight and at an angle that accords with the screen (i.e. horizontally, vertically, or above all at 45 or 135 degrees) are not reproduced accurately."[9] The simple takeaway is that Carlson's alleged handwriting irregularities are an optical illusion created by the low-resolution halftone images he relied on, and they vanish when we compare photographic reproductions of the manuscript with a much higher resolution.[10]

If Carlson had detected actual evidence of handwriting anomalies in the Mar Saba manuscript, this would have been a major contribution to the scholarly debate over Smith's discovery. Instead, all he appears to have discovered was the "statistical noise" associated with examining a 100 dpi photographic reproduction under magnification. It is possible that Carlson made an inadvertent methodological error by choosing to rely so heavily on the reproductions from Smith's Harvard volume to the exclusion of other witnesses to the manuscript that were of much higher quality, perhaps not fully understanding how much distortion these low-resolution images would produce. But given the fact that Carlson's other major arguments for forgery rely on his knowledge of obscure technological and linguistic details (a skill set that must have served him well as a patent lawyer), it is difficult to believe that his use of the poorest-quality photographic reproductions available for the manuscript that Smith discovered was a simple oversight.

Fact-Checking the Forgery Hypothesis: The Contributions of Scott Brown

Remember that Carlson's forensic examination of the manuscript, according to a number of reviewers, was the strongest part of his argument. But he also identified several breadcrumbs that he believed Smith planted to reveal himself as the forger of the manuscript. Before we discuss these, however, we should pause momentarily to recognize the extraordinary contributions of one scholar who has done more than anyone else to contest these and other arguments for forgery presented by Carlson, Jeffery, Quesnell, and others. This is Scott Brown, whom we have already mentioned. Brown wrote his dissertation on the Mar Saba Clementine at the University of Toronto, published as *Mark's Other Gospel: Rethinking Morton Smith's Controversial Discovery* in 2005—the same year Carlson's book was released. Now, Brown's book is valuable enough on its own for his thorough presentation of the history of scholarship on this text. But even more beneficial to scholars are the

numerous journal articles that Brown wrote *after* his book was released, dismantling virtually all the major arguments propping up
the forgery hypothesis. These articles tend to be quite long and
detailed, so much so that some readers have expressed dissatis-
faction at what they perceive to be Brown's tendency to devote so
much attention to minutiae that the big picture, the dismantling of
arguments in favor of the forgery hypothesis, occasionally becomes
obscured.[11]

While this extreme attention to detail is admittedly a drawback
of Brown's approach, we would argue that it is a very understand-
able weakness, perhaps even a noble one, in light of the types of
claims that Brown has tasked himself with refuting. Many of the arguments that have been marshaled in favor of the forgery hypothesis, especially those involving breadcrumbs (Brown's preferred term
for these arguments is "folklore"), tend to resemble conspiratorial
modes of thinking. Namely, an author finds a perceived incongruity,
very often small and easily overlooked, which then becomes seen as
a hidden sign or clue pointing toward a concealed reality—Smith's
forgery of the Mar Saba manuscript, in this case. Then, in order
to make this perceived incongruity fit the forgery hypothesis, the
author develops an ingenious explanation of its significance that
very frequently gets a number of key accompanying facts and details wrong. Therefore, when a researcher like Brown decides to
refute this argument and all of its misrepresentations in their entirety, the process can require much more time to present than the
initial flawed argument did. Such is the unfortunate lot of those who
attempt to argue against pernicious conspiracy theories and other
types of misinformation on the basis of sound reason and evidence.
If it is any consolation to Brown, we liken his efforts at responding
to the various arguments of the forgery hypothesis to the mytholog-
ical fifth labor of Hercules, which involved cleaning out the messy
Augean stables. Yet all of Brown's shoveling has made our work in
this book much less daunting.

We will only briefly examine several other arguments by Carlson that rely on the concept of internal evidence; readers who desire
additional arguments and more detailed refutations should consult
Brown's numerous articles. Although there is a second argument by
Carlson that also involves hidden clues in the manuscripts studied

by Smith, we will cover that one a little later. Instead, it is appropriate to introduce first a textbook example of the conspiratorial logic, infused with numerous factual errors, that undergirds most of the arguments presented by Carlson and other recent advocates of the forgery hypothesis.

Carlson's "Morton Salt" Clue

This textbook example involves a passing reference by the author of Clement's letter to, of all things, salt. Though it would hardly seem to be a likely place to discover a clue pointing to Smith's forgery of the manuscript, Carlson nevertheless seizes upon it. In the letter, Clement complains that the Carpocratians have corrupted the Secret Gospel by interpolating into it additional material that, according to Clement, excessively sexualizes the relationship between Jesus and the young man whom he raised from the dead—above all, the phrase "naked man with naked man." The relevant part of Clement's criticism is as follows: "For true things mixed with fictions are effaced, so that, as it is said, even salt loses its saltiness." The statement about salt losing its saltiness is an allusion to Jesus's "you are the salt of the earth" saying as found in Matthew 5:13 and Luke 14:34.

So what is of interest in this seemingly banal passage in Clement's letter? According to Carlson, its description of salt is anachronistic and makes sense only in the twentieth century: "It presupposes salt-making technology that did not exist in Clement's place and time. The imagery in *Theodore* involves mixing an adulterant [such as potassium iodide for the prevention of goiter] with salt and spoiling its taste. For salt to be mixed with such an adulterant, it would have to be loose and free-flowing, but free-flowing salt is a modern invention."[12] But this is not all, since the company that invented free-flowing salt in the early twentieth century was . . . the *Morton* Salt Company. According to Carlson, once the anachronism is recognized, it is only a matter of figuring out what hidden clue is waiting to be uncovered: "This anachronism involves the kind of minor detail that may well have easily been overlooked by its twentieth-century creator, but it is more likely a deliberately embedded clue. Morton Smith, the putative discoverer of *Theodore*, shares his given name with Morton Salt, the company that invented the type of salt *Theodore* invokes."[13]

As with Carlson's claim that there were handwriting anomalies in the manuscript, if it were certain that the letter of Clement contained anachronisms that could only be explained by a very recent date of composition, this would be a discovery of monumental significance. Unfortunately, as Scott Brown has demonstrated with characteristic thoroughness, virtually all of what Carlson claims about this passage and salt-making technology is wrong. First and most fundamentally, the rhetorical point that Clement is making here has nothing to do with the modern process of mixing salt with additives. To illustrate this, Brown rewrites the passage from Clement to say what Carlson believes it means: "For the true things, being mixed with inventions, are falsified, with the result that, as the saying goes, even the salt, *being mixed with adulterants, tastes less pleasant.*"[14] But Carlson's interpretation misunderstands Clement's metaphor; so Brown also rewrites the passage to make Clement's point more clear: "For the true things *which the Carpocratians say about the longer text*, being mixed with inventions, are falsified, with the result that, as the saying goes, even the 'salt' [the goodness and value of the longer gospel] loses its savor [is lost]."[15]

Thus, the only property of salt that Clement cares about in this passage is that it can, as Jesus taught, lose its flavor and become useless—just as the longer gospel loses its value when the Carpocratians add passages to it that excessively sexualize its content. Foreign elements are being added to the Secret Gospel: they are not being added to salt. Since Jesus's saying about salt losing its saltiness has, understandably, perplexed many modern readers, Brown helpfully explains the ancient context of this saying: "The table salt produced by Morton Salt, and other salt companies, is a highly refined form of a stable chemical compound, sodium chloride. Pure salt cannot lose its savor. The imagery in the letter presupposes an impure form of salt that can lose its sodium chloride without the compound disappearing altogether. Many of the salts used in antiquity were of this sort."[16] One of the most common ways that these ancient impure salt compounds could lose the distinctive flavor provided by the sodium chloride was, not surprisingly, by getting wet—for instance, from rainwater or dampness where they were stored. This is the ancient context presupposed by the saying of Jesus, and seemingly also by the author of Clement's letter.

A Bald Swindler? Or a Plucked Huckster?

Not only is the understanding of Morton Smith's process of composition that is demanded by the arguments of the forgery advocates so complex and intricate that it must be judged fantastically implausible. We have also seen, thanks mostly to the efforts of Scott Brown, that these ingenious breadcrumbs frequently crumble under the weight of their discoverers' flawed readings of texts and inaccurate representations of the data. Two more brief instances of this may be noted in Carlson's book before we move on to address Peter Jeffery's contribution to the debate over the Secret Gospel. In addition to detecting handwriting anomalies in the manuscript containing the letter of Clement, Carlson believed that Smith had hidden a clue referring to himself in a second manuscript that he also forged, which appears in the corner of a photograph found in the popular Harper version but not in the scholarly Harvard volume.[17] The photograph in question contains manuscript fragments in several languages and was intended by Smith to show both the richness of the manuscript material that remained at Mar Saba and the frequent repurposing of these materials as bindings for more recently written texts.

The manuscript that catches Carlson's eye is the latest one, a Greek manuscript only a few centuries old, for which earlier manuscript fragments were used as bindings. The photograph in *The Secret Gospel* shows only a small portion of the handwriting in this manuscript, but Carlson regards the first part of the handwriting (there appear to be three different hands) as suspiciously similar to the Mar Saba Clementine. With only a few representative letters, Carlson confidently builds a case in just three sentences that whoever wrote this also wrote the letter of Clement.[18] Carlson's curiosity was evidently piqued enough by the resemblance in handwriting that he then examined Smith's catalogue of the Mar Saba manuscripts from the tower library, which—as we've noted—exists only in a modern Greek translation. On the basis of the photograph and Smith's caption for it, Carlson was able to determine that this was manuscript 22 in the catalogue. In Smith's entry, Carlson noticed that one of the manuscript's owners was a certain M. Madiotēs, whose handwriting Smith dated to the twentieth century (though this name does not appear in the cropped photograph). No one by this surname, however, could be found by Carlson in the online Greek telephone directory. How does Carlson account for the presence of this odd name? By arguing that it is actually Morton Smith's secret identity, "the bald swindler": "Rather, the name is a pseudonym built on the root *mad-*. Few modern Greek words begin with *mad-*, but one of them is the verb *madw*, which literally means 'to lose hair' and has a figurative meaning of 'to swindle.'"[19]

For Carlson's "bald swindler" argument, we would seemingly need to assume that Morton Smith intended for someone to be able to solve each step of the puzzle, one by one. First, to spot the similarity in handwriting that existed between the Mar Saba Clementine and the barely visible Greek handwriting in this cropped photo. Then, to take the crucial next step of consulting Smith's modern Greek manuscript catalogue in the hopes of identifying the one in the photo. Next, having found the entry, to recognize that there was something odd about the surname Madiotēs and use the online Greek telephone directory (which raises the question of how Smith expected scholars to solve his puzzle prior to the invention of the internet; the libraries having a printed Greek telephone directory must have been few and far between) to verify that it was not a real name. Finally, to search through a dictionary of modern Greek, discover a verb with the unusual beginning of *mad-* that could mean both "to lose one's hair" and, metaphorically, "to swindle," and—at last—recognize that this must be a reference to the bald Morton Smith. To put it charitably, this is an exceedingly complicated riddle for Smith or anyone else to devise. Though such a scenario is not to be regarded as completely impossible, it can hardly be considered a likely explanation.

Carlson's exceedingly clever hypothesis about this hidden clue also runs into a number of stubborn factual difficulties that undermine its ingenuity. Allan Pantuck and Scott Brown have identified a host of such problems by utilizing Smith's archives at the Jewish Theological Seminary of America. For one, in Smith's personal copy of his modern Greek catalogue of the Mar Saba manuscripts, he has made a number of annotations and corrections; this was a common practice of Smith's when he received copies of his own work, so that he could more easily revise his work if it happened to be printed again. In the Mar Saba catalogue, one correction he made for the entry on manuscript 22 was to change "Madiotēs" to "Madeotas." Such a minor change may not seem very significant at first glance, but it becomes very difficult to make sense of if the name in question is a pseudonym Smith gave himself. As Pantuck and Brown correctly point out: "Smith's decision to correct the spelling of this name . . . in his private papers makes sense if M. Madeotas is a real name that appears on this page of the manuscript, but is hard to explain if he invented the name himself: why correct a pretend name that does not appear on the page?"[20] Second, it was discovered that the name Madiōtēs, which is quite similar to Madiotes, *did* appear in a Greek telephone directory, indicating that the name may not be quite as fictitious as Carlson supposed.[21]

Third, once the uncropped version of this photo (located in Smith's archives at Jewish Theological Seminary) is studied, several other difficulties emerge.[22] The name in question appears, on closer examination, to be Modestos, a far more common Greek name; even more significantly, manuscript 22 later mentions a monk named Modestos living at Mar Saba in 1916, with whom it is tempting to identify the Madiotēs/Modestos who has signed his name on the first page of the manuscript. Fourth, the hand that signed this name is markedly different from the small bit of handwriting that Carlson singled out as resembling that in the letter of Clement. The signature is very likely twentieth century; the handwriting that Carlson focused on could certainly be eighteenth century, but it is not nearly similar enough to the handwriting in the letter of Clement to believe that both manuscripts were written by the same scribe. In any case, there is no reason to suppose that the hand that wrote the Modestos signature is the same individual who wrote either the letter of Clement or the earlier portions of manuscript 22.

Fifth and finally, even if the name *did* read "Madiotēs," "Madeotas," or "Madiotēs," Carlson is somewhat disingenuous when he claims that the Modern Greek verb *madō* means "to lose hair."[23] A consultation of two recent Modern Greek–English dictionaries demonstrates that the verb *madw* primarily means "to pluck." Since it can metaphorically mean "to fleece" (to steal, swindle, or defraud), its dominant meaning is "to remove hair or feathers, as from an animal." Moreover, it is a transitive verb (that is, it takes a direct object such as "chicken" or "sheep") and does not appear to be commonly used in an intransitive sense (that is, as a verb lacking a direct object), as in "I am going bald." So it can hardly function as a straightforward, familiar synonym for "bald," as Carlson claims. Instead, there is a totally unrelated Greek adjective, *phalakros*, that is most commonly used as the equivalent of "bald," as well as a cognate noun, *phalakrotēta*, that means "baldness" or "the state of being bald."[24] If Madiotes is not a real name but a pseudonym, a better translation might be "plucked huckster." This may not readily call to mind Morton Smith in the way that "bald swindler" does; but it is nevertheless a more accurate rendering of the underlying Greek than what Carlson proposes.

How might we characterize the persuasiveness of Carlson's arguments that Morton Smith forged the Mar Saba manuscript? As we noted at the beginning of this overview, most reviews of Carlson's book were favorable, and reviewers were nearly unanimous in their praise of his handwriting analysis that seemingly revealed signs of forgery. But when it came to evaluating Carlson's alleged clues that Smith had left behind, reviews were far less positive. For instance, Michael Kruger, who teaches at a conservative evangelical Christian seminary, first declared that Carlson's "legal/forensic approach breaks new ground and undoubtedly should end the 'stalemate' over this apocryphal Gospel within the academy"—in other words, that scholars should now accept that Smith's discovery is a forgery. But a few sentences later, Kruger admits deep misgivings about the breadcrumbs that Carlson claimed to have found, describing them as "a great deal more subjective and esoteric than the other parts of his book. Drawing a connection, for example, between Morton salt and Morton Smith seems to be somewhat speculative and without the possibility of external corroboration."[25] Similarly, Bruce Chilton's review asserts that Carlson "does demonstrate . . . that 'Secret Mark' is *someone's* forgery, and that Smith is the likely culprit,"[26] but also regards the Madiotes clue as an instance where "argumentative skill gets ahead of Carlson's expertise" and rejects the Morton Salt clue

as "supposititious."[27] If reviewers who are inclined to view the Secret Gospel as a forgery are this dismissive of Carlson's proffered
breadcrumbs, then this in itself demonstrates how hard it is to take
this part of Carlson's argument seriously. Furthermore, as Viklund
and Paananen demonstrated eight years after Carlson's book was
published, even his strongest argument—detecting signs of forgery
in the handwriting—is based on shoddy data (namely, low-quality
halftone photographic reproductions) that he has interpreted incorrectly. Such, then, is the upshot of what many scholars have regarded as the strongest case for Morton Smith's forgery of the Mar
Saba manuscript.

"I Pray for the Late Morton Smith—May God Rest His Anguished Soul"

When we come to the second book-length argument for the forgery
hypothesis, Peter Jeffery's *The Secret Gospel of Mark Unveiled*, we are
confronted with the unusual combination of a book whose literary
merits have received much more effusive praise than Carlson's but
whose case for forgery has generally been viewed as less persuasive
than his predecessor's. What accounts for this surprisingly mixed
reception? Certainly Timo Paananen is correct to suggest that Jeffery's extremely harsh treatment of Smith probably unsettled some
scholars who were otherwise favorably disposed to the idea that the
Secret Gospel was a forgery: "Whereas Carlson talked of Smith in
a rather neutral, low-key manner, giving the impression of almost
sympathizing with the master hoaxer in his greatest moment of
leg-pulling, Jeffery started by praying 'for the late Morton Smith—
may God rest his anguished soul' . . . and ended by lamenting 'the
tragic paradox of the man' who 'wasn't a good Christian . . . wasn't
even a very good Gnostic.'"[28] But perhaps more decisive was the fact
that Jeffery showed no interest in basing any of his arguments for
forgery on data from the manuscript itself,[29] unlike Carlson, whose
appeal to observations of handwriting anomalies won him rave reviews. Yes, Carlson's alleged signs of forgery would be refuted years
later; but when his book was published, it appears that many scholars who had long been skeptical of the authenticity of the Secret

Gospel were simultaneously overjoyed and relieved that someone was finally making a case for forgery on the basis of something that resembled—at least on the surface—empirical evidence.

When it comes to the matter of breadcrumbs, which loomed so large for Carlson and several others before him, Jeffery treats this material somewhat differently. On the one hand, he certainly creates space in his interpretation for Smith to have intentionally deposited clues pointing to himself as the creator of the Secret Gospel. But Jeffery is arguably more interested in what we might call "accidental breadcrumbs": signals he believes Smith has inadvertently transmitted throughout his writings that reveal important insights about his psychological and emotional disposition. Jeffery's interest in detecting this type of breadcrumb is demonstrated time and again throughout the first chapter of his book, which recounts and interprets Smith's story of discovering the manuscript as found in *The Secret Gospel.*

Jeffery first highlights a number of places in *Secret Gospel* where Smith seemed mostly uninterested in the sort of material he was likely to discover in the tower library. Smith was particularly disparaging of later liturgical manuscripts, and if we combine this with Smith's more cynical attitude toward the Byzantine liturgy in 1958 as compared with his first visit to Mar Saba,[30] we can perhaps catch a glimpse of what may initially have interested and infuriated Jeffery, a historian of Christian liturgy, enough to write a book on a topic that was rather far afield from his main research focus. When Jeffery reaches the point in *Secret Gospel* where Smith first discovers the letter of Clement, he uses an unexpected word to characterize Smith's reaction: "bipolar."[31] But soon enough, it will become clear that Jeffery has chosen this descriptor because he believes that Smith suffered from serious mental illness, perhaps depression or bipolar disorder. Consider Jeffery's version of Smith's stay at Mar Saba:

> For almost three weeks . . . Smith had been excusing himself from services to study manuscripts in his room—manuscripts that only discouraged him, that fulfilled his "worst expectations," in which he "discover[ed] nothing of importance." Yet when he finally found something genuinely interesting, with his stay at the monastery almost over, he left the book

on his desk and floated off to church, so excited by his discovery that he forgot he didn't go to church anymore. We
will meet this strange combination of euphoria and amne-
sia again, at important junctures throughout Smith's tale—a
weird, giddy forgetfulness that punctuates his narrative with
eerie predictability, and points—as memory lapses do—to
even larger denials.[32]

As readers may have predicted, this psychological interpretation of Smith's "find narrative" allows Jeffery to gainsay the veracity
of Smith's report of what transpired at Mar Saba in 1958. There
are at least three significant problems with Jeffery's psychological
analysis of Morton Smith, the first of which several reviewers of his
book already raised. First and most broadly, there is the question
of whether it was either beneficial or appropriate for Jeffery, not
being a trained mental health professional, to perform a diagnosis
on Smith—and only on the basis of Smith's writings, not through an
in-person evaluation.[33]

Jeffery evidently received enough criticism on this point that it
features prominently in an FAQ that he published on his Princeton
website after his book was released. Despite his admission that he
is not a trained therapist, he nevertheless insists that his work as a
suicide hotline counselor gave him more than enough experience
to recognize that Smith was mentally ill simply by reading *Secret
Gospel*. Jeffery writes, "The book is, in fact, the weirdest publication
I ever read, full of many of the kinds of things we are trained to look
for: sudden and extreme changes of mood that seem like excessive
reactions to the events that provoked them, an exaggerated sense of
self-importance, memory lapses at key points, hostility disguised as
humor, bizarre theories about what constitutes truth, sanity, or reality. The fact that some of these also appear in the Mar Saba letter of
Clement, as well as in Smith's own voice, is surely relevant."[34]

The second and third criticisms of Jeffery's psychologizing of
Smith are closely connected to each other. The second is that, as
is clearly seen at the end of the previous quotation, Jeffery comes
very close to suggesting that Smith's mental illness is ultimately
the driving force behind his forgery of the Mar Saba Clementine,
since he alleges that some of Smith's psychological characteristics

also appear in the text of the letter itself. Moreover, Jeffery reveals in his FAQ his belief that Smith's creation of the manuscript was not a mischievous hoax, which was Carlson's perspective, but rather a serious moral failing: "A fraud like the Secret Gospel ought to be exposed and condemned in the harshest terms, along with the numerous misrepresentations of evidence and history that Smith wrote to support it."[35] In so doing, he insinuates the very old but very damaging stereotype that people who suffer from mental illness are frequently a danger to themselves and others.

Smith's Sexuality and Why It Matters (to Jeffery)

Our third criticism of Jeffery's psychologizing pertains to the way in which his book treats Morton Smith's identity as a gay man. Before we come to the substance of our critique, it is appropriate to say something about the information that we have amassed on Smith's mental health and sexual identity throughout our research. In our extensive interviews with individuals who were both friends and colleagues of Smith, we never heard anyone assert or even speculate that he suffered from bipolar disorder, depression, or any other mental health condition.[36] In contrast, it appears to have been widely known that Smith was gay. He was not "out" in the sense of having a long-standing partner or making some other public declaration about his sexual identity—though we must bear in mind that Smith's career played out in a time when many LGBTQ+ people were forced to remain closeted. Nevertheless, most of his friends and colleagues did mention his sexuality in our conversations with them, which leads us to believe that Smith's identity as a gay man was something of an "open secret": most people connected with his field of study knew this about him—including, presumably, many of his enemies.

While Jeffery is aware of the fact that Smith was gay, it remains unclear whence his information about this part of Smith's life comes. It is also quite difficult to find in his book a clear and unambiguous statement of Smith's sexual identity—though it is strongly implied in numerous passages. But Jeffery is more forthright in his FAQ: "It seems to me perfectly reasonable to assume that Smith, finding himself unable to live as a homosexual Christian within the structures available at the time, experienced such a 'dark night.' And with no competent spiritual guidance (as his 1949 article demonstrates), the most honest step he could take was an angry rejection of Christianity itself, at least as he knew it. Since I have listened to many other people who, though desiring to be faithful Christians or Jews, find themselves quite unable to conform to conventional Judeo-Christian patterns of heterosexuality, I believe I have a good sense of what Smith was experiencing."[37]

Recall that the second objection to Jeffery's psychological analysis of Smith was his tendency to associate mental illness with harmful behavior—specifically, his fraudulent claim to have discovered the Mar Saba Clementine. The third objection, in much the same vein, is Jeffery's close linking of Smith's sexual identity with the mental health conditions from which he alleges that Smith suffered. As with the stereotypical connection between mental illness and criminality, there is a lengthy and destructive discourse that regards homosexuality as intrinsically a psychological disorder.

Even if he does so inadvertently, Jeffery reproduces this discourse in several ways. Most notably, he has a propensity for excessively sexualizing both the narrative of the Secret Gospel and Smith's writings on it. In so doing, he comes uncomfortably close to insinuating that same-sex attraction is necessarily characterized by an unhealthy obsession with sexual activity. This stereotype imagines gay people as flaunting their sexuality by virtue of their mere existence, while simultaneously downplaying far more overt displays of heteronormativity—such as crude or even violent sexual humor that is explained away as harmless "locker-room talk"—simply because it is heterosexual in nature.

Before we discuss the chief instance of Jeffery oversexualizing the content of the Secret Gospel, it is important to bear in mind that his interpretative perspective has not emerged entirely out of thin air. After all, we still have the undeniably homoerotic depiction of the relationship between Jesus and the young man that stands at the center of the Secret Gospel's narrative. Moreover, Smith himself was by no means reluctant to joke about this feature of the text—most notably in his "Cops Arrest Rabbi in Park with Naked Teenager" quip that he frequently included in oral presentations of his discovery. It is also entirely possible that Smith went uncomfortably farther on several occasions with jokes that he cracked. For instance, Jeffery has noted that Smith's way of describing the hypnotic effect that the Byzantine hymns had on him as a young man on his first visit to Mar Saba—"I knew what was happening, but I relaxed and enjoyed it"—is probably to be construed as a rape joke, an interpretation with which we agree.[38]

Despite the fact that Smith was hardly squeamish about making dirty jokes, Jeffery believes that Smith went much farther than even the above examples when he forged his discovery. He argues that the entire narrative of the Secret Gospel is packed with subtle sexual references that go well beyond the nighttime, scantily clad rendezvous between Jesus and the young man at the end of the story. According to Jeffery, the very act of the young man emerging from his tomb, restored to life, is to be read not as a literal miracle of resuscitation but metaphorically as "an anguished young man 'com[ing] out of the closet' for his first (homo)sexual experience."[39] Also significant is the remark that Jesus "stretched forth his hand and raised him, seizing his hand," in response to which Jeffery declares, "The pointless duplication of hands is a sure sign that something's afoot."[40] Even the beseeching of Jesus by the sister of the dead man could be construed as sexual "if the Secret Evangelist was an English-speaker who wanted to imply that, while 'coming, she bent down to kiss Jesus,' the woman was 'coming' in the slang English sense—that is, 'experiencing sexual orgasm.'"[41] Piling all these sexual innuendos upon each other, Jeffery then argues that the Secret Gospel fragment becomes a very recent and familiar type of story: an "extended double entendre—a popular kind of joke among literate North American males of the twentieth century. But it is in the nature of such jokes that the teller can deny that the sexual elements were really intended: 'blaming' the audience for detecting them is part of the humor."[42]

In contrast to the remarks from *Secret Gospel* that Jeffery regarded as inadvertently disclosing that Smith suffered from mental illness, his interpretation of the entire Secret Gospel narrative as an "extended double entendre" is more in line with the breadcrumbs that Carlson, Ehrman, and others claim to have discovered. That is, Jeffery seems to believe that Smith intentionally inserted clues into the text that could potentially reveal it as a forgery and him as its creator. As with the other examples of breadcrumbs we have examined, Jeffery's "extended double entendre" hypothesis appears far-fetched, especially since it imagines both a woman and a man to be having almost simultaneous sexual encounters with Jesus. But even if we temporarily assume that Jeffery is correct, and that Smith forged a text full of sexual innuendo, what does Jeffery then regard as Smith's reason for concocting this forgery?

When it comes to the question of motive, Jeffery has several explanations, some of which seem to be at odds with each other. On the one hand, if Smith essentially composed a lengthy dirty joke, it would seem to follow that it was a sort of prank: certainly more of a mean-spirited trick than Carlson's notion of a hoax designed to test whether Smith's colleagues would be sharp enough to spot it.[43] Jeffery apparently endorses such a view when he states—in a much-quoted passage from the final pages of his book—that Smith's forgery was "arguably the most grandiose and reticulated 'Fuck You' ever perpetuated in the long and vituperative history of scholarship."[44] Such a prank would necessarily have had among its chief victims those scholars with whom Smith was closest and with whom he corresponded extensively over several decades. But, perhaps realizing that the idea of inflicting a vengeful prank on one's most loyal supporters might seem implausible, Jeffery proceeds—on the very next page—to suggest that a combination of Smith's mental illness and his identity as a gay Christian man was the impetus for him to create this forgery. "One could say," says Jeffery, "that Smith did not know what he was doing. I conjecture that the letter of 'Clement' may have begun as a purposeful, even a wistful, attempt to set the historical record 'straight' (or rather 'gay')—but that it quickly fell afoul of Smith's nasty sense of humor, which in turn became the transparent mask of his considerable rage—I suspect without his fully realizing or understanding what was happening."[45]

Despite making bold claims such as these about what was going on in Smith's head throughout his book, Jeffery nevertheless insists that he is refusing the temptation to do "armchair psychoanalysis dressed up as objective scholarship."[46] It is difficult to understand how the quotation at the end of the previous paragraph is not an example of the precise thing that Jeffery says he refrains from doing. He seems concerned to explain away this glaring contradiction in his FAQ when he states: "I did not, for example, engage in 'armchair psychoanalysis' . . . ; on the contrary I refrained from publishing my opinion on what Smith's most likely diagnoses were. I simply noted the many curious symptoms so that readers could draw their own conclusions."[47] Whether readers find Jeffery's self-exoneration convincing, the fact remains that he—like Carlson, despite their differences in argument and tone—bases most of his case for forgery on highly speculative breadcrumbs whose correctness is nearly impossible to verify.

Even when Jeffery seems to be on firmer ground by appealing to anachronisms in the letter of Clement and the Secret Gospel that would point to a date of composition in the twentieth century, logical flaws can be identified without much difficulty. Jeffery is not content simply to assert that Smith was a gay man, but also devotes a significant amount of attention to identifying the particular gay subculture to which Smith may have belonged. This was a school of thought sometimes referred to as "Uranian Venus," composed of scholars, artists, and authors who were classically trained at elite English-speaking universities, men who came to believe, as Jeffery describes it, "that homosexuality virtually endowed a man with a superior artistic sensibility, and the creative person's perennial demand for artistic freedom came to represent the homosexual's desire for affectional freedom, like those ancient Greeks whose morality was aesthetic, not theocratic, unhampered by divine revelation or Mosaic law."[48]

It is by no means implausible that such a way of thinking might have exerted a significant influence on Morton Smith's self-understanding as a gay man. And, if we factor in Smith's Christian upbringing and stint in the priesthood, it is certainly possible or even likely that the conflict between these two identities gave rise to painful psychological turmoil for Smith—even if we resist the urge to push our "armchair psychoanalysis" further than this. But while this would help us to understand better the difficulties that Smith may have experienced as a closeted homosexual in the mid-twentieth century, this contextualizing does not by itself strengthen Jeffery's case for Smith's forgery of the Mar Saba Clementine at all. So why does Jeffery bring it up?

The answer is Oscar Wilde, the celebrated author and playwright who was imprisoned for two years at the end of the nineteenth century on the charge of "gross indecency"—that is, homosexual activity—and died shortly thereafter. Wilde, unsurprisingly, identified with the Uranian Venus subculture; he also would attain the status of a martyr for gay communities through his imprisonment and untimely death.[49] But one of Wilde's greatest achievements was his play *Salomé*, a retelling of the story of John the Baptist's murder that, according to the sixth chapter of the Gospel of Mark, was set in motion by Herodias, the illicit wife of Herod Antipas, and her daughter. Though the daughter, who dances so seductively that Herod promises to give her anything she asks for, is not identified by name in Mark, the Jewish historian Josephus states that one of Herodias's daughters was named Salome.[50] The urge to have a name for this notorious biblical villainess was so strong that, from the Middle Ages onward, the dancing daughter was commonly referred to in literary works and artistic representations as Salome—hence the name of Wilde's play.

A woman named Salome also appears in a number of ancient Christian writings—including, of course, the second and much briefer fragment of the Secret Gospel excerpted in the letter of Clement: "And the sister of the young man whom Jesus loved and his mother and Salome were there, and Jesus did not receive them." The reason for this apparent rejection of a group of women by Jesus is not at all obvious and has given rise to a range of explanations by scholars. In Morton Smith's opinion, the text had been tampered with by Clement himself to suppress further material about Salome. He writes in *Secret Gospel*, "The story was going to tell of a conversation between Jesus and Salome, but Salome, in early Christian literature, was a very shady lady. Matthew, Luke, and John all deleted her name from their gospels. All sorts of heretics, but worst of all the Carpocratians, appealed to her as an authority. We have one story that she tempted Jesus (how, is not told), another that she inquired about his getting onto her bed—a sufficient reason for inquiry, no doubt, but also a sufficient reason for Clement's cutting her conversation with Jesus out of the secret Gospel." Smith adds a footnote about the identity of Salome at the end of the first sentence that becomes especially significant for Jeffery: "This one should not be confused with the Herodian princess celebrated by Oscar Wilde. The name was common."[51]

Smith thus explains in this note that the Salome who appears in the Secret Gospel is not the same as the daughter of Herodias who precipitates the execution of John the Baptist. But Smith also reveals that he is familiar with Oscar Wilde's play *Salomé*—and this is what matters for Jeffery. Although Jeffery concedes that no other evidence exists that Smith was especially fond of Wilde's works, he nevertheless suspects that he was: "He must have enjoyed Wilde and other 'Uranian' writers as an English major at Harvard, but so have millions of other people around the world."[52] For Jeffery, there are three compelling indications that Wilde's *Salomé* was a source used by Smith in his composition of the letter of Clement and the Secret Gospel. First, there is the shared presence of a woman named Salome. Second and more specifically, Wilde's Salomé is described in his stage directions as "dancing the dance of the seven veils"; the letter of Clement states that the Secret Gospel "lead[s] . . . the hearers into the innermost sanctuary of the truth that is veiled seven times." Third, the letter of Clement states that Mark the Evangelist "did not disclose the things not to be uttered" (Smith's translation; we translated this phrase above as "did not yet disclose the ineffable things") when he wrote the Secret Gospel, but only hinted at them, leaving the oral transmission of these hidden truths to be provided to advanced Christians by church leaders. While Jeffery notes that the word translated by Smith as "things not to be uttered" is used elsewhere in Clement's authentic works, he appeals to the title of an obscure modern Greek study of ancient Greek obscenities as evidence that this word "can also refer to words that should not be spoken because they constitute 'obscene, silly, and vulgar talk.'"[53] Jeffery therefore believes that Smith alludes, through the use of this term, to "the love that dare not speak its name," a reference to homosexuality that first appeared in the poem "Two Loves" by Lord Alfred Bruce Douglas, Wilde's partner, which was then made famous through Wilde's impassioned explanation of it during his trial.[54]

The collection of breadcrumbs that emerges for Jeffery out of the work and life of Oscar Wilde is ingenious. But so is the hidden reference to free-flowing table salt invented by the Morton Salt Company; and so is the Greek pseudonym meaning "bald swindler" that Smith buried in the modern Greek translation of his Mar Saba manuscript catalogue. Despite their ingenuity, Carlson's theories are so subjective that they cannot be treated as serious evidence in favor of Smith's having forged the manuscript, and Jeffery's links to Oscar Wilde will not fare much better. Jeffery's first piece of evidence (the presence of a woman named Salome in both texts) and his third (that "things not to be uttered" is a coded reference to "the love that dare not speak its name") are particularly superficial as connectors between the Secret Gospel and Oscar Wilde. The references to seven veils in both texts, Jeffery's second piece of evidence, is perhaps a bit more solid than the other two, but not by much. Yes, Jeffery is technically correct that Clement's other writings never explicitly mention a tradition about the holy of holies in the Jerusalem temple being separated by seven veils. But there are a number of other passages where Clement uses the metaphor of secrets hidden behind veils, so the imagery from the letter of Clement is not nearly as strange as Jeffery would lead his readers to believe.[55] Moreover, even if we were to conclude that something in the letter was so unlike Clement that the letter could not have been written by him, Morton Smith should not then automatically become the most likely author, certainly not with all we know about the prevalence of ancient Christian pseudepigraphy. Jeffery is but one of a number of writers on the Secret Gospel who jumps to this rash conclusion.

How Many Breadcrumbs Are Enough?

We have not responded to every single argument in favor of the forgery hypothesis here. For instance, we will not be examining the alleged parallels between Morton Smith's discovery and an evangelical Christian thriller published in 1940 called *The Mystery of Mar Saba*. It also features the discovery of an early Christian writing that threatens to destroy the foundations of Christian belief by stating that Joseph of Arimathea had reburied Jesus's body elsewhere. Yet the manuscript turns out to have been a malicious forgery created by the Nazis in order to demoralize the British war effort. Part of the reason for omitting it from our discussion is that it was one of a relatively small number of breadcrumbs that did not originate with Ehrman, Carlson, or Jeffery. We are confident that if we analyzed it here, readers would find it no more persuasive than any of the other

ones we have covered—though we will provide the necessary documentation in the accompanying note for any readers who wish to
examine it for themselves.[56]

To conclude: as is evident from the space we have devoted to the
books by Carlson and Jeffery, their arguments in favor of the forgery
hypothesis are exceedingly complex. Some readers may have, quite
understandably, become fatigued by our presentation of so many alleged breadcrumbs, only to see us dismantle them again and again as
speculative and flawed. We would prefer to be able to write a book
about a fascinating but perplexing text like the Secret Gospel without becoming bogged down in refutations that border on pedantic.
Nevertheless, Carlson's and Jeffery's studies continue to be viewed
favorably by many scholars who have not gotten into the weeds of
the Secret Gospel debate. Moreover, even though several scholars
had already done the hard work in exposing the serious weaknesses
of the case for forgery, their efforts have, for a variety of reasons,
not succeeded in changing the current consensus in biblical studies:
that the Secret Gospel is, more likely than not, a modern forgery
perpetrated by one of the most gifted and controversial scholars of
the twentieth century.

Part of the way forward, we propose, is not just to refute the
arguments for forgery point by point—though that task cannot be
completely avoided and ignored. It is also important not to be awed
by the quantity of arguments—the sheer number of alleged clues,
jokes, anachronisms, and other such breadcrumbs—and instead to
keep one's eye always on their quality. Do any of these breadcrumbs
actually stand out as probable, or do they inevitably collapse like
a house of cards when even modest scrutiny is applied to them? If
they collapse time and again, as we have argued that they do, then
one ought to make a choice about whether *any* newly discovered
hints allegedly buried by Smith are likely to be more viable than all
those that came before. Samuel Schoenbaum, evaluating the various
hypotheses that Shakespeare's plays were written by someone other
than the Bard, gives an assessment that is blunter than we would feel
comfortable saying ourselves, but nevertheless seems worth repeat-
ing: "It is difficult to see why a great heap of rubbish should possess
any more value than a small pile of the same rubbish."[57]

CHAPTER SEVEN
The Handwriting

I F WE ARE TO MOVE BEYOND conspiratorial thinking about the *Letter to Theodore* and the Secret Gospel of Mark, we must approach this text and its accompanying manuscript the way we would any other. When it comes to working with manuscripts, we studied with François Bovon, longtime professor at the University of Geneva and then Harvard Divinity School, where he served as a committed mentor to countless students. Bovon had many academic interests, but chief among them was tracking down unpublished Christian writings and making them available to the scholarly world. In 1974 Bovon had an experience—not unlike Smith's discovery at Mar Saba—while working at Mount Athos, a mountainous peninsula in northeastern Greece that, as a conglomeration of twenty monasteries, has been for centuries an important hub of Greek Orthodox monasticism. While perusing the manuscript holdings of the Monastery of Xenophontos, Bovon discovered a text that had gone unnoticed in the stacks, a writing thought not to have survived into the modern period: the complete version of the apocryphal Acts of Philip, a lengthy account of the miraculous deeds of the apostle Philip that includes dragon-slaying, talking animals, and women who dressed as men so they could serve as leaders in a male-dominated church.

Like Smith, Bovon quickly realized that he had discovered something special. Yet unlike Smith, who needed to complete an inventory of Mar Saba's holdings and couldn't dedicate too much in-person attention to any given manuscript, Bovon chose to maximize his in-person time with the manuscript. He writes about his time with the manuscript in an article that has become a veritable "field guide" for those hunting for undiscovered textual treasures. "You enter a library," Bovon writes, "perhaps a little shyly the first time, and ask for manuscripts."[1] Once you present the librarian with your credentials and the requested item is located, you get to see the manuscript. "At last," continues Bovon, whose love for ancient books is undeniable, "filled with mixed feelings of joy, anxiety, and excitement, you sit at a small table with the manuscript, a pad of paper, a magnifier, and a pencil."[2]

Under ideal circumstances, the first step toward understanding the *Letter to Theodore* would be to conduct an autopsy—that is, to pack a notepad, magnifying glass, and a pencil; fly to Jerusalem; and spend some quality time with the manuscript. But there's one thing that has prevented us from following Bovon's advice: the manuscript has vanished. No one has reported seeing it in person since 1983, and all subsequent attempts to view or even locate the manuscript have met with failure.

Let's rewind in time and follow the trail until it goes cold.

Who Saw the Manuscript, and When and Where Did They See It?

As we already know, Morton Smith first came across the *Letter to Theodore* in the summer of 1958 while cataloguing books in the tower library at Mar Saba. He found the *Letter to Theodore* inscribed on the endpages of Voss's 1646 edition of the letters of Ignatius. Smith took the book back to his room to study, where he deciphered the first few sentences. He took photographs of the *Letter to Theodore*—"three times for good measure"—and even snapped a couple of the Voss edition, before returning it to the tower library.

One might think that there would have been a steady stream of scholars eager to view the *Letter to Theodore* in person after 1960, when Smith introduced it to the world at the annual meeting of the SBL, and again in 1973, when he published not one but two books about the discovery. But apparently the manuscript remained where Smith left it, in the tower library, from 1958 until the spring of 1976, when a small group of scholars made a pilgrimage to Mar Saba in search of the manuscript now at the center of so much controversy.

As we mentioned in chapter 5, news of the 1976 sighting broke only recently, when Guy Stroumsa, a prominent scholar of religion who has held posts at Hebrew University and the University of Oxford, realized during a conversation with an American colleague that he was one of a very small number of scholars ever to have seen the *Letter to Theodore* in person. In the preface to his 2008 publication of the letters between Morton Smith and Gershom Scholem, Stroumsa gave an account of his journey to Mar Saba:

> In the spring of 1976, a party of four, including the late David Flusser, Professor of New Testament, the late Shlomo Pines, Professor of medieval Arabic and Jewish philosophy, both at the Hebrew University of Jerusalem, Archimandrite Meliton, from the Greek Patriarchate in Jerusalem (at the time a research student at the Hebrew University) and myself (then a graduate student at Harvard University), drove (in my car) from Jerusalem to Mar Saba monastery, in the Judean wilderness, in the quest for Clement's letter. Together with Flusser and Pines, I had been intrigued by Morton Smith's sensational description of his find, and we wanted to see the text with our own eyes. When we reached the monastery, with the help of one of the monks, whose name I have forgotten, we began searching for Isaac Vossius' edition of the Letters of Ignatius on the very dusty shelves of the library in the monastery's tower. The young monk and Archimandrite Meliton explained to us that most books from the monastery's library had been moved to the Patriarchate library in Jerusalem after too many thefts had occurred. We did come with great expectations, and indeed the monk soon found the book, with "Smith 65" inscribed on its front page. There, on the blank pages at the end of the book, were the three manuscript pages of Clement's letter, exactly

as described by Smith. The book had clearly remained where Smith had found it, and where he had replaced it after having made his photographs. It was obvious to all of us that the precious book should not be left in place, but rather should be deposited in the library of the Patriarchate. So we took the book with us back to Jerusalem, and Father Meliton brought it to the library. We planned to analyze the manuscript seriously and contemplated an ink analysis. At the National and University Library, however, we were told that only at the Police Headquarters were people equipped with the necessary knowledge and tools for such an analysis. Father Meliton made it clear that he had no intention of putting the Vossius book in the hands of the Israeli police. We gave up, I went back to Harvard, and when I returned to Jerusalem to teach, more than two years later, I had other commitments.[3]

It would seem that while the world pored over the text of the *Letter to Theodore*, wrestled with its erotic retelling of Mark's Gospel, and debated its authenticity, the manuscript remained where Smith left it, tucked away in the library of the great tower gathering dust. Years later Flusser recalled that they struggled at first to locate the book, but finally found it "in the middle of a pile of books, carelessly thrown together on the floor, all covered with dust." "What kind of scholar," he wondered, "could have permitted this? Walked off, leaving his great discovery to such a fate?"[4] As we have discussed, Smith had his reasons for leaving the manuscript behind—chief of which being that it wasn't his to take. Stroumsa, Flusser, and the rest of the party sought a more suitable home for the book, in part because they reasoned that such an important manuscript deserves a more dignified dwelling, and in part because books in the tower library had a habit of disappearing. So they arranged to relocate the manuscript written within the Voss volume to the Patriarchal Library in Jerusalem. Flusser remembers that they did encounter one bump in the road. When the team of scholars attempted to leave with the book, "Abbot Seraphim," an old friend of Smith who presided over Mar Saba, "raised hell," demanding that "they would have to request it, and he would send it."[5] But the abbot's request stemmed less from

a desire to prevent the team from taking the book than from a concern for due process—because in the end, Flusser recalls, they requested the book and he allowed them to take it.[6] Stroumsa and
the others did discuss the possibility of subjecting the manuscript
to scientific analysis—the kinds of tests that can help determine the
age of a manuscript (that is, the age of the writing surface and its
ink)—but Father Meliton did not want the manuscript to leave the
Patriarchal Library and enter into the custody of the Israeli police.

Soon after the manuscript arrived in Jerusalem, sometime in
1976, Kallistos Dourvas, librarian at the Patriarchal Library from
1975 to 1990, received the new volume and added it to the collection of manuscripts from Mar Saba. A receipt from the transfer, signed by Dourvas among others, has recently surfaced.[7] The
paleographer Agamemnon Tselikas discovered it in the archives of
the Patriarchal Library in Jerusalem. The document describes the
letter of Clement as "unpublished and without any doubts about
its authenticity." It remains unclear whether "authenticity" means
that they regarded it as a genuine letter of Clement or that they did
not believe it to be a modern forgery. What is clear, however, is that
those documenting the transfer in 1976 were already well aware of
the controversy Smith's discovery had generated.

Upon receiving the manuscript, the librarian took the remarkable step of separating the *Letter to Theodore* from the Voss volume.
Dourvas's plan was to keep printed books in one section of the library
and manuscripts in another, so separating the Voss edition from the
Letter to Theodore inscribed on its endpages seemed natural. Dourvas
then photographed the loose pages containing the *Letter to Theodore*.[8]
These images suggest, however, that at least one of the three pages
of the *Letter to Theodore* was carelessly torn from the book, not a
method preferred by most librarians or conservationists. Dourvas
claims that despite his initial intention to separate manuscripts from
print editions in the Patriarchal Library, he never completed his re-
organization of the collection. The *Letter to Theodore* thus remained
with the Voss edition at least until he left his position at the library in
1990, though, once divided, Voss's edition and the *Letter to Theodore*
were catalogued as separate items in the collection.[9]

In January 1980 Thomas Talley of General Theological Seminary, who considered the *Letter to Theodore* to be an important new

source about the development of early Christian rituals in Alexandria, traveled to the Patriarchal Library in search of the manuscript. Father Meliton was there and told him that he himself had relocated the Voss edition and the *Letter to Theodore* from Mar Saba to the Patriarchal Library a few years prior. Talley also met with Kallistos Dourvas, who confirmed that he was present when the manuscript arrived at the library. He also told Talley that the manuscript was no longer attached to the Voss edition, and that it was not available for viewing because it was being repaired.[10]

The Final Eyewitness: Quentin Quesnell

Though there would be several subsequent attempts to see the *Letter to Theodore*, the last documented sighting of the manuscript occurred in 1983, when none other than Quentin Quesnell, then chair of the Religion Department at Smith College, traveled to Jerusalem in search of the *Letter to Theodore*. As you will recall, Quesnell was an outspoken critic of Smith and had faulted him for failing to make the manuscript available for others to examine. For unknown reasons, however, Quesnell did not tell many people that he had indeed seen the manuscript in person.

News of Quesnell's autopsy became widely known only recently. A few weeks after Quesnell returned to the States from Israel, he attended a conference at Princeton Theological Seminary, where he told Adela Collins, then professor in New Testament at McCormick Theological Seminary before moving on to posts at Notre Dame, the University of Chicago, and ultimately Yale Divinity School, about his recent trip. Years later, when Collins was working on a commentary on the Gospel of Mark, she phoned Quesnell to verify the details of his trip. For years all that was known publicly about Quesnell's inspection of the manuscript came from a brief note buried deep in Collins's commentary.[11] But thanks to the investigative work of two scholars who consulted Quesnell's archival papers at Smith College, a fuller picture has recently emerged.[12] His visit unfolded as follows.[13]

On June 1, 1983, Quesnell brainstormed strategies for gaining access to the manuscript with M. Armand, the Vatican representative for pilgrimages, who recommended that he "barge in on the Patriarch and demand . . . to speak to 'le secrétaire en chef,'" because, Armand reasoned, "this is the only way to get results from them." The next day he went to the library and managed to make contact. In a letter to his wife about that day, he reports somewhat uneventfully that he "got into the Patriarchate this morning, talked to the officials and to the librarian." However, George Dragas, a friend of Kallistos Dourvas who was also present that day, remembers Quesnell's initial visit differently.[14] It seems that Quesnell did heed the advice of Armand, at least on his initial approach, because Dragas remembers when a "rude American" bounded into the library and demanded to see the manuscript. Dourvas, not one to bow to impertinent demands, apparently told Quesnell to apologize, go outside, and come back with a better attitude, which he apparently did, since, as he told his wife, "I've been promised the ms. for Monday morning."

Quesnell also noted some of what Dourvas told him about the manuscript that day. These remarks by Dourvas are some of the most tantalizing material that we have come across while writing this book, and they suggest that Dourvas had insider information about the origins and history of this manuscript. Although we very much wish that we could have learned more from Dourvas, he died in 2016 before we began this project. In addition to confirming his role in relocating the manuscript from Mar Saba to the Patriarchal Library, Dourvas told the American that he was sure that the manuscript was produced in the eighteenth century, and that it was not composed by Clement of Alexandria but was written by someone else in response to certain "heretics and heretical schools" active in Mar Saba. Intriguingly, Dourvas also told Quesnell that "he remembers someone noting in some publication that someone did report seeing this in the 16th? 17th? century." It must have been hard for Quesnell—one of the most outspoken proponents of the forgery theory—to hear the librarian claim that the text not only is ancient but also may have been mentioned in a sixteenth- or seventeenth-century source. To his credit, however, Quesnell went to Jerusalem with an open mind. As he would tell his wife, "Perhaps I'll be convinced too when I see it. Maybe. This is what this is all about."

As promised, Quesnell was able to view the manuscript the following Monday, June 6. He examined the manuscript for most of the morning and noted that the *Letter to Theodore* had been removed from the Voss edition: "The manuscript itself is now two free sheets that they have removed from the printed volume they were a part of. The two sheets are kept in a plastic binder, which you are asked not to open."

He would spend many hours with the manuscript during his lengthy visit, carefully examining the letterforms under magnification. He even attempted his own re-creation of the handwriting, which was about as good as one could expect from someone with, in his own words, "no previous experience or practice in modern Greek handwriting." Though he wanted to have scientific testing done on the paper and ink, his requests were denied, and he was forced to settle for a set of color photographs, which he requested on June 20 and received a few months later, on September 5.

Quesnell could not have known that he'd be the last on record to see the *Letter to Theodore*, but the writing was already on the wall during his visit. He reports that Dourvas was insistent that "he does not want others to come," and on another day Quesnell notes that "the librarian shudders any time I suggest more people coming." Dourvas regarded the *Letter to Theodore* as a pious text produced by monks at Mar Saba during a particularly trying time in the monastery's history, and he may well have wanted to prevent visitors from seeing it in order to insulate the manuscript from the circus Smith's work had generated. Smith himself reported in 1985—during Dourvas's tenure as librarian at the Patriarchal Library—"that the Patriarchate of Jerusalem refuses to make the manuscript available for study."[15] Whatever the reason for this policy, no one has reported seeing the manuscript since June of 1983.[16]

What to Do When a Manuscript Goes Missing

For the foreseeable future, no one is likely to be able to view the manuscript in person, and those who want to study the manuscript will have to rely on the photos that survive. This may sound like a setback—and to be honest, it is—but in truth it is not uncommon for scholars to study texts from manuscripts that cannot be located or, even worse, have been destroyed. One of the more striking instances of a disappearing manuscript involves another ancient letter that surfaced under strange circumstances before going up in smoke.[17] The Letter to Diognetus, which survived into the modern period only in a single manuscript, is an important early Christian apologetic text; that is, it was written in part to defend Christianity from its critics, both Jews and non-Jews. The text was not known to have existed until it surfaced sometime around 1436 in Constantinople in a most unexpected place: in a fishmonger's shop, among a pile of papers for wrapping fish. To this day scholars have no idea how the Letter to Diognetus ended up where it did, but fortunately a young cleric named Thomas d'Arezzo rescued the manuscript from the pile of papers by purchasing it from the shop owner and placing it in capable hands. By the late 1500s the manuscript had been transcribed—that is, copied out by hand by scholars trained in deciphering manuscripts—at least three times, and the first print edition of the text appeared in 1586. It's a good thing the Letter to Diognetus was transcribed and published, because the manuscript was incinerated during the Franco-Prussian war in 1870, when a fire ripped through the library in Strasbourg where the manuscript was being kept. Had it not been for the transcription and publication of the text, the world would have lost this important early Christian writing for good.

No other manuscript has emerged under such fishy circumstances, but many have been similarly found, then lost or destroyed, often as collateral damage during times of war. We should consider ourselves fortunate when transcriptions or print editions of otherwise lost manuscripts survive. Though the manuscript containing the Letter to Diognetus is long gone, its text lives on in various scholarly editions and continues to contribute to our understanding of early Christianity. But it is even more fortuitous when we have images of lost manuscripts—ideally high-quality images, since we saw in chapter 6 what can happen when poor-quality images are misinterpreted—to accompany these transcriptions and editions. When images do survive, manuscripts can be consulted virtually again and again as new meanings and interpretations are proposed. Therefore, while it may be tempting to lament the absence of the *Letter to Theodore* or to regard its disappearance as evidence of its inauthenticity, we should remember that we are lucky to have multiple sets of photographs—including color photographs—of the Mar Saba text.

To return to Bovon's guide to working with newly discovered manuscripts, he actually recommends that studying the handwriting and deciphering the text of the manuscript should be done remotely, with the aid of photographs. "The writing is very important," he notes, "fortunately, once you are at home, you can examine it more closely and describe it from your microfilm copy."[18] Time spent in person with the manuscript should be dedicated to gathering data that cannot be collected with ease remotely, such as the size of the manuscript, the material it is written on, the nature of the book (its structure, number of pages, quires, etc.), the layout of the page, decorations, and other paratextual features of the manuscript. Fortunately, Smith and Quesnell were able to do this work during their own inspections of the manuscript. So now—with the aid of images—it is time to examine the nature of the handwriting. Quesnell's images make possible close paleographic analysis, so to this task we now turn.

A Fresh Paleographic Analysis

While we have experience working with ancient Greek handwriting, we do not consider ourselves to be experts in modern Greek handwriting. And unlike some scholars who have published their opinions about the style of handwriting found in the *Letter to Theodore*, we do not think it would be appropriate or intellectually honest for us to offer authoritative judgments on the paleography of the *Letter to Theodore*. For this reason, we have decided to do what Smith himself did and contact today's leading experts in Late Greek cursive writing to get their thoughts on the handwriting. Recall that Smith contacted several of the top experts in Greek handwriting, and that they all dated the hand to sometime between the late seventeenth and early nineteenth century, with most preferring the eighteenth century. One, Vanghelis Scouvaras, offered an even more precise date, the middle of the 1700s, and gave Smith an image of a manuscript from that period that he found to be written in the same writing style, which Smith reproduced in his Harvard monograph.[19] Smith reported these expert findings on several occasions; nevertheless, skeptics, most of whom having no formal training in Late Greek handwriting, have disputed their conclusions.

As we have already established, in the absence of a physical manuscript, scholars can work from images. In situations when an in-person examination of the manuscript is not possible—because the manuscript has been lost or destroyed or is otherwise not accessible to scholars—it is imperative that scholars work with the best images available. Anyone who has studied an image of a manuscript long enough knows that poor lighting and failure to clean the manuscript before imaging can give rise to misreadings, as shadows and flecks of dirt begin to resemble meaningful ink traces. Smith's images were good, but they were not excellent. Smith had experience photographing manuscripts—recall that he returned home from his Fulbright in Athens with more than five thousand images of manuscripts!—but he was still an amateur using an ordinary camera. The so-so quality of Smith's photos was partially beyond his control, since he had no access to professional lighting at Mar Saba. And though Smith photographed the manuscript "three times for good measure," he was only able to publish one set of photographs in his 1973 books. Recall too that Harvard cropped the images of the manuscript without Smith's consent, so those disseminated widely to the public were not as complete as the prints he retained.

If the quality of Smith's images left some scholars eager to study the manuscript frustrated, it left others with nagging suspicions. Recall that imperfections in low-quality photographic reproductions gave rise to the theory of the so-called forger's tremor (see chapter 6). But the good news is that before the manuscript vanished, Quesnell ordered another set of images from the librarian. These images are superior to Smith's; they are higher quality, in color, and taken by a professional photographer with a better camera. And while we still lament the patriarchate's unwillingness to allow scholars to view the manuscript and perhaps even produce high-resolution, digital images of these three endpages, we are nonetheless grateful that we have access to Quesnell's photos.

Since skepticism about the date of the handwriting endures, and given the inevitability of developments within the discipline of paleography over the past sixty years, we contacted several of the world's leading experts on later Greek handwriting, and three were generous enough to offer an assessment of the manuscript: Panagiotis Agapitos (University of Cypress, Department of Byzantine and Modern Greek Studies), Erich Lamberz (Bavarian Academy of Sciences, Munich), and Zisis Melissakis (Institute of Historical Research, National Hellenic Research Foundation). We sent each one Quentin Quesnell's 1983 color images and asked them three questions: (1) What date would you give to this sort of hand? (2) Are there any particularly interesting or unusual features about this hand? And (3) how likely do you think it is that such a hand could have been forged in the twentieth century? We present their responses below. We also summarize the views of a fourth expert, Agamemnon Tselikas (director of the Paleographic Institute, Cultural Foundation of the National Bank of Greece, Athens), who recently published his own fresh analysis of the handwriting.

Dr. Panagiotis Agapitos assigned the hand to the "second half of the 18th century, probably in the third quarter (ca. 1750–1775), rather than in the later part of the century."[20] He also directed our attention to several manuscripts from the period that resemble the *Letter to Theodore*: two from the Benaki Museum in Athens and one from the Monastery of St. John the Evangelist on Patmos. Dr. Agapitos says that Benaki Old Collection 21, a manuscript written in 1759, shares many of the Mar Saba manuscript's general characteristics.[21] But he finds more striking parallels between the Mar Saba manuscript and the other two—or, to be more precise, the notes written on them. Benaki Exchange Fund 313 is a manuscript copied in 1674, but the note at the top of the page dates to 1756 and is written, according to Dr. Agapitos, in "a hand very close to the 'Mark Text.'"[22] Another very similar hand appears at the bottom of Patmos 285.[23] While the body text is written in what Dr. Agapitos calls "a restrained cursive," the note at the bottom of the page, dated to 1744, is in the "fluid, cursive style of private hands," the same style of informal writing we find in the *Letter to Theodore*.

When we asked Dr. Agapitos to clarify what he means by "private hand," he said that the term refers to someone who copies texts, but not as a professional. The term "is not related to the social or other standing of the scribe; he might be a monk or layman," but he is not someone who copies texts for a living. In the case of the *Letter to Theodore*, Dr. Agapitos thinks that it may have been copied by a monk with a personal interest in the text, or, if the *Letter to Theodore* is an eighteenth-century composition, written in the informal hand of the person who composed it.

When asked about unique features of the hand, Dr. Agapitos pointed to two features that, in his expert opinion, "cancel the hypothesis of 20th-century forgery": (1) the consistent use of the calligraphic post-Byzantine π (a development from the liturgical scripts of the sixteenth/seventeenth century); (2) the use of the highly traditional abbreviations for τὴν, τῆς, and τῶν. He characterizes the style of handwriting in the *Letter to Theodore* as a cursive and fluid style with a mix of older and newer letterforms[24]—exactly what one would expect from a "private Early Modern Greek hand, rather than a professional scribe."

When asked about the possibility that the manuscript is a twentieth-century forgery, Dr. Agapitos responded in no uncertain terms: "I think it practically impossible that the handwriting could have been forged in the 20th century. Literate persons, who (not having Modern Greek as their native tongue) learned to write sentences in the Greek alphabet used in the nineteenth century a slightly cursive but formalized and vertically oriented script, while in the twentieth century they used (and still use) a more typescript-like standardized script (called the Cambridge font). The script of the few pages in the 17th-century book are far too complex, far too symmetrical and balanced throughout to have been written by an amateur user of the Greek script." Dr. Agapitos concluded with this summary of his assessment: "All in all, my suggestion is a private hand of the 18th century, probably between 1740–1770."

When we presented Quesnell's photographs to Dr. Erich Lamberz, he responded concisely and unambiguously: "(1) The writing of the note is very likely to date back to the 18th century. (2) The hand does not show any unusual forms for this time. (3) I consider it impossible that it is a 20th-century forgery."[25]

Dr. Zisis Melissakis prefaced his response by saying that he was aware that Dr. Tselikas had already evaluated the handwriting of the Mar Saba manuscript in *Biblical Archaeological Review*, but that he had not read the account and would read it only after conducting his own analysis of the handwriting.[26] After looking at the photographs and creating his own independent transcription of the text,

Dr. Melissakis concluded that the cursive script "seems to be dated to the 18th century, most probably in the second half and maybe at the end of this century." However, when Dr. Melissakis began to work through the text line by line and letter by letter, he noticed some "rather unusual forms of letters and ligatures" (including α, ζ, ι, ξ, π, φ, ψ, εν). He also noticed some inconsistencies in word-division conventions but conceded that he has "seen this phenomenon in a few other 18th c. manuscripts." He also noted that while abbreviations commonly used in the eighteenth century appear in the manuscript, they do not appear consistently, and remarked that it is odd to see words like "God" and "Jesus" written out in full rather than appearing in the more common, abbreviated form.

Though Dr. Melissakis still judges the hand to be eighteenth century, the unusual letter forms, ligatures, and scribal features leave open the possibility that the *Letter to Theodore* is a "forgery." In his opinion, however, the "forger" would have had to be active in the early decades of the nineteenth century: "Therefore I conclude that if the script of this manuscript is a forgery, it could not be a forgery of the 20th c., but an imitation dated to the 19th c. (first half, not after 1820–1830), when the Greek script changed, but its system of abbreviations and the forms of letters and ligatures were not yet completely forgotten." In other words, Dr. Melissakis rules out Morton Smith—or anyone else from the twentieth century— as a suspect. If the Mar Saba letter is a forgery, it is the work of a nineteenth-century scribe emulating a style of handwriting en vogue only a generation earlier.

Dr. Melissakis ends his evaluation of the handwriting with a call for a fresh codicological analysis—that is, an in-person study of the Voss edition itself and the endpages containing the *Letter to Theodore*.

Agamemnon Tselikas published his analysis of the language and handwriting of the *Letter to Theodore* in 2009 as part of a special issue of *Biblical Archaeological Review*, a periodical that brings to the general public recent discoveries and trends in biblical studies.[27] Linguistically, Tselikas found occasional grammatical and stylistic problems in the text: an accusative where one expects the nominative, missing accents, unnecessarily dense sentences, and other infelicities here and there. Most significantly, Dr. Tselikas identified one instance of a modern Greek word used where we'd expect an ancient one: when the heretic Carpocrates is said to have procured a "copy" of the Secret Gospel, the Greek word used for copy is *apographon*. However, Dr. Tselikas claims that *apographon* is the modern Greek term for a copy of a book. The ancient Greek term, he asserts, is *antigraphon*.

According to Dr. Tselikas, at first glance the handwriting appears to hail from sometime between the late seventeenth and late eighteenth century. The scribe appears to be "experienced" and maintains control of his pen. On closer examination, however, Dr. Tselikas finds some letterforms that are "completely foreign or strange and irregular," not in keeping with the "generally traditional way and rule of Greek writing." Yet he does find hands similar to the *Letter to Theodore* in "some manuscripts of the 18th century on the island of Cephalonia in Greece." Dr. Tselikas remains suspicious, however, since Morton Smith is known to have studied these manuscripts.

In the end, Dr. Tselikas concludes that the *Letter to Theodore* is likely a forgery, and while he finds it conceivable that Smith could have done the job, he suspects Smith may have worked with an accomplice, a scribe more capable of emulating this particular archaic Greek style, but who nevertheless worked under Smith's direction.

Dr. Tselikas's assessment remains the most detailed and the most prominent today. In fact, one of the paleographers we contacted—Dr. Agapitos, who initially concluded that the *Letter to Theodore* is written in "a private hand of the 18th century, probably between 1740–1770"—revised his position after reading Dr. Tselikas's article. "It seems to me now," he wrote to us some weeks later, "that the text was composed by Morton Smith with help of some Greek-speaking person." He concluded: "It is a fairly successful forgery . . . but it looks like forgery nonetheless."[28]

What, then, are we to make of the mixed results from our experts? One initially dated the hand to 1740–1770 but then became convinced that Smith forged the manuscript with the help of a native Greek speaker. A second dated it to the eighteenth century, ruling out the forgery hypothesis as impossible. A third dated it to the eighteenth century but admitted that it could be an early nineteenth-century forgery. The fourth found close parallels with some eighteenth-century manuscripts from Cephalonia but ultimately concluded that Smith forged the manuscript, perhaps with the help of someone more skilled in Greek handwriting.

Paleography is more an art than a science. And the judgments of expert paleographers often rest on their expert intuition, which we should take seriously because it has been refined over years of working with manuscripts. However, at times paleographers can locate "hard evidence" for dating a hand. In the case of the *Letter to Theodore*, perhaps the most damning potential evidence of forgery lies in Tselikas's observation that the scribe uses a modern Greek term in place of an ancient one. He claims that the ancient Greek word for a copy of a text is *antigraphon*, but that the manuscript reads *apographon*, the modern Greek term. Might the actual author of the text, someone familiar with modern Greek, have slipped up here? Did Smith—or, better, his alleged Greek-speaking co-conspirator— slip up and write *apographon* when he meant to write *antigraphon*?

It is possible that the scribe simply updated the language of the text he was copying to reflect current usage. We know that scribes did occasionally change the language of a text to make it more contemporary. Consider, for example, Luke 4:17, where Jesus is said to "unroll" a scroll of Isaiah. Later scribes apparently changed the verb from "unroll" to "open" in light of their preference for the codex, the book in its modern format.[29] Still, such instances of language updating are rare and, when they do occur, often involve place-names that have changed over time. And why would the scribe of the *Letter to Theodore* update only this word and not others? Thus, we find it unlikely that a scribe changed *antigraphon* to *apographon* to reflect contemporary use.

Nevertheless, it remains unlikely that this is the smoking gun forgery proponents have been looking for, since Tselikas seems to be mistaken. In antiquity words with the root *apograph-* can refer to copies of books, and while modern Greek words with the *apograph-* stem can refer to copies, they are used in a bureaucratic context to refer to legal documents, inventories, censuses, and surveys. Had the scribe wanted to update antiquated language, he would likely have used a term built on the *antitup-* stem.[30]

Therefore, we have to rely on the instincts of the experts we contacted and the two conclusions they reached: (1) that the hand hails from the late eighteenth or early nineteenth century, and (2) that

Smith forged it in the twentieth century, likely with the help of a native Greek speaker who was also skilled in emulating eighteenth-century Greek handwriting. When we add these new assessments to those Smith solicited prior to his 1960 SBL presentation, we must conclude that the weight of expert opinion favors authenticity. Even those who suspect foul play have to posit a co-conspirator who was more proficient in Greek and Late Greek handwriting than Smith was.

At present, the overwhelming evidence from the initial paleographic assessments and this more recent round suggests that even if Smith did compose the *Letter to Theodore* and the Secret Gospel, he likely did not copy it out in the manuscript. It would take an expert forger to fool the world's leading manuscript experts—those Smith consulted and those we consulted who were convinced that the hand predates the twentieth century. Even Dr. Tselikas's table of comparable letterforms from Smith's handwritten Greek and the handwriting of the *Letter to Theodore* is short—a paltry six examples of letterforms that show only passing resemblance. No, these analyses—despite their diversity—make clear that if the *Letter to Theodore* is a modern forgery, it must have been copied by someone else, a native Greek intimately familiar with eighteenth-century Greek hands. But there are no obvious candidates for producing such a forgery, and the weight of evidence still suggests the hand that copied the *Letter to Theodore* and the Secret Gospel of Mark belongs to the second half of the eighteenth century. So the burden of proof rests on those who suspect the manuscript to be a modern forgery, and the one piece of hard evidence that has been produced—the appearance of an allegedly modern Greek term in the manuscript—does not hold up.

CHAPTER EIGHT

The Author

I F THE *LETTER TO THEODORE* is not likely a twentieth-century forgery, then it must be old. But how old? Scholars approach a question like this by establishing two points, the *terminus post quem* and the *terminus ante quem*—that is, the time *after which* and *before which* a text must have been composed. At the outset, we know that the *Letter to Theodore* was likely composed sometime between the second and the eighteenth century. It could not have appeared prior to the lifetime of Clement of Alexandria, to whom it is attributed, and it must be at least as old as the moment it was copied into Voss's edition—that is, sometime in the second half of the eighteenth century. But this is a remarkably broad swath of time, a span of sixteen centuries that saw the fall of the Roman Empire, the rise of Byzantium, the Crusades, and even the birth of the modern printing press. So if we hope finally to arrive at a clear sense of what Morton Smith discovered over sixty years ago at Mar Saba, we'll need to narrow down a more precise date of composition for the text.

Did Clement Write the *Letter to Theodore*?

Let's start with the *terminus post quem*, the date after which it must have been written. Is the name on the manuscript correct? Did

Clement of Alexandria actually compose the *Letter to Theodore*? As we have seen, Morton Smith came to believe that he had discovered an authentic letter of Clement. He arrived at this conclusion not in haste but after conducting a careful comparison of the language of the letter—its words, phrases, metaphors, and grammatical constructions—with the language in texts that Clement is known to have composed. Even though this process was aided by the recent publication of a concordance to Clement's works, the comparison nevertheless took Smith about two years to complete. Smith presented the evidence meticulously in his 1960 SBL talk, and then again in even more detail in his 1973 academic book. He deserves praise for the care with which he worked to establish Clement as the author of the letter, and despite having some prominent critics, he amassed a host of ardent supporters who were convinced that Clement did in fact compose the letter.

But one wonders whether Smith, by painstakingly noting the linguistic parallels between the *Letter to Theodore* and Clement's genuine works, simply retraced the steps of the text's real author. Yes, striking parallels like those presented by Smith could indicate that Clement composed the *Letter to Theodore*, but they also could suggest that whoever composed the letter had access to Clement's writings and used them to imitate the Alexandrian theologian's style. Similarities in language between the *Letter to Theodore* and Clement's known writings can't establish definitively that Clement composed the letter. They leave open a second possibility: someone familiar with Clement's writings composed the letter in Clement's literary style.

Smith was well aware that linguistic similarities alone could not establish definitively that Clement authored the text. He stated sensibly in his SBL presentation that the *Letter to Theodore* is either a "genuine letter" or a "careful imitation." Yet, as we know, Smith ultimately came to the former conclusion. The occasional differences in language and outlook between the *Letter to Theodore* and Clement's known writings made Smith even more confident that Clement had in fact composed the text. "It would be hard to explain," Smith reasoned, "why an imitator should endanger the success of his efforts by inserting details of content which seem to contradict well known passages of Clement's works."[1] Smith was confident: Clement was the author of the *Letter to Theodore*.

But was Smith right? Did the teacher from Alexandria actually compose the letter? There is strong evidence to suggest that Smith was too quick to rule out the alternative possibility, that the *Letter to Theodore* was the work of a later author, someone familiar with Clement's writing style, which the author emulated faithfully, though not perfectly. As we have seen, comparing the language of the letter with Clement's own language can get us only so far. If we want to move beyond the stalemate—that the letter was composed by Clement or someone who knew his style well—we'll need to shift the question from "Does the author's language resemble Clement's?" to "What writings did the person who composed the letter make use of?" We can demonstrate that Clement did not compose the letter if, for example, the author used sources written after Clement's lifetime. Clement could not have drawn on a source composed, say, a century after his death.

The *Letter to Theodore* and Eusebius, "the Father of Church History"

What then is the latest source used by the author of the *Letter to Theodore*? The *Ecclesiastical History* of Eusebius of Caesarea, an innovative and popular history of the church composed in the 320s CE (that is, more than a century after the death of Clement of Alexandria), was likely one of the sources used in the composition of the *Letter to Theodore*. In three key instances the author deviates from Clement's style precisely because he is no longer drawing on Clement's writings but on Eusebius's *Ecclesiastical History*.

Some of what the author of the *Letter to Theodore* knows about Carpocrates he apparently learned from Eusebius. True, Clement does mention Carpocrates in his surviving writings. In *Stromateis* 3.2 he discusses Carpocrates and his followers, the so-called Carpocratians, at length. Yet his report derives not from any firsthand knowledge of Carpocrates or his teachings but from the writings of Carpocrates's son, Epiphanes, treatises "which," Clement reports, "I have at hand." Though Epiphanes died at the tender age of seventeen, he nonetheless lived long enough to enjoy a some-what successful literary career. His book *Concerning Righteousness* was popular enough for Clement to have gotten his hands on it. In fact, Clement's knowledge of the teachings of the Carpocratians is limited to what he has read in *Concerning Righteousness*, and to give the impression that his is a comprehensive knowledge of the sect, he repeatedly presents what Epiphanes has written as representa-tive of the teachings of Carpocrates and his followers as a whole. He characterizes Epiphanes as a student of his father and extrapo-lates Carpocrates's own views from what he has read in Epiphanes's book. After a lengthy refutation of Epiphanes's *Concerning Righteous-ness*, Clement concludes that "these then are the doctrines of the excellent Carpocratians." Clement presents this writing by the son of Carpocrates as representative of the teachings of the remaining members of the sect, either because he believes this to be the case or because he wants others to believe that he knows more than he really does.

By comparison, the author of the *Letter to Theodore* does not seem to rely on Epiphanes's *Concerning Righteousness* for his knowl-edge of the Carpocratians. In truth, whoever composed the *Letter to Theodore* also does not seem to know much about the actual teach-ings of Carpocrates or his followers. Much of what he reports, that they have "unspeakable teachings" and pride themselves on wicked knowledge, is vague and formulaic polemic—but he does give an interesting, and indeed telling, explanation for how Carpocrates got hold of the Secret Gospel of Mark. Apparently Carpocrates, at the instigation of demons, used deceitful arts to enslave a presbyter who had a copy of the Secret Gospel. This detail, completely absent from Clement's report in *Stromateis* 3.2, is oddly specific and presumably requires access to traditions about Carpocrates beyond what could be found in the book written by his son, Epiphanes. Irenaeus, the only other author prior to Clement to discuss Carpocrates, also says nothing about Carpocrates's demonically inspired ability to enslave unsuspecting Christians. This story is found nowhere in the surviv-ing accounts of Carpocrates's life, save one. It is most likely a para-phrase of Eusebius's report about Carpocrates in the *Ecclesiastical History*, a work that, as we have seen, was composed over a century after Clement's death.

Eusebius cites Irenaeus as his source for his knowledge about Carpocrates and his followers: "Irenaeus . . . writes that Carpocrates was a contemporary of these [heretics just mentioned]."[2] What follows is Eusebius's somewhat faithful summary and paraphrase of Irenaeus's more lengthy presentation of the teachings of Carpocrates and his followers. Among the additions that Eusebius makes to Irenaeus's account, one in particular sheds light on the sources used by the author of the *Letter to Theodore*. Inspired perhaps by Irenaeus's claim that the Carpocratians are "sent forth by Satan . . . so that many turn away their ears from the preaching of the truth,"[3] Eusebius introduces his own, novel notion that a "malignant demon . . . making use of . . . these deacons/ministers . . . enslaved those that were so pitiably led astray by them to their own destruction."[4] To be sure, there are a few uncertainties in what Eusebius says. Is Carpocrates the demon? Who are these deacons/ministers? Are they menacing demigods or people who unwittingly participate in the demon's plot? But these details do not matter at present. What matters is that the author of the *Letter to Theodore* seems to be familiar with Eusebius's elaboration on Irenaeus and uses it to craft an account of how Carpocrates got hold of the Secret Gospel of Mark. According to the *Letter to Theodore*, Carpocrates procured a copy of the Secret Gospel after being instructed by the "foul demons" and using his own "deceitful arts" to "enslave a certain presbyter" who had a copy.

The similarities between these two accounts are clear to us. Anyone who has ever caught a clever student cheating on an essay or during an exam will find the pattern familiar. The author of the *Letter to Theodore* has reworded Eusebius's account—"malignant demon" becomes "foul demons," "deacons" becomes "presbyter," the Greek word for "enslaved" is swapped out for a synonym—to create what can pass as an original and authentic legend about Carpocrates and his demonically inspired coercive act. That the author of the *Letter to Theodore* would turn to Eusebius for information on Carpocrates may seem odd, since it was Clement's writing, not Eusebius's, that he was attempting to emulate. However, when we recall that Clement knew nothing about the Carpocratians beyond what he found in a book by Epiphanes, Carpocrates's son, the motivation for consulting Eusebius becomes clear: the real Clement simply didn't know enough about Carpocrates to be useful to the author of the *Letter to Theodore*.

There are other reasons to believe that the author of the *Letter to Theodore* made use of Eusebius. Recall in the *Letter to Theodore* that Mark's Secret Gospel is called "a more spiritual gospel." The expression is strange and, to our knowledge, unparalleled in ancient Christian literature. Yet the designation is also odd within the context of the *Letter to Theodore*, since Mark's first gospel, canonical Mark, is not referred to as a "spiritual gospel," as one would expect the forerunner to the "more spiritual gospel" to be termed. One gets the impression that something is missing from the *Letter to Theodore*, that it is building on another tradition about a "spiritual gospel."

Eusebius again helps us understand what's going on in the *Letter to Theodore*. In *Ecclesiastical History* 6.14 he discusses the order in which the gospels were written by making use of an influential but now largely lost work of Clement of Alexandria, the so-called *Hypotyposeis* or *Outlines*. Eusebius reports that Clement believed that Matthew and Luke wrote their gospels first. Mark followed, being urged by followers of Peter to set down Peter's preaching that he gave in Rome. Then John, "the last to be sure" (*mentoi . . . eschaton*), decided to compose a "spiritual gospel," one focused not exclusively on the "outward facts," as the previous three had been, but on the deeper spiritual significance of Jesus's life and teachings.

Thus in a passage attributed to Clement of Alexandria we find mention of a "spiritual gospel." Might this "spiritual gospel" help us understand the "more spiritual gospel" in the *Letter to Theodore*? Yes, but how? One could perhaps argue that this passage from Clement's *Outlines* quoted in Eusebius suggests that Clement did in fact compose the *Letter to Theodore*, that since Clement did refer to a gospel as a "spiritual gospel," he could refer to another, more esoteric one as a "more spiritual gospel." This was Morton Smith's thinking. However, the hypothesis leaves some important questions unanswered. Why would Clement imply in the *Letter to Theodore* that canonical Mark, not John, was the "spiritual gospel" if he believed John to have been the "spiritual gospel"? Why not just mention John, the "spiritual gospel," in the *Letter to Theodore*? Why would Clement state in the *Outlines* that John was "the last for sure" if he knew that the Secret Gospel of Mark was in fact the last gospel written? It doesn't add up.

There is a simpler explanation: the author of the *Letter to Theodore* has read this passage in Eusebius. The author of the letter seems to have created a text that could plausibly pass as authentic to readers well versed in Eusebius's *Ecclesiastical History*. The *Letter to Theodore* makes the most sense when read as an expansion on the passage from Clement quoted in Eusebius. Readers who already know from Eusebius that Clement believed that Matthew and Luke composed their gospels first, followed by Mark, and then John composed his "spiritual gospel" would then learn from the *Letter to Theodore* that Mark composed a gospel "more spiritual" than John's, the Secret Gospel of Mark. The most plausible scenario, the one that makes the most sense of the language in the *Letter to Theodore*, is that someone designed it to look like an expansion on Eusebius's excerpt from Clement's *Outlines*.

A third and final example further suggests that the author of the *Letter to Theodore* knows Eusebius's *Ecclesiastical History*. One of the striking features of the letter is a detail that was pointed out by Pierson Parker in the *New York Times* immediately following Smith's debut of the manuscript at the SBL meeting in 1960. Parker found the *Letter to Theodore* to be historically valuable, though not on account of the excerpt from the Secret Gospel of Mark it contained. Instead, he believed it preserved the earliest known account of Mark the Evangelist's alleged journey to Alexandria in Egypt. There can be little doubt that the early Jesus movement expanded rapidly in the years following Jesus's death. Paul alone brought the message of the gospel to Asia Minor, Greece, Rome, and possibly even Spain. Yet the origins of Christianity in Egypt have remained a mystery to historians. While there was a vibrant Christian community in Egypt in the second half of the second century, to which Clement belonged, the years leading up to this are murky. Who brought the teachings of Jesus to Egypt, and when?

The earliest report of the first Christian mission to Egypt emerges in writing only in the fourth century, and it comes from Eusebius himself. In *Ecclesiastical History* 2.16.1 he claims that "they say that this Mark was the first that was sent to Egypt, and that he proclaimed the gospel which he had written, and first established churches in Alexandria itself." But with the discovery of the *Letter to Theodore*, we may have, as Parker pointed out, a tradition placing Mark in Alexandria that predates Eusebius by more than a century and hails from an author active in the same city. Presumably someone like Clement would be likely to possess accurate, or at least ancient, local knowledge.

Yet it is strange that Clement does not mention elsewhere in his voluminous writings that Mark brought Christianity to Egypt. According to Eusebius's quote from Clement's *Outlines* discussed above, Clement knew that Mark was a student of Peter and reported that he composed his canonical gospel while in Rome, but said nothing about Mark continuing on to Alexandria.[5] One would think that a tradition linking his own city to one of the authors of the canonical gospels—and a disciple of Peter to boot!—would be worth sharing widely, not burying in a private letter.

It is not impossible that Clement believed that Mark traveled to Alexandria following his stay in Rome, and that he, for whatever reason, chose to reveal this crucial information only in a private letter to an otherwise unknown Theodore. But there is a more likely explanation. Once again, it appears that the author of the *Letter to Theodore* knows Eusebius's *Ecclesiastical History* and has borrowed some ideas from it to make the *Letter to Theodore* seem authentic. Unlike the other two instances of borrowing, however, the notion that Clement knew about Mark traveling to Alexandria comes from a misreading—whether deliberate or accidental, we can't know—of Eusebius. Since this misreading could emerge only from a reading of Eusebius, the *Letter to Theodore*'s dependence on Eusebius seems highly likely in this instance.

As a standalone sentence, Eusebius's report in 2.16.1 about Mark traveling to Alexandria sounds like hearsay: "*They say* that this Mark was the first that was sent to Egypt." This sentence follows directly after a passage in which Eusebius is quoting Clement and Papias, another early Christian author who wrote about the apostles and the composition of the canonical gospels; thus it might sound as if Eusebius is continuing his paraphrase of Clement and Papias. However, Eusebius uses the expression "they say" frequently in his writings, so we can track when and possibly why he decides to use it. Without exception, he uses the formula "they say" when, as one scholar has put it, he "had no clear written authority."[6] In other words, Eusebius likely heard that Mark made it to Alexandria or read it in a source he could no longer locate. Rather than leave the tradition out of his history of Christianity, he chose to flag it as a rumor by prefacing the report with his stock expression "they say." An inattentive or perhaps even opportunistic reader, however, could understand Eusebius's (intentionally?) ambiguous "they say" to mean that Clement and Papias both maintained that Mark the Evangelist brought Christianity to Alexandria. But Eusebius most likely got this information from some other source, not from Clement.

Therefore, given what we now suspect—that the author of the *Letter to Theodore* is making use of Eusebius, and that someone could get the impression from a misreading of Eusebius that Clement thought that Mark made it to Egypt—the most likely conclusion is that the author of the letter is again making use of Eusebius's *Ecclesiastical History*. What remains unclear, however, is whether he has simply misunderstood Eusebius or has deliberately misrepresented him. Yet in either scenario the author seems to be familiar with Eusebius.

That a late antique author would make use of Eusebius's *Ecclesiastical History* to give the impression that he had access to more sources than he really did is, in itself, not surprising. Authors frequently cited sources that they knew only secondhand from Eusebius. For example, John of Scythopolis, a sixth-century Palestinian bishop, claims that he is citing authors like Philo, Irenaeus, and even Clement, when in fact he is only using Eusebius's excerpts of these authors.[7] Even Eusebius himself misled readers, giving them the impression that he had direct access to more sources than he really did.[8] What's innovative about the *Letter to Theodore*, then, is that its author apparently used Eusebius's *Ecclesiastical History* to compose— one might even say forge—a fictitious letter. However, as we will see, the author's motivations for composing the letter—and perhaps even the Secret Gospel itself—are likely more complicated than a term like "forgery" implies.

So if the *Letter to Theodore* builds on traditions in Eusebius's *Ecclesiastical History*, a work composed sometime in the 320s CE, it cannot be an authentic letter of Clement of Alexandria, who died around 215, over a century earlier. This means that we are likely dealing with a pseudepigraphic letter—that is, a letter composed in someone else's name—and that we can move forward our *terminus post quem*, the date *after which* the *Letter to Theodore* was composed, from the second century to the fourth. Recall what A. D. Nock said to Morton Smith in his off-the-cuff assessment of the text when Smith showed it to him: "It must be something medieval; fourth or fifth century, perhaps. They made up all sorts of stuff in the fifth century."[9] It seems that Smith should have listened to Nock.

If the *Letter to Theodore* was likely composed in the fourth century at the earliest, what about the Secret Gospel of Mark? The author claims to offer excerpts from another gospel by Mark the Evangelist. But is he right? Or is he being dishonest about the authorship of the Secret Gospel as well?

Ancient Rewritings of the Gospel of Mark

Even though the *Letter to Theodore* seems to hail from the fourth century or later because its author has consulted Eusebius's *Ecclesiastical History*, it remains possible that the excerpts from the Secret Gospel embedded within it could belong to a first-century writing. After all, the author of the letter does claim that Mark the Evangelist composed the gospel, and even if the author is not actually Clement, the information he gives about Mark's other gospel may still be accurate. Yet the likelihood that he falsely claimed to be Clement of Alexandria gives us reason to suspect that what he says about the great antiquity of the Secret Gospel is also not true.

So when was the Secret Gospel actually composed? In the first century, perhaps even earlier than the canonical version of the Gospel of Mark? In the second century, when a number of apocryphal gospels came into existence? Later than this, and if so, how much later? Despite the very late date of the manuscript, two pieces of evidence—apart from the author's likely dependence on Eusebius's *Ecclesiastical History*—point toward a date sometime after the fourth century. The first of these has been mentioned in passing by a few commentators, but the full implications of this evidence have yet to be explored. The second piece of evidence, which is even stronger than the first, has to our knowledge not yet been considered.

The first reason to suspect that the Secret Gospel was written around the fourth century or somewhat later comes from the fact that the text reports the existence of an expanded version of the Gospel of Mark specifically. Is there any discernible reason why the author of this document would have claimed to possess a secret, longer edition of Mark's Gospel, rather than of Matthew, Luke, or John? In fact, yes: the choice of Mark was by no means random, since this particular gospel was rewritten in antiquity far more than any of the other three. Although the first rewritings of Mark seem to go back to the first century CE, the most tangible instances of rewritings are found in manuscripts produced in the fourth and fifth centuries.

Mark is generally thought to have been the first of the New Testament gospels to be written. Mark also stands in a peculiar relationship to the Gospels of Matthew and Luke, since it seems that these two authors relied heavily on Mark in the composition of their gospels. In other words, Matthew and Luke copied most of Mark's Gospel into their own gospels without citing their source. Matthew and Luke tend to be viewed as distinctive literary creations, but their extensive use and editing of their predecessor qualifies them as the first of many early Christian "rewritings" of Mark's Gospel. Though they were the first to rewrite Mark, they were not the last.

Other ancient rewritings exist, though they are not as thoroughgoing as Matthew and Luke. Many of these smaller rewritings aimed to remedy Mark's strange ending, which we already mentioned in chapter 5. On the basis of manuscript evidence and Mark's distinctive literary characteristics, it appears that this gospel ended abruptly and unexpectedly: when the women discover Jesus's empty tomb, an angel announces that he had been raised from the dead and the women flee from the tomb in terror, not breathing a word of what they saw and heard to anyone (Mark 16:1–8). Now *that* is a shocking ending: no appearances of the risen Jesus to his followers, no instructions on what they are to do now. Just amazement, terror, and silence, despite the good news that Jesus is inexplicably alive again.

Many contemporary biblical scholars love this ending, but it is clear that many ancient readers of Mark found it to be inadequate, with Matthew and Luke as the first on record to come to this conclusion. A little later, a copyist added his own ending to the gospel (Mark 16:9–20), a patchwork retelling of resurrection appearances gleaned from Matthew, Luke, and John. Jesus appears to Mary Magdalene and then to the disciples before sending them out into the world to spread the gospel, equipped with the power of the Spirit so that they can drink poison and handle snakes without danger. Then the scribe has Jesus ascend into heaven. Certainly this is an ending that is more crowd-pleasing and less polarizing than Mark's original ending. This so-called Longer Ending may have been written as early as the second century,[10] but the earliest manuscripts that contain this ending of Mark are from the fourth and fifth centuries. In addition, Christian writers from this period like Eusebius and Jerome say that nearly all the manuscripts that they have seen lack the Longer Ending. So even if the Longer Ending was actually created in the second century, the manuscript evidence suggests that it was still a relatively novel rewriting in the fourth and fifth century.

Even after the creation of this Longer Ending, Christian scribes continued to tinker with Mark's ending and other problematic features of the gospel. A brief addition to Mark's original ending (appropriately called the Shorter Ending) states quite tersely that the women told Peter and the other disciples that Jesus had been raised from the dead, and that Jesus then sent the disciples out into the world to preach the gospel; this ending appears in one fourth-century Latin manuscript by itself, while a number of other manuscripts combine it with the more popular Longer Ending. Different still is an important Greek manuscript housed in the Smithsonian, copied in the fourth or fifth century and fittingly known as Codex Washingtonianus (abbreviated as W): it provides additional dialogue between the risen Jesus and the disciples beyond that found in the Longer Ending. Whereas the Longer Ending simply reports that Jesus shamed his disciples for not believing the reports of his resurrection, Codex W allows the disciples to defend their disbelief by saying, "This age of lawlessness and unbelief is under Satan." In other words, the devil made them do it. This additional dialogue is often referred to by scholars as the "Freer Logion," since Codex W was purchased in Egypt by the American railroad magnate Charles Lang Freer and donated to the Smithsonian as part of his funding of the Freer Gallery of Art.[11]

Two further examples will suffice to show how much ancient evidence exists for the rewriting of Mark. The same fourth-century Latin manuscript that contains the Shorter Ending by itself also adds the following strange report just before the women arrive at Jesus's tomb in 16:4: "But suddenly at [or perhaps 'until'] the third hour of the day there was darkness over the whole circle of the earth, and angels descended from the heavens, and as (Christ) was rising in the glory of the living God, at the same time they ascended with him, and immediately it was light." This addition is not found in any other manuscripts, and since it occurs after the death of Jesus but right before the discovery of the empty tomb, it has usually been interpreted as a description of Jesus's resurrection—an event described nowhere in the New Testament gospels. But the mention of darkness over the earth sounds much more like an account of the crucifixion, and a few scholars have suggested that this is an alternative version of the death of Jesus where Jesus is raised back to life while he is on the cross and then ascends directly into heaven, without any burial. Odd as it may sound for Jesus to ascend into heaven right from the cross, there are some scattered hints throughout other writings that some early Christians believed this.[12]

One last example is particularly important for our purposes, since it shows that early Christian scribes were not simply content to supplement the ending of Mark's Gospel—though the peculiar ending of the gospel certainly attracted a great deal of attention. Revisions to Mark could take place wherever a reader or a scribe felt that the content was flawed, objectionable, or incomplete in some way. Again, the Gospels of Matthew and Luke provide the most extensive evidence of this, with rewritings great and small distributed throughout the entirety of the portions of their gospels where they rely on Mark. But one example found in manuscripts of Mark is especially striking. In Mark 1:40 a leper comes and kneels before Jesus, begging to be healed of his affliction. In most English translations, Jesus is reported as being "moved by compassion" by this request—exactly the sort of reaction that we would expect from Jesus. But a few important early manuscripts instead say that Jesus "became angry" or "was indignant" in response to the leper's request for a cure. Why in the world would Jesus get mad at a poor leper? It is difficult to explain his reaction, but many scholars are convinced that this is the original reading, which a later copyist changed to "moved by compassion." This makes a great deal of sense, since it is much easier to imagine a scribe changing an unpleasant reaction by Jesus to a much nicer one. In spite of the problems posed by Jesus getting angry at a leper, a few brave recent translations of the Bible have opted for this reading, since it appears most likely to be the original one.[13]

Why Did the Author of the Secret Gospel Rewrite Mark?

So, we have seen a number of instances where ancient readers attempted to "fix" problems in the text of the Gospel of Mark or "improve" on its narrative. Some of these instances concern things that readers felt *should* have been present in Mark, like appearances of the risen Jesus. Other passages seem to have been changed because of how readers felt Jesus *should* or *should not* behave. Confronted with so many ancient rewritings of Mark's Gospel, it might be illuminating to read the alleged excerpts from the Secret Gospel of Mark in the *Letter to Theodore* as yet another rewriting of Mark. Viewed from this perspective, what problems in Mark's narrative or portrayal of Jesus might the rewriting in the Mar Saba manuscript have attempted to remedy? And might the characteristics of this rewriting point to a specific kind of reader of Mark, living in a particular place and time?

There are at least three difficulties with Mark's Gospel that the excerpts from the Secret Gospel apparently intend to resolve. The first has to do with some confusing, perhaps even contradictory, geographical information in Mark 10, which is where the expansion in the Secret Gospel is said to be located. At this stage in Mark's story, Jesus is journeying from Galilee to Jerusalem for the Passover festival and is said in 10:1 to be crossing over to the other (eastern) side of the Jordan River. Although the Jordan is not especially wide or deep, it is significant enough as a geographical marker that biblical narratives often note when a person or group crosses it. But the next geographical notice, in Mark 10:46, has Jesus coming into Jericho, which is on the western side of the Jordan. When did he cross back to the other side of the river? Mark does not tell us. Even more strangely, right after saying that he entered Jericho, Mark tells us that Jesus left Jericho. What did he do while he was there? Again, Mark does not explain.

Some scholars believe these geographical problems in Mark 10 were created when the contents of the Secret Gospel—which they believe was older than the version of Mark's Gospel that has come down to us—were excised by an ancient editor who regarded the material from the Secret Gospel as objectionable.[14] But we have already seen a number of instances where Matthew, Luke, or other ancient readers of Mark rewrote parts of the gospel that they considered to be deficient. It is just as plausible, if not more so, that the geographical problems in Mark 10 were yet another instance of the original author's lack of polish. In that case, we could imagine that a reader who was keenly aware of Palestinian geography might have spotted the issue and took the liberty of expanding the text to describe Jesus's travels more completely. Even better, these holes in Mark's narrative provided this careful reader with the perfect opportunity to place a story about Jesus raising a young man from the dead in a setting on the other side of the Jordan—namely, the village of Bethany where John 1:28 says that John the Baptist did his work. This reader of Mark, who seems to have known all four New Testament gospels very well, probably opted for Bethany across the Jordan because it had the same name as the village where John 11 reports that Jesus raised Lazarus from the dead—a narrative with many resemblances to the one found in the Secret Gospel. The imaginative reader was even able to use Mark's curious reference to Jesus entering and leaving Jericho as the setting for the second excerpt from the Secret Gospel, where Jesus rejected the female relatives of the young man.

The second difficulty with Mark that the Secret Gospel attempts to resolve concerns one of the most mysterious passages in the New Testament. When Jesus is arrested in the garden of Gethsemane according to Mark, all of his disciples immediately flee. But they are not the only ones who flee: Mark also reports, "A certain young man was following him, wearing nothing but a linen cloth. They caught hold of him, but he left the linen cloth and ran off naked" (14:51–52). Questions about this passage abound. Who is the young man? Why was he out in the middle of the night wearing only the equivalent of a bedsheet? Why does Mark feel that this information is important enough to narrate at such a pivotal moment in his story of Jesus—and yet does not even supply the youth's name?

In the nearly two thousand years since Mark's Gospel was written, no one has been able to explain satisfactorily the meaning of this strange incident.[15] Matthew and Luke did not even try: neither of them includes this story from Mark in their gospels. Matthew and Luke seem to have used Mark independently of one another, and it is rare for them to change Mark in exactly the same way. But there are a handful of instances where they both decide to omit the same passage from Mark, and nearly all of these cases involve material that is either embarrassing, confusing, or—as seems to be the case with the fleeing naked youth—both. One of the oldest and most popular explanations of this scene is that the unnamed young man is a kind of "artist's signature" in the gospel. In other words, the young man was actually the evangelist himself, who had a fleeting acquaintance with the historical Jesus decades before he wrote his gospel. As intriguing as this idea might be, it is just as speculative as all the other explanations for Mark's strange incident. We simply do not know what this passage means.

Yet the reader of Mark who wrote the *Letter to Theodore* solved this puzzle in a particularly novel way: by creating a new story earlier in the gospel that explained who this young man was. In the Secret Gospel, the young man is raised from the dead by Jesus, desires to remain with him, and receives secret teachings from him— wearing nothing but the same linen cloth that he will shed several days later when he flees from the scene of Jesus's arrest. Is this young man to be identified with Lazarus, whose resurrection John's Gospel reports as also taking place in a village called Bethany? It is tempting to think so, especially since there are a number of affinities between the Secret Gospel excerpt and the Lazarus narrative. Nevertheless, it is important to observe that just as Mark's Gospel leaves the young man in the linen sheet unnamed, so does the Secret Gospel. The reasons for this omission will become clear a little later.

The third problem that the author of the Secret Gospel endeavored to solve pertains not only to Mark's Gospel but to John's as well. Both of these gospels mention several individuals who Jesus is said to "love," though the reasons for and nature of his love for them are never made clear.[16] In Mark 10, only a few verses before the Secret Gospel addition, we find the famous story of a rich man asking Jesus what he must do to receive eternal life. After the man tells Jesus that he has kept all the commandments since he was a boy, Jesus is said to "look" at the man and "love him" (*ēgapēsen auton*; Mark 10:21). What is the meaning behind this strange reaction of Jesus? Interpreters ancient and modern have grasped at straws seeking a solution. It might mean that Jesus regards the man as an excellent potential disciple. Or it might mean that Jesus finds him to be naïve and has compassion for him, since in a moment Jesus will tell this rich man to do something that Jesus knows he cannot: sell all his possessions and give the money to the poor. In this case, the meaning would be something akin to a patronizing expression used in the American South, "Bless his heart." Or might Jesus's "love" for this man have been more complex and intense than either of these two interpretations would have it? We don't know; Mark doesn't tell us.

The mystery of Jesus's love for this man deepens when we turn to John's Gospel. As many know, this gospel has much to say about love. Think, for instance, of such passages as "For God so loved the world" (John 3:16) or "Just as I have loved you, you also should love one another" (John 13:34). But in addition to these well-known verses, the Gospel of John refers to two specific individuals that Jesus loves: one of them is definitely a man and the other probably is. The first of these is Lazarus, whom Jesus raises from the dead in John 11. At the beginning of the story, messengers report Lazarus's dire condition to Jesus by saying, "Lord, he whom you love is ill" (John 11:3). The specialness of their relationship is underscored by Jesus weeping at the sight of Lazarus's tomb, a reaction that causes a nearby crowd of mourners to exclaim, "See how he loved him!" (John 11:36). The reasons for Jesus's love for Lazarus are, at least potentially, less mysterious than the love he has for the rich man, since Jesus seems to have a long-standing relationship not only with Lazarus but also with his sisters, Mary and Martha. Yet even though Jesus is said to love the whole family, it is his deep affection for Lazarus that is reinforced throughout the narrative.

A few chapters later in John's Gospel, an enigmatic new character will be mentioned for the first of several times. During the Last Supper, we learn of an unnamed disciple of Jesus, referred to only as "the disciple whom Jesus loved." This mysterious disciple appears in several pivotal scenes at the end of Jesus's life: he or she stands at the foot of the cross with Jesus's mother and Mary Magdalene when all the other disciples have fled; runs alongside Peter to verify Mary Magdalene's report of the empty tomb; and recognizes the risen Jesus standing on the seashore while fishing with other disciples. Scholars refer to this enigmatic figure as the "Beloved Disciple," and no consensus exists about his or her identity. The most popular solution, however, is that the Beloved Disciple is John the son of Zebedee, since this prominent follower of Jesus is never mentioned by name in the gospel that would eventually be attributed to him. But many other candidates for the Beloved Disciple have been proposed, including Lazarus, Mary Magdalene, and Nicodemus.

As with the other instances in the Gospels where Jesus is said to "love" a particular person, the nature of Jesus's love for the Beloved Disciple remains unspecified. Nevertheless, during the Last Supper scene where this character is introduced, details about the disciple's placement at the meal suggest that he and Jesus have an unusually close relationship. In John 13:23–25 this disciple is described not simply as reclining next to Jesus but actually as "resting on his breast" and then as "lying back on his chest" when he is prompted by Peter to ask Jesus a question.[17] In effect, the disciple seems to be using Jesus's torso as a pillow. To be sure, the body positioning that would be used in the ancient custom of reclining at a meal would in itself likely be regarded as overly intimate by many modern, Western observers. Even so, the closeness of Jesus and the Beloved Disciple goes far beyond the conventions of ancient meal practices and borders on the erotic.

Is the Secret Gospel Homoerotic?

It therefore appears that a thoughtful and creative reader carved out a space in Mark 10 for a new story about an intimate encounter that Jesus had with a younger male disciple. Although the story itself has never before appeared in precisely this form, it builds on traditions about Jesus that existed earlier: traditions about a mysterious young man who ran away naked at Jesus's arrest, about a very close friend whom Jesus raised from the dead, and about Jesus's unexplained love for several men throughout the Gospels. Such a reader would probably not have viewed this creation as an "invented" or "forged" narrative; rather, this was simply an exercise in "filling in the gaps," in pulling together subtle details scattered throughout the Gospels and making the meaning of these details clear.

We would be justified in surmising that this rewriter of Mark was particularly concerned about same-sex relationships between men. This is, of course, precisely what several recent commentators on the Secret Gospel have pointed out. They have argued that this concern about homosexuality is thoroughly modern and reveals that the author of the letter of Clement is none other than Morton Smith. In reaction to the allegations of forgery, those who believe this document to be an authentic ancient letter of Clement have frequently insisted that there are no homoerotic elements in the text: the young man coming to Jesus at night nearly naked is nothing more than a standard description of early Christian baptismal practices.

As has so often been the case in the history of research on the Secret Gospel, both of these well-entrenched positions are likely incorrect. On the one hand, the defenders of the authenticity of Secret Mark are wrong: the description of the relationship between Jesus and the young man in this expanded version of the Gospel of Mark is undeniably homoerotic. Jesus grasps the man by the hand. The young man "looks" at Jesus, "loves" him, and "begs" Jesus "to be with him." Jesus accepts the man's entreaty to come stay in his house, and stays for nearly a week. Jesus then tells the young man to come to him at night wearing nothing but a linen cloth. They stay together throughout the night, with Jesus imparting secret teachings to the man. As we have seen, there are certainly a number of suggestively homoerotic passages throughout the Gospels of Mark and John, but in the Secret Gospel these elements are emphasized by combining them. Attempts to minimize or explain away the homoeroticism of the Secret Gospel are simply not persuasive.

On the other hand, partisans from both the forgery and authenticity camps are wrong in their shared assumption that the presence of homoerotic elements automatically means that the text originated in the twentieth century. Yes, it is true that the precise contours of what is termed "homosexuality" become fully articulated only in medical literature from the nineteenth century onward, and earlier cultures generally lacked the concept of a stable, unchanging "sexual orientation." Nevertheless, references to same-sex desire and sexual activity can be found in the literary and material records of virtually every known human culture.[18]

But even if same-sex pairing is a recurring phenomenon throughout history, the "rules" that govern such relationships are time-bound. Consider, for example, ancient Greece, where same-sex relationships were common. Yet the conventional wisdom among scholars has been that Greeks deemed same-sex relationships appropriate not on the basis of modern notions of romantic love or compatibility—frequently regarded as the standards for successful relationships today, same-sex or otherwise—but according to the extent to which sexual practices in the bedroom played by the same rules as those governing the culture more broadly. If in the public square a master has dominion over a slave, a slave-holder is expected to play an active role in the bedroom, and a slave a passive one. Violation of these culturally bound "rules" would result in behavior deemed deviant.[19]

So we can shift our attention from the mere fact that the Secret Gospel includes a scene in which Jesus and a young man engage in some sort of same-sex relationship to observe how their relationship is characterized. What, we can ask, are the cultural "rules" of the relationship? In doing so, we get a better sense of the outlook of the author and gain access to some clues as to when the Secret Gospel was written, by whom, and for what reasons.

The main point of the Secret Gospel of Mark is plain enough. The author seeks to sanction a particular kind of same-sex relationship by adding a scene to the Gospel of Mark in which Jesus has an intimate relationship with a young man. The two are not equals—Jesus is older and wiser, and let's not forget that he brought the young man back from the dead—but they forge a bond none-theless, or perhaps because of their asymmetry. The young man "loves" Jesus and wants to be "with him," an invitation Jesus accepts when he stays at the young man's house. Yet there are boundaries in their relationship; while their union may be intimate, even erotic, it is not explicitly sexual:[20] despite the best efforts of the licentious "Carpocratians" to pervert the teachings of Jesus, the expression "naked man with naked man" does not appear in the Secret Gospel, "Clement" insists. Jesus mentors the young boy, first by whispering an instruction in his ear, then by staying up all night teaching him the secrets of the kingdom of God. This final detail reveals another aspect of their relationship: it is cast in the language of Christian spirituality. The same-sex relationship between the young man and Jesus is presented as a legitimate—even ideal—expression of faith.

This model of same-sex coupling—an erotic but not necessarily sexual relationship between two Christian men, one a mentor, the other a novice—does not hail from the twentieth century, not with all we know so far about the manuscript, the sources the text uses, and its desire to rewrite part of the Gospel of Mark. It must come from another culture, another era. But where, and when?

CHAPTER NINE

The Monastery

W E SUSPECT ONE OF THE major reasons that skeptics doubt the authenticity of the *Letter to Theodore* and the Secret Gospel of Mark has nothing to do with the circumstances of the manuscript's discovery. Long-lost writings surface in libraries from time to time, especially those—like what Smith found in the tower library at Mar Saba in 1958—that are disorganized and lack a comprehensive catalogue. Nor is the format of the *Letter to Theodore* alone enough to arouse suspicion: while most manuscripts survive apart from print volumes, Smith uncovered several other examples at Mar Saba of printed books with handwriting on the blank pages. Nor, we would venture, is the nature of the handwriting alone enough to cause people to suspect the *Letter to Theodore* and the Secret Gospel are forgeries. Most paleographers—those consulted by Smith and those we contacted—consider the style of handwriting to be typical of the late eighteenth century, and those who expressed doubts nevertheless often admit that Smith must have had a highly skilled accomplice, someone capable of emulating an antiquated, difficult style of cursive Greek handwriting to a high degree of accuracy.

It is rather the *content* of the *Letter to Theodore*—of the Secret Gospel of Mark, to be more precise—that initially leads scholars to doubt the authenticity of the text. Jesus and a nearly nude young man stay up all night discussing the "mystery of the kingdom"? This must be a joke, right? The shocking content of the Secret Gospel raises red flags for scholars, causing them to scrutinize seemingly innocuous details—the circumstances of the manuscript's discovery, its format, handwriting style, and so on—and setting in motion a wild-goose chase for additional evidence of forgery. Smith's other discoveries, those with less shocking content, have not been subject to the level of scrutiny that the *Letter to Theodore* and the Secret Gospel have.

But if we take a step back, Jesus's intimate evening with the young man is not necessarily the most shocking detail in the Secret Gospel. What's truly stunning is that Jesus brings a dead person back to life. Even in homophobic societies, Jesus's intimacy with the young man merely violates a religious or cultural norm, but his ability to reanimate a corpse violates the most basic laws of nature. The only reason we don't regard the resurrection scene as shocking is that Jesus is well known to have raised people from the dead. Most famous—and one of the chief inspirations for the scene in the Secret Gospel—is the raising of Lazarus, who had been entombed for four days before Jesus brought him back to life (John 11:17). So if we read Jesus's miraculous act of bringing the young man back to life in the Secret Gospel without raising an eyebrow, it is because resurrection has become normalized within Christian tradition.

Therefore, in our quest to contextualize the Secret Gospel of Mark, we must ask ourselves whether there is a time and place in which telling a story about Jesus spending time with a young man would be less shocking. Was there a time in the history of Christianity when such a scene would be less controversial than it has been in the twentieth and twenty-first centuries?

The Writings of Clement in Late Antique Palestine

Our search for the context should start, logically, in the place where this manuscript was discovered: the Mar Saba monastery in the Judean desert. No one outside the monastery seems to have known about the *Letter to Theodore* or the Secret Gospel, so it may be that the text was composed in-house and never left the premises. Recall too that even though the monastery's holdings have dwindled in the modern era because of a fire, the relocation of many of its books to Jerusalem, and intermittent theft, Mar Saba once boasted one of the largest libraries in the region. Yet Mar Saba was no island, in spite of how desolate its surroundings might appear. In its heyday—the fifth to eighth century CE—Mar Saba was a destination for monks in the area who wanted to consult the library's rare books, often while writing their own. Additionally, the monastery, like many in and around Jerusalem, was strategically located near places connected to events that occurred in the Bible. Pilgrims traveling to holy sites frequently visited the monastery.[1] Since traveling monks and other pilgrims most likely introduced books into the library at Mar Saba in late antiquity, we should also look to the broader milieu of Palestinian monasticism for clues as to the origins of the *Letter to Theodore* and the *Secret Gospel*.[2]

We have good reason to suspect that whoever composed the *Letter to Theodore* had access to Eusebius's *Ecclesiastical History* and some of Clement's genuine writings. He or she also seems to have known Clement as "the Stromatist" and as a letter writer. Therefore it is worth considering at the outset whether these texts would have been available in the region. Let's start with Clement's writings, since the availability of his writings in the area has received some attention in the scholarly literature on the *Letter to Theodore*. Morton Smith himself uncovered evidence for a collection of letters of Clement at Mar Saba. The *Sacra Parallela*, attributed to John of Damascus, who resided at Mar Saba from 716 to 749, mentions "the 21st letter of Clement" and "a letter of Clement."[3] Smith argued on the basis of these references that the *Letter to Theodore* could have come from this collection of genuine letters of Clement located at Mar Saba. However, since we believe the *Letter to Theodore* not to be an authentic letter of Clement, the references in the *Sacra Parallela* instead suggest to us that Clementine literature may have been on site. Moreover, if the author of the *Letter to Theodore* were a monk at Mar Saba, he would have known Clement as—among other things—a letter writer, and thus could have expected a long-lost letter of Clement to pass as plausibly authentic.

But the author of the *Letter to Theodore* must have known Clement's other writings too, since his emulation of the Alexandrian theologian's style is so skillful that after two years of careful linguistic study, Smith was convinced that Clement was the author. Unfortunately, the manuscript evidence for Clement's writings is sparse and late. We don't have early, physical copies of Clement's writings from the region, hard evidence that he was being read in Palestine in late antiquity. However, we do know that Jerusalem was home to a well-stocked library; in fact, Jerusalem was home to the first Christian library on record. It was founded in the third century by Alexander, the bishop of Jerusalem and a former student of none other than Clement himself.[4] His teacher's writings would almost certainly have numbered among the stacks, especially considering that Clement dedicated one of his books to Alexander.[5] We also know that Alexander was in possession of at least one letter written by Clement, which he circulated among Christians who, he claimed, were already familiar with Clement's writings.[6]

Clement's writings would likely also have been available at the famous library of Caesarea, located about sixty miles northwest of Mar Saba. Among the library's holdings were many of Origen's books. While there is good reason to doubt that Clement and Origen both belonged to a catechetical school in Alexandria, Origen was certainly influenced by Clement and even cites him occasionally.[7] Thus Clement's writings were likely among Origen's holdings. Any writings of Clement that Origen didn't have, however, may have been acquired by Pamphilus, presbyter and avid bibliophile who is largely responsible for amassing tens of thousands of books at the library of Caesarea.

Smith himself makes a passing observation that he marshals in support of his argument that the *Letter to Theodore* is authentic, but it also further strengthens the case for the availability of Clement's writings in the region of Palestine in late antiquity. In the midst of a complex case he is making for the authenticity of the letter, Smith notes that Clement was not popular enough among early Christians to be the namesake of a forgery. Yet, as Smith correctly points out, there is an exception: "a cluster of citations" that point to a surge of interest in and access to Clement's writings in the late fifth, sixth, and seventh centuries.[8] Among the six authors he names, all hail from the East, and two, Antiochus of Mar Saba and John Moschos, have direct ties to Mar Saba. To Smith's list we should add John of Damascus, who also knew Clementine literature and resided at Mar Saba for a time, and Sophronius, who also cites Clement's writings and will reappear again in this chapter because of his close relationship with John Moschos. It would seem that Clement's writings were particularly popular at Mar Saba in the monastery's heyday.

Eusebius's *Ecclesiastical History* would also have been readily available in Palestine. A student of Pamphilus, Eusebius made use of the library of Caesarea when writing his own books, and when the library holdings dwindled during the persecution of Diocletian, two of his own students, Acacius and Euzoius, built it back up.[9] It is hard to imagine that they didn't ensure that their teacher's writings were included. *Ecclesiastical History*, the work likely known by the author of the *Letter to Theodore*, was especially popular. Many late antique Christian writers, particularly church historians, made use of it.[10]

In short, someone at Mar Saba or in the region would have had access—perhaps *unrivaled* access—to the writings of Clement and Eusebius. Furthermore, the evidence from John of Damascus and Alexander indicates that Christians in and around Mar Saba would also have known Clement as, among other things, a writer of letters.

Two additional details help us triangulate late antique Palestine as the likely context for the composition of the *Letter to Theodore*: the letter's designation of Clement as "the Stromatist" and its interest in the Carpocratians. Alone they do not demonstrate unequivocally that the *Letter to Theodore* hailed from this particular time and region, but as part of the cumulative case we are making, they are noteworthy. It should come as no surprise that Smith commented on both of these issues extensively in his monograph. He cites several other authors who call Clement "the Stromatist," and even includes a collection of primary sources that mention the Carpocratians. Smith's diligent work actually strengthens the case for the *Letter to Theodore* as a late antique composition.

Clement seems not to have been known as "the Stromatist" before the fifth century, when it became a common designation for him. For this reason, Smith concluded that a later scribe may have added a heading to the letter: "The heading is conventional and might be the work of any excerpt down to the time of the present [manuscript]; it cannot be used to date the collection from which the text was taken."[11] But if the *Letter to Theodore* was a late antique composition, then we need not assign the heading to a later scribe; it could be the work of the author himself. The author may call Clement "the Stromatist" precisely because that was Clement's designation at the time. What for him was a banal designation may in fact be a fingerprint that allows us to locate, in time if not in place, the actual author. Two of the first authors to call Clement "the Stromatist" had ties to Palestine in the fifth through seventh century, and one was John Moschos, onetime resident of Mar Saba.

As for the interest of this text in the Carpocratians: part of what led Smith to believe that Clement of Alexandria composed the *Letter to Theodore* was the discussion of the Carpocratians therein. The Carpocratians, as we have seen, were an early Christian sect active only in the second century. Why would someone mention them in later centuries? Even during Smith's "dark night of the soul"—when he had his doubts about the authenticity of the *Letter to Theodore*—he found solace in the idea that the Carpocratians simply would not have been of interest to an eighteenth-century monk. "Who, at that time, could have made up such a thing? What monk knew anything about Carpocrates? What motive could there possibly have been for the invention of such a document?"[12] It turns out later monks were interested in the Carpocratians, and Smith includes these later discussions of the heretical sect in his monograph. In light of the present argument, it becomes significant that three of the sources Smith includes are from late antique Palestine, and two have a connection to Mar Saba: John of Damascus and Sophronius.[13] It seems that later monks—though perhaps not as late as the eighteenth century—did have an abiding interest in the Carpocratians.

But it is not enough to argue that the *Letter to Theodore* and the Secret Gospel could have been composed in late antique Palestine on the basis of the availability of source texts alone. To make a more compelling case for the text's origin in this time and place, we must consider several additional questions: Does the author of the Secret Gospel make use of literary tropes peculiar to the region at that time? Does the message of the Secret Gospel participate in conversations taking place in and around Mar Saba? The answer to both questions is yes.

Death and Resurrection in John
Moschos's *Spiritual Meadow*

We have already seen how the Secret Gospel belongs to a long tradition of rewriting Mark that began with Matthew and Luke and continued for centuries. But there are aspects of the vignette in the Secret Gospel that fit well within the storytelling conventions of late antique Palestinian monasticism, conventions present even within the walls of Mar Saba.

Stories of death and resurrection abound in monastic authors, who were eager to give accounts of God's ability to accomplish miraculous deeds. Tombs are also a fixture in this literature, since many hermits took up residence in tombs. Both themes coalesce in an account that is as comical as it is terrifying. According to one legend, when a hermit named Macarius attempted to leave the cave he had dwelt in for three years, a corpse in the tomb—Macarius was unaware that he had been living with a roommate!—came to life and prevented him from leaving. Apparently, the mummy wanted Macarius to stay since his presence had brought comfort to the mummy, easing suffering he experienced even in death.[14]

But some of the most intriguing parallels to the Secret Gospel from the literature of the region are found in a seventh-century text known as the *Spiritual Meadow*. Several of its stories likely help us hone in on where and when the Secret Gospel—and the *Letter to Theodore* that frames it—was composed. The *Spiritual Meadow* was the work of John Moschos, who was born in the middle of the sixth century, likely in Damascus. He eventually left his family and joined the Monastery of Saint Theodosios, located not far from Mar Saba. John Moschos then traveled around the region and south to Egypt, conducting interviews so he could document the piety of past and present generations of monks. His research travels included a stint at Mar Saba. The *Spiritual Meadow* is something of a hagiographical notebook filled with the stories, teachings, and people he encountered during his travels. Among those he interviewed were residents of, in his words, the "monastery of our holy father Saba."[15] One might think of John Moschos's *Spiritual Meadow* as an archive of monastic legends or tales told at Mar Saba and the surrounding region.

A recurring theme in the *Spiritual Meadow* is resurrection, present in accounts of people dead and entombed who miraculously come back to life when another person comes into contact with them. These scenes often also include a more or less subtle erotic subtext. Resurrection stories in the *Spiritual Meadow*, then, may provide us with the elusive white whale of Secret Gospel scholarship, comparable examples of ancient literature that resemble the Secret Gospel in form and meaning. The parallels between the Secret Gospel and the resurrection narratives in the *Spiritual Meadow* are quite remarkable. Equally remarkable is the fact that no previous studies of Morton Smith's discovery show an awareness of these similarities.

The first example of such a story comes in chapter 11 of the *Spiritual Meadow*, and it is a story told to John Moschos by a priest named Peter, a leader at the monastery of Mar Saba. John likely heard the story while visiting the monastery. Peter told of a certain Hagiodoulos, an elder at the nearby monastery of Gerasimos, who was unaware that one of his beloved monks had died. When the time of mourning had come, Hagiodoulos saw the body of the monk and began to grieve. He then told the dead monk, "Arise, brother, and greet me." The deceased then "arose and greeted him," and the elder told him to "rest" or, as another manuscript has it, "give me the kiss of peace." After the kiss, the man dies again and returns to his resting place.

There are differences between this resurrection story and the Secret Gospel of Mark, chief among them that the young man in the Secret Gospel comes back to life until presumably he eventually dies a natural death, whereas Hagiodoulos's subordinate returns immediately to the grave. However, we find it striking that within the walls of Mar Saba a story circulated about a cherished man who miraculously emerged from his grave at the command of a male superior so the two could share a final moment together, perhaps even a "kiss of peace."

John Moschos recounts two additional resurrection stories that share even more striking affinities with the scene in the Secret Gospel. The first appears in chapter 77, when a monk living in Alexandria tells Sophronius and John Moschos how he lost his eyesight:

> When I was younger I really hated working, so I became dissolute. When I found myself without anything to eat, I began to steal. One day, after I had accomplished many wicked things, I stood in the market and I saw a well-dressed corpse on the way to be buried. I followed the procession in order to see where they were going to bury the body. They went to the back of St. John's Church, and laid the body in a tomb, and then departed. Once I saw that they had left, I went into the tomb and stripped the body of its clothing, except for a single linen cloth. As I was about to leave the tomb, taking many things, my wickedness said to me: "Take the linen cloth as well, because it is possibly valuable." So I turned back, wretched man that I am, and stripped the body of the linen cloth, and left it naked. Then the dead man got up before me, and stretched out his two hands toward me, and with his fingers scratched my face and gouged out both of my eyes. Then I pitifully left everything behind and, in great pain and affliction, left the tomb. Behold, I have told you how I became blind.

Despite some differences, it is difficult to read this story without the scene in the Secret Gospel coming to mind. True, Jesus does not appear in this scene, and there is no mention of blindness in the Secret Gospel, but many of the other themes in this story bear more than a passing resemblance to what we find in the Secret Gospel: a wealthy deceased person in a tomb, a miraculous resurrection, a linen cloth draped over his body, a coyness toward nudity. What are we to make of these curious parallels?

A third resurrection scene appears in the very next chapter, and this one allegedly took place in "Theoupolis," or the Divine City, likely a reference to Jerusalem. In this passage the leader of a monastery relates to John and his companion the tale of a recent event that led a young man to become a monk:

Two days ago I heard that the young daughter of a top-
ranking person in this city had died and been buried in many
clothes in a tomb outside the city. Now I was already in the
habit of this unlawful act (of grave robbing). At night I went
to the tomb and began to disrobe the body. I stripped her of
all she was wearing, not even sparing her undergarment, but
removing that from her as well, leaving her as naked as she
was when she was born. As I was about to leave the grave,
she got up before me and reached out her left hand. She
grabbed my right hand and said: "Oh, man, was it necessary
to strip me naked? Do you not fear God? Do you not fear
the judgment that is sure to be repaid? Ought not you to
have pity on me in my death? Should you not be ashamed of
my biological sex? But as a Christian, how can you condemn
me to present myself naked before Christ, because you did
not respect my biological sex?"

Here we find the now familiar premise: a wealthy person—in
this instance a woman—dies, and a grave robber attempts to steal
the deceased person's possessions. Unlike the thief from the first
story, however, this one takes the linen cloth during his first pass,
"leaving her as naked as she was when she was born." The girl then
miraculously comes back to life, grabs the hand of the grave robber,
and chastises him not only for his greed but also for his wanton dis-
regard for modesty.

It should be clear from these last two scenes that we find in the
Spiritual Meadow the same peculiar convergence of themes found
in the Secret Gospel of Mark. Stories about dead wealthy people
coming back to life become the occasion for addressing concerns
about sexuality, the body, and propriety in the presence of God.
True, these stories are not identical to the one told by the author
of the Secret Gospel, and it is not our intention to argue that John
Moschos composed the Secret Gospel. After all, Moschos's Greek
style differs from that of the Secret Gospel and the broader *Letter to
Theodore*, and one struggles to explain why someone like John, who
openly writes about these matters in *Spiritual Meadow*, would feel
compelled to hide behind a pen name in the *Letter to Theodore*. Yet
the parallels are striking enough to suggest that the Secret Gospel

and the *Letter to Theodore* may well have been composed around the same place and time as the *Spiritual Meadow*: late antique Palestine.

Same-Sex Monastic Couples in Ancient Christianity

Apart from this proliferation of resurrection stories in ancient Christian monastic literature, there is a second set of materials from the same collection of writings that helps us contextualize the Secret Gospel within this milieu even more securely. Let us begin with a closer look at Mar Saba and its fifth-century founder. Saint Sabas exercised a considerable influence on Christian monasticism in the Middle East, but recall that his tenure as the leader of the monastery was fraught with controversy. On at least two occasions, groups of monks opposed his rule and left to found their own communities. A major source of the tension seems to have been that Sabas was not a very deep or sophisticated thinker, whereas many of the monks at Mar Saba were highly educated and conversant with a broad spectrum of ancient Christian theological thinking.

To understand better the dynamics of the relationship between Sabas and the monks under his authority, it will be helpful to know something about the living arrangements within this monastery in antiquity. Monastic life often followed one of two models. Those who preferred to live mostly in isolation from other people practiced eremitic, or desert, monasticism. Saint Antony is perhaps the most famous example of a hermit living a solitary life in the desert.[16] Others, however, preferred to live holy lives in community, and organized themselves into cenobitic, or communal, monasteries. One of the first to establish a cenobium was Pachomius, who oversaw a federation of monasteries in Egypt in the middle of the fourth century.[17]

But there was a third living arrangement, blending elements of the eremitic and cenobitic models, in which monks would live in small groups of two or more.[18] This "third kind" of monastic living was not uncommon, though it did trouble some church leaders who preferred the more traditional models. Upon encountering monks living in these semi-eremitic pairs and small groups, John Cassian complained that among the three kinds of monks in Egypt, "two are admirable, [yet] the third is a poor sort of thing and by all means to be avoided," adding that it is also "reprehensible."[19]

Part of what worries John Cassian about this kind of monasticism is his impression that they lack the discipline of the other monks. But he also finds their autonomy troublesome; they are, in his words, "not subject to the will of the Elders."[20] While one could argue that the hermits are likewise not subject to the will of the elders, Cassian claims that at least they were initially trained by the proper monastic authorities. Cassian clearly considers groups of two or three independently minded monks cohabiting in the desert to be problematic. Many other Christians shared his view.[21]

Sabas initially set up his monastery as a *lavra*, a loose collection of individual cells—often built out of caves—where monks lived either singly or in small groups. Many of these ancient cells remain visible in the area today, including immediately surrounding the walls of Mar Saba. The lack of a central space tended to mean that monks had more autonomy and less oversight from an abbot or superior. With this sort of structure (or lack thereof), one might imagine that some independent-minded monks would be particularly averse to someone—*anyone*—telling them what to do or not to do.

Nevertheless, Sabas did attempt to institute a set of rules for the *lavra*. One particularly intriguing rule, formulated in several slightly different forms, was this: "Our father Sabas would never allow an adolescent to live in his community who had not yet covered his chin with a beard, because of the snares of the evil one."[22] The "evil one" mentioned is, of course, the devil, but what sort of "snares" would be associated with a boy or a young man living with the monks at Mar Saba? As a number of scholars of late antiquity have demonstrated, there seems to have been a widespread concern that older monks frequently exhibited sexual desire for pubescent or prepubescent boys.[23]

Sabas may well have established this rule on the basis of his own experience as a young monk. Recall that Sabas himself was prevented from joining the monastery of Euthymius as a young man because his youthfulness could distract the older monks from their spiritual pursuits.[24] It wasn't personal; Euthymius once let some younger brothers join his monastery, but came to see the youngest as a liability. He warned the older brother not to let his younger brother near his dwelling because a "feminine face" could arouse the "warfare of the enemy."[25] By the time Sabas arrived, Euthymius had adopted a policy known from Scetis in Egypt not to let young boys join.[26] He recommended that the young Sabas stay with Theoctistus until he was older and more mature.[27] Theoctistus would serve as a spiritual mentor to Sabas and prepare him for monastic life.

It is tempting to view this phenomenon as differing little from recent sexual-abuse scandals in religious organizations. However, there are problems with pushing the equation of the two too far. First, we don't know how often such relationships were sexual. Frequent prohibitions against same-sex intercourse in monastic literature reveal that at times they were sexual, but doubtless many were not. Second, as is well known, there was the long-standing influence of Plato's notion that the pairing of an older man and a younger boy was the ideal relationship on both an intellectual and a sexual level. This does not make such a relationship any less problematic or exploitative, but this ideology was still quite pervasive when ancient Christian monastic communities were forming in the fourth and fifth centuries, even if a number of Christian leaders were strongly opposed to it. Third, it would be a mistake to understand this homoerotic desire as "homosexuality," if by that we mean a biologically based attraction to people of the same sex. Our modern concept of sexual orientation was not operative in the ancient world, and there is ample evidence that the same monks who desired young boys often also lusted after women.

But beyond these considerations, it is even more important to realize that this concern about adolescent boys in monasteries is actually part of a much more complex social practice that scholars of ancient Christianity have only recently begun studying. This practice, referred to in Greek sources as *adelphopoiēsis*, literally "brother-making," appears to have involved two male monks (though we know of a few instances of female pairs) who develop a strong emotional bond and make a vow to bind themselves together for a time, if not for the rest of their lives.[28] Such agreements often also involved cohabitation. Sabas's mentors, Euthymius and Theoctistus, themselves shared this bond; according to one biographer they loved each other and "grew so united . . . in spiritual affection that the two became indistinguishable in both thought and conduct and displayed, as it were, one soul in two bodies."[29] If this sounds like an ancient example of same-sex marriage, it has certainly been characterized as such by some scholars (though not all) who have written about this phenomenon.[30]

The literary sources describing monks in these relationships have been studied extensively by such scholars as Derek Krueger and Claudia Rapp, and these descriptions are nothing if not erotically charged. One monk in such a pair, after visiting an older, venerable monk who praised their relationship, remarked that the encounter had "incited in us an even more ardent desire to preserve the perpetual love of our union." Another couple, after cultivating a close friendship, decided they "would no longer part from each other," and the abbot who consecrated their relationship was "astounded by the love both had for each other." When this same couple was confronted with the difficult reality of being separated from each other for some time, "they kissed each other's breast and drenched them with their tears."[31]

The sentiments above are highly erotic; should we therefore assume that these partnerships were sexual in nature? Although one might expect the answer to be an unequivocal yes, it is actually quite difficult to regard all such relationships as involving sexual intercourse or even contact. Some of them certainly were, and we frequently hear of church authorities expressing their disapproval of this behavior. One superior railed against what he described as "evil friendship": "You anxiously glance this way and that, you watch until you have found the opportune moment, then you give him what is (hidden) under the hem of your garment, so that God himself, and his Christ Jesus, will pour out the wrath of his anger on you and on him."[32] Accusations also are found that monks who are sleeping on the same mat or under the same blanket are engaging in sexual activity. One monastic rule goes so far as to prohibit monks from looking at their *own* naked bodies!

Yet we also must remember that celibacy was an esteemed and desirable virtue in many ancient Christian communities. Sources indicate that some monks entered into same-sex partnerships as a way of managing sexual arousal, even if the relationships were still emotionally intimate. Addressing this ambiguity, Krueger writes, "Although the stories in question predate the nineteenth-century invention of homosexuality, a decoding of Moschos's and Leontios's idealizations of same-sex monastic companionship reveals a powerful erotic substrate even as it assumes and endorses shared chastity and celibacy."[33] Krueger includes John Moschos among those who idealized same-sex relationships because he himself had a lifelong partner named Sophronius, who was a younger companion and eventual patriarch of Jerusalem. Moschos even dedicated the *Spiritual Meadow* to Sophronius, his "beloved," and presented him with the stories therein as "the finest flowers from the unmown meadow, woven . . . into a crown."[34] Some of these partnerships were, it seems, suffused with actions and language of desire and homoeroticism, but nevertheless lacked any overtly sexual consummation. In many instances, we simply cannot know if or to what extent the relationships were sexual, because the sources fall short of being explicit.

Amidst these suggestive yet evasive stories about same-sex monastic couples in late antique Palestinian monasticism, the Secret Gospel fits astonishingly well. It too uses rather ambiguous language, such as the desire of the young man to be "with him [i.e., Jesus]" (*met' autou*), a phrase that is used in some monastic tales to refer to sexual intercourse. There are also instances of monks who used their isolation to remain naked, not unlike the nearly naked young man who comes to Jesus at night (we are never told what Jesus is wearing—or not wearing). The opaque reference to Jesus teaching the man "the mystery of the kingdom of God" could refer to the sort of edifying instruction and words of wisdom that younger monks frequently sought from older monks, but it could also refer to sexual intimacy. Or it could refer to both.

It is therefore possible to understand the Secret Gospel—and the *Letter to Theodore* as a whole—as a document composed by a monk in the fifth, sixth, or seventh century to provide a powerful argument in favor of same-sex monastic partnerships. The Secret Gospel, then, would not have been an expanded edition of Mark created by the evangelist himself, nor a second-century complete apocryphal gospel that was known by Clement and excerpted. The Secret Gospel probably never had any independent existence apart from the letter ascribed to Clement: what we find quoted in the letter is likely the entirety of the Secret Gospel. As we pointed out earlier, this monk would not have regarded what he was doing as dishonest or as "forgery," but rather as elucidating a hidden or lost truth. In this case, the truth was that Jesus himself had legitimated these same-sex pairings through the special relationship he had with one younger, male, "beloved" disciple. This may be why the Secret Gospel does not use the name Lazarus or another proper name to refer to the young man. The young man may well have been an exemplum for future Christians to follow. This sort of creative reinterpretation is not that different from when Matthew the Evangelist insists that Isaiah 7:14 was actually a prophecy of Jesus's virginal conception and birth, even if Isaiah himself thought he was writing that verse about something during his lifetime. Nor is it very different from scribes who added, deleted, or changed passages in New Testament writings because they instinctively *knew* that the text they were copying had been corrupted somehow and needed to be fixed. In every one of these cases, a reader has rewritten or even "liberated" an ancient text to speak to a situation in that reader's own time that is in desperate need of clarity.

The monk who composed the letter of Clement and the Secret Gospel was likely well aware of, perhaps even enmeshed in, the controversy surrounding the practice of same-sex monastic pairs— otherwise he would not have written the document. But as strongly as he felt that this practice was instituted by Jesus, he was not naïve to the fact that such relationships could also potentially serve as a cover for satisfying base sexual urges. This perhaps explains why the Carpocratians—a well-known example of a licentious Christian sect—are presented in the letter as corrupting the Secret Gospel by adding overly salacious passages like "naked man with naked man." The monk who composed the document may well have been in such a same-sex partnership, and this partnership may even have had a sexual dimension to it, though we cannot be sure one way or another. But even if it had this dimension, it was in no way "just" about sex. His attempt to legitimize same-sex monastic couples also did not condone male monks entering into partnerships with women, since the temptations were far too great. Sabas himself did not permit monks even to glance at a woman.[35] Herein may lie the key to understanding the overlooked but equally enigmatic "second fragment" of the Secret Gospel, where Jesus refuses to receive the female relatives of the young man. Even a hotly debated practice such

as same-sex monastic partnerships had its limits on which all dis-
putants agreed, and heterosexual cohabitation was beyond the pale.

Brother-making became an official ritual within the church by
the eighth century. Scores of *euchologia*, or prayer books, survive that
include a blessing to be read during the ceremony in which brothers
formalized their relationship before God and the priest. *Euchologia*
with prayers for the brother-making ceremony have been found
in libraries throughout Palestine and indicate that the practice
was well known, and even common, in the region.[36] Claudia Rapp
re-creates the ceremony vividly: "Imagine the following scene: Two
men enter a church together. They step in front of the table on
which the Gospel is laid out, and place their hands on it, one on
top of the other. The priest speaks prayers over them, asking that
God may grant them his peace, love, and oneness of mind. Then
they embrace and from now on are regarded as 'brothers.' What
has been performed here is the ritual of *adelphopoiesis*, literally the
'making of brothers.'"[37]

As we have already seen, prior to the eighth century, monks
were still pairing up, even if they did not formalize their partnership
through an official church ceremony. If the *Letter to Theodore* does
date from sometime before the eighth century, it may well represent
an initial, alternative strategy for sanctioning brother-making relationships. Rather than make official the bond between men in a
church ceremony, which involved, among other things, placing their
hands jointly on a gospel book, the author chooses to rewrite the
gospel itself, creating a secret version of Mark that locates the origins of same-sex intimate relationships within the ministry of Jesus.
By the eighth century, once the church began to recognize *adelphopoiēsis* as a legitimate, even beneficial institution, gospel rewriting
would no longer be necessary. Even if Scripture did not explicitly
sanction the practice, the church did.

Returning to Mar Saba

Given what we know about same-sex monastic couples, this practice was widespread throughout ancient Christianity, being attested
in Egypt, Syria, Palestine, and beyond. Therefore, the monk who

composed this text could have potentially lived anywhere and was not necessarily an inhabitant of the *lavra* at Mar Saba. Nevertheless, it is most reasonable to regard Mar Saba as its most likely place of composition for several reasons. First, we know from the rules of Sabas that he was concerned with this practice, or at least concerned with the impact it could have on adolescent monks living in community. So it would make sense for a monk at Mar Saba to tread into this controversy, especially given other instances of opposition to Sabas's leadership. Second, it would account for the fact that this letter of Clement and the Secret Gospel are completely unknown and unattested in other ancient Christian literature apart from this manuscript. If the document was composed at Mar Saba and was utilized as part of a debate at this particular monastery, then it would have had an "in-house" function and would not have been widely disseminated, if at all.

Third and finally, an origin at Mar Saba might help to make sense of a series of cryptic statements that the former librarian of the Greek Orthodox Patriarchal Library in Jerusalem made to Quentin Quesnell, the arch-skeptic of Morton Smith's discovery, during his visit to Jerusalem in 1983. Recall that, according to Quesnell's diary, the librarian, Kallistos Dourvas, was confident that this manuscript had been at Mar Saba for quite some time prior to Smith's 1958 discovery. Quesnell noted that, concerning the manuscript, the librarian "feels sure it is 18th c[entury]."[38] Recall too that a recently discovered transfer document signed by Dourvas in 1976, when the Voss edition with the *Letter to Theodore* still attached was relocated from Mar Saba to the Patriarchal Library in Jerusalem, characterizes the manuscript as "unpublished and without any doubts about its authenticity." During Quesnell's 1983 visit, Dourvas also told him that "he remembers someone noting in some publication that someone did report seeing this in the 16th? 17th? century."[39] Though Dourvas considered the manuscript to be a genuine eighteenth-century document, he did not consider the *Letter to Theodore* to be the work of Clement. Quesnell reports that the librarian "says there were heretics and heretical schools often at M[ar] S[aba] and this fragment is part of a response to one of their books. He doesn't think it is from S[aint] Clement."[40]

We have thus far not been able to locate any further evidence that someone saw the *Letter to Theodore* in the sixteenth or seventeenth century. Nor do we know why Dourvas was so sure that the letter of Clement was a pseudepigraphic, in-house production written against the views of other residents of Mar Saba. Sadly, we are not able to follow up with Dourvas himself about these statements: like so many other key players in the Secret Gospel saga, he was already dead by the time we began this project. Dourvas died in 2016, after he had apparently been relieved of his duties as head of the Patriarchal Library for unclear reasons and transferred to a small parish in a Greek village near the border with Bulgaria.[41] In any case, Dourvas believed that this enigmatic and fascinating text was not forged by Morton Smith but created by a monk in late antiquity embroiled in an ecclesiastical controversy. And so do we.

CHAPTER TEN

The End

URING THE FINAL YEARS of his life, Morton Smith shifted his attention from Jesus to the apostle Paul. He devoted his time to a final monograph meant to be something of a sequel to *Jesus the Magician*, a book with an equally provocative title: *Paul the Possessed*. This book was never published, and we have few clues about what he planned to argue. We can imagine, however, that it would have been an engaging and controversial book—as is his entire corpus. By 1990 Smith's health was declining and he began to suffer from several ailments, including very painful shingles. Smith lamented the fact that his chronic pain made it difficult for him to research and write. He disclosed to a friend the effect his health was having on his work: "The really bad thing is that I can't work sitting at a desk for any length of time."[1]

During Smith's final months, he did his best to continue his academic research and writing. He met regularly with graduate students, who would routinely visit him in his cramped apartment and assist him with research. But by the summer of the following year, the regular research visits became wellness checks, until one day Smith told his graduate student that a visit the following week would not be necessary. On July 11, 1991, Smith was found unresponsive in his apartment. Though his obituary records the cause of death as heart failure, the true cause was a cocktail of prescription medication recommended by the Hemlock Society, a right-to-die organization that promoted access to the drugs needed for voluntary euthanasia. Hemlock, as you may know, is the name of the plant Socrates took to end his own life.

Smith's decision to die by suicide was not one he made in haste, nor was it one brought on by mental illness, as Peter Jeffery might imagine. Smith's decision was rational, thoughtful, and born out of his own belief that all people have the right to die. Years earlier he shared his thoughts on euthanasia in a letter about Plato to Grace Goldin, accomplished poet and wife of the prominent scholar of Judaism Judah Goldin. In the letter Smith questioned the premise that "life is *per se* good, therefore death is absolutely and always evil."[2] Smith agreed with Plato that "in many circumstances death is preferable to life," a view he also playfully labels "biblical," since the Mosaic law at times calls for capital punishment. "I have on my desk a note about the Society for the Right to Die," Smith continued, "which I intend to join as soon as I can find time; I think our most important and basic freedom needs its defense." In a subsequent letter to Grace, he restated his view: "But I do think death is a right—and often denied to those who want and need it most and whom it would most benefit."[3] Nearly eight years later, when Smith could no longer sit at his desk and do the one thing he loved the most, he exercised that fundamental right. Without the ability to read, write, and think about antiquity for a sustained period of time, death became preferable to life.

Photographs of Smith's apartment at the time of his death make clear the depth of his commitment to the discipline. Bookcases line the hallways of his apartment (fig. 6) and surround his modest twin-size bed (fig. 7). Even Smith's kitchen cabinets are packed with academic volumes (fig. 8). Behind boxes of Cup-a-Soup and canned pineapple stands a row of *Analecta Sacra* volumes, and above the refrigerator where most keep spare appliances, dry goods, or fine glassware, Smith placed several file boxes labeled "magic," meticulously alphabetized. Even Smith's oven was filled with books. While many scholars have a library in their home, Smith made his home into a library. Such was his commitment to scholarship.

Figure 6. The walls of Morton Smith's apartment. Photo: T. Alwood.

Figure 7. Morton Smith's bedroom. Photo: T. Alwood.

Figure 8. Morton Smith's pantry. Photo: T. Alwood.

In his obituary, which ran in the *New York Times* two days after his death, Smith was remembered as a talented yet controversial scholar. Despite the fact that he wrote seven books, co-wrote two, and published well over one hundred articles during his lifetime, his Mar Saba discovery and the stir it caused in the field occupied more than half of the announcement. Smith would be remembered most of all for his work on the Secret Gospel. The obituary ends with the note that Smith had "no immediate survivors." Yet his legacy does live on in his scholarship, and also in his colleagues and students, whom we have found share a deep reverence for Smith. Without their willingness to share memories, anecdotes, letters, photographs, and even Smith's sketches—which they chose to hold onto all these years—this book could not have been written.

One thing we found surprising when conducting interviews and reading Smith's correspondence was that no one who knew Smith well ever suspected him of forging the *Letter to Theodore*. His commitment to discovering the truth about the past—apparent in his teaching, writing, conversations, and even the state of his apartment—all but rule out this possibility. It is true that Jacob Neusner knew Smith well yet nonetheless accused him of forgery, but Neusner appears to have done so out of spite, not on the basis of well-grounded suspicions. Embarrassed by his former mentor, he wanted to hit Smith where it would hurt the most: his commitment to good history. The people closest to Smith knew him to be someone who loved the past too much to tamper with it. This testimony should count for something, and we recommend that those who are quick to accuse him of forgery pause to take seriously Smith's cloud of character witnesses.

Smith himself was by no means innocent in all of this. The jokes he told in presentations about the Secret Gospel—even in his 1960 presentation, when he first introduced the manuscript to the scholarly world—were designed to ruffle the feathers of his more pious colleagues in the field. And many felt provoked, even if they hesitated to admit it publicly. It is difficult to conduct nuanced scholarly research, especially on a text as complicated as the *Letter to Theodore*, under these conditions. Smith also argued for an interpretation of the Secret Gospel that we and many others have found implausible, in his dating of the text to the first century and his interpretation of Jesus's encounter with the young man as a mystical, baptismal ritual. By making such bold claims, he pushed an argument for the antiquity of the letter that many found unlikely, which then led them to suspect the text to be modern.

Finally, Smith should have given more serious consideration to A. D. Nock's hunch that the Mar Saba writing is a late antique apocryphon. Smith was well aware that Nock was peerless in his knowledge of antiquity and that his suspicion grew out of years of experience in the field, but still he chose to reject Nock's advice. One wonders how scholarship on this text would have unfolded differently had Smith taken seriously his nagging suspicion that Nock was right, and accepted his invitation to publish an article in the *Harvard Theological Review* on the Secret Gospel as a late antique—or in Nock's parlance "medieval"—apocryphal text. Would the *New York*

Times and other media outlets have reported on Smith's SBL talk? Would critics ever have accused him of forging the text? Would the Patriarchal Library still allow scholars to consult the manuscript? One wonders. Alas, Smith did not heed the warning of his trusted mentor, so here we are. But we regard these missteps as errors in judgment, not moral failings of the kind that would be required of Smith had he in fact forged the manuscript.

Of course, our case for the antiquity of the *Letter to Theodore* and Secret Gospel of Mark does not—and cannot—rest solely on appeals to Smith's character. We believe that the Greek handwriting used in the Mar Saba manuscript would have been too complicated for Smith or any other twentieth-century co-conspirator to emulate, and that Smith's Greek was likely not good enough to compose the letter and the Secret Gospel. Smith also dedicated years of his life to the interpretation of the text, as can be seen in his conference presentations, correspondence, and publications. Why would he make so much effort—much of it in unpublished letters that he didn't expect would ever be made public—to a letter he himself fabricated? Smith's peculiar interpretation of the Secret Gospel also makes it unlikely that he forged it. Had Smith wanted to fabricate a text that could prove that Jesus abandoned the Mosaic law and embraced a "libertine," mystical tradition that opened the door for Greek culture to enter into the Galilee, he could have done a much better job. But neither can our case for the antiquity of this text rely heavily on the immense time and effort that Smith devoted to making sense of it.

We suspect that the main reason the authenticity of the Mar Saba manuscript remains in doubt is that scholars have struggled to imagine a place and time in Christian history from which a text like this could plausibly emerge. We sympathize with these concerns, with which we too have grappled. But in an effort to make progress in answering these questions, we have set forth what is both a completely novel interpretation of this writing and one that we believe has a strong possibility of being correct. We have argued that a monk living in Palestine in late antiquity—perhaps even within the walls of Mar Saba—may have composed the *Letter to Theodore* and the Secret Gospel to provide scriptural justification for those who would choose to live a life of holiness with a spiritual partner of the same biological sex. If our argument is persuasive, then the *Letter to*

Theodore adds to the growing body of evidence for same-sex relationships in late antique monasticism and opens the door for new
work on the place of Christian apocryphal writings in the history of
sexuality. But to return to the initial point, if we've found a plausible
context for the *Letter to Theodore* and the Secret Gospel of Mark,
then there is no longer a need to go out in search of a forger—
especially when no credible evidence for forgery exists.

At the same time, we are open to the possibility that there is an
even better context to be found for the *Letter to Theodore* and the Secret Gospel of Mark, a place and time in which the text settles even
more naturally than it does in late antique Palestinian monasticism.
We welcome such research. Our chief aim in this book is not to
solve the Mar Saba mystery once and for all. Such a goal is not possible given the complexity of the topic and the limited evidence that
survives. Instead, our intention is to refocus the debate on the evidence we do have, and to encourage more research into promising
avenues, while also calling attention to what we consider to be dead
ends. We especially encourage scholars of late antiquity and those
interested in the history of sexuality to join what has largely been
until now a rather circumscribed investigation into the origins and
significance of the *Letter to Theodore* and the Secret Gospel of Mark.

Finally, we insist that if more progress is to be made on the Mar
Saba Clementine, scholars need to have access to the manuscript
itself. As we have stated, there is no reason to suspect that the manuscript is anywhere other than the Patriarchal Library in Jerusalem,
though we remain unsure whether it was accidentally lost or deliberately hidden. We have attempted to contact the library multiple
times without success. We hope that the patriarch will decide to
make a concerted effort to locate the manuscript and make it again
available for scholars to examine. We would also like to see scientific
tests done on the manuscript, to test the age and composition of
the ink. We have been reassured by experts that such tests can now
be done without causing any damage to the manuscript. If we are
correct that the Mar Saba manuscript was produced by monks in
pursuit of holiness, then the *Letter to Theodore* and the Secret Gospel
of Mark belong to the rich heritage of Greek Orthodox literature,
and these materials merit preservation and careful study. With this
sentiment we are confident the patriarch will agree.

Notes

Chapter One. The Announcement

1. We are grateful to Christopher Hooker for sharing with us scans of the original program from the session (now available online: https://s3-us -west-2.amazonaws.com/pittsarchives/rg100/web/programbooks/SBL _19601228.pdf). A copy of the original program is kept in the Society of Biblical Literature Archives in the Pitts Theological Library at Emory University.

2. Robert Kraft (professor emeritus at the University of Pennsylvania), who was in attendance, recalls that the presence of the press that evening was "obvious, and unusual" and that Smith certainly "showed an awareness of their presence," perhaps even engaging in a "certain amount of posing" for the cameras. Robert Kraft, email correspondence, February 29, 2020.

3. Smith's list (incorrectly dated 12/29/1961) from his Biographical File (box 291, folder 21), University Archives, Rare Book & Manuscript Library, Columbia University Libraries.

4. Sanka Knox, "A New Gospel Ascribed to Mark," *New York Times*, December 30, 1960.

5. Typescript of Smith's presentation in his Biographical File (box 291, folder 21), University Archives, Rare Book & Manuscript Library, Columbia University Libraries.

6. On page 5 of the transcript of his SBLE talk, Smith writes, "The answer, then, reads as follows," before leaving a blank space so he can read Clement's *Letter to Theodore* and the Secret Gospel from a separate sheet.

7. Robert Kraft, email correspondence, February 29, 2020.

8. Helmut Koester's teaching notes, generously shared with us by Cavan Concannon.

9. Robert Kraft, email correspondence, February 26, 2020.

10. Sanka Knox, "Expert Disputes 'Secret Gospel,'" *New York Times*, December 31, 1960.

11. Bruce Buckley, "Wrangle over 'Secret Gospel' Begins," *Morningsider*, January 6, 1961.

Chapter Two. The Find

1. The report comes from Nicephorus, *Ecclesiastical History* 4. Estimates of the number of Isidore's letters that survive range from two thousand to more than three thousand.
2. Letter 28 (March 31, 1951) to Gershom Scholem, scholar of Jewish mysticism. All letters between Smith and Scholem can be found in Stroumsa, *Morton Smith and Gershom Scholem*.
3. Letter 31 (January 26, 1953) to Scholem.
4. Letter 31 (January 26, 1953) to Scholem.
5. Between 1955 and 1958, Smith held positions at Brown, Drew (a visiting position, not permanent), and Columbia; see letter 36 (May 14, 1954) to Scholem.
6. Smith, *Clement of Alexandria*, ix.
7. See Smith's lengthy account of the mission in box 13, item 2, of his archived papers at Jewish Theological Seminary.
8. Smith, *Secret Gospel*, 9; Smith, *Clement of Alexandria*, ix.
9. These quotes appear in Smith's reviews published in *Journal of Biblical Literature* 89, no. 1 (1970): 82–84; *Journal of Biblical Literature* 91, no. 4 (1972): 548–550; and *Journal of the American Oriental Society* 102, no. 3 (1982): 544–546.
10. Letter 84 (August 15, 1967) to Scholem.
11. Shaye Cohen, email correspondence, May 19, 2019.
12. When we asked Cohen to clarify how he went about destroying Smith's private papers, he responded, "I dumped the correspondence, in installments, down his apartment building's garbage disposal. I assume the correspondence is at the bottom of a landfill somewhere." Shaye Cohen, email correspondence, May 20, 2019.
13. Smith's summary of his career, May 30, 1985. Box 1, item 7, from Smith's papers at Jewish Theological Seminary.
14. Letter from Saul Lieberman to Mr. R. H. Smith, September 28, 1949. Box 1, item 11, from Smith's papers at Jewish Theological Seminary.
15. Theodor Gaster quoted in Baumgarten, *Elias Bickerman*, 209.
16. Shaye Cohen quoted in Smith's obituary printed in the *New York Times*, July 13, 1991.
17. Smith's dissertation was eventually published as *Palestinian Parties and Politics That Shaped the Old Testament*.
18. Smith, *Secret Gospel*, 1.
19. Smith, *Secret Gospel*, 1–2.
20. Smith, *Secret Gospel*, 2.
21. Smith, *Secret Gospel*, 3.

22. P. Brown, "Holy Man," 83.

23. Patrich, *Sabas*, 7.

24. Cyril of Scythopolis, *Life of Sabas* 87.10 (*Lives of the Monks*, 95).

25. This policy, adopted by some Palestinian monastic communities, seems to have originated in Scetis in Egypt. See Cyril of Scythopolis, *Life of Sabas* 114.12 (*Lives of the Monks*, 123); and Patrich, *Sabas*, 14, 40, 263–264, 274.

26. Patrich, *Sabas*, 8.

27. Potter, "Spirituality of the Judaean Desert," 437.

28. Smith, *Secret Gospel*, 3.

29. Edward M. Chapman, "A Night with the Monks of Mar Saba," *The Congregationalist and Christian World*, June 3, 1905, 755–757, at 756.

30. Smith, *Secret Gospel*, 4.

31. Smith, *Secret Gospel*, 6.

32. Interview with Tom Alwood, December 29, 2020.

33. Tom Alwood reports seeing what may be a torn patch on the blank page indicating there was once a photo glued to the page. Tom Alwood, email correspondence, January 13, 2021.

34. "Pantalemon's house" likely refers to the dwelling of one of the leaders at Mar Saba, Panteleimon, who resided there sometime from the 1920s until his death in 1947.

35. "Never revisit a place that fascinated you when you were young—you discover not only its changes, but your own. Electricity had been introduced, and not even the magic of the Byzantine liturgy can survive direct illumination. Perhaps that was just as well; it enabled me to blame the lighting for my own failure to respond *at forty-three as I had at twenty-six*." Smith, *Secret Gospel*, 10 (emphasis ours).

36. Smith, "Monasteries and Their Manuscripts," 173; Smith, *Secret Gospel*, 33, 35.

37. Smith's sketchbook also includes a photograph and accompanying sketch of Hagia Sophia, possibly another example of Smith creating a sketch from a photo.

38. If Smith has correctly captured the shadows in his sketches, he sketched the tower from "Pantalemon's house" in the morning and the view from the tower around midday.

39. See his comments in Smith, *Secret Gospel*, 8.

40. Smith, *Secret Gospel*, 4.

41. Patrich, *Sabas*, 191.

42. *Vita Stephani Sabailae* (10, 354, ed. Ciaritte), cited in Patrich, *Sabas*, 192.

43. Patrich, *Sabas*, 192 (and other sources cited therein).

44. In addition to Cyril of Scythopolis, John Moschos, Sophronius, Antiochus Monachus, John of Damascus, and Theodore Abu Qurrah all took up residence at Mar Saba. Patrich, *Sabas*, 192.

45. Smith, *Secret Gospel*, 4. See also Smith, *Clement of Alexandria*, 288.

46. Smith, *Secret Gospel*, 4. Smith, *Clement of Alexandria*, 288. Papadopoulos-Kerameus, Ιεροσολυμιτικη Βιβλιοθηκη, 3:316.
47. Smith, *Secret Gospel*, 5.
48. Smith, *Secret Gospel*, 11.
49. Smith, *Secret Gospel*, 11.
50. Smith, "Ελληνικὰ χειρόγραφα."
51. Smith, *Secret Gospel*, 11.
52. Smith, *Secret Gospel*, 12.
53. Smith, *Secret Gospel*, 13.
54. Smith, *Secret Gospel*, 13.

Chapter Three. The Vetting

1. Smith, *Secret Gospel*, 19.
2. Translation is our own.
3. Smith, *Secret Gospel*, 18.
4. For more on the Hitler diaries, see Hamilton, *Hitler Diaries*. The most recent and thorough investigation into the Gospel of Jesus's Wife saga is Sabar, *Veritas*, and his earlier article "The Unbelievable Tale of Jesus's Wife," *Atlantic*, July/August 2016.
5. Smith, *Secret Gospel*, 18–19 (emphasis ours).
6. This information comes from Papias of Hierapolis, a second-century church leader in Asia Minor, as quoted in Eusebius, *Ecclesiastical History* 3.39.15.
7. For a discussion of the figure of Mark and his alleged authorship of the Gospel now bearing his name, see Collins, *Mark*, 1–6.
8. For a discussion of the various interpretations of these verses, see Collins, *Mark*, 693–695.
9. Letter 63. All letters between Smith and Scholem can be found in Stroumsa, *Morton Smith and Gershom Scholem*.
10. Smith, *Ancient Greeks*.
11. Letter from Smith to Hans Dieter Betz dated August 1, 1983. Jewish Theological Seminary archives, box 1, folder 11.
12. Letter from Smith to Hans Dieter Betz dated August 1, 1983. By 1982 Smith estimated that he had spent $135,000 on books (more than $350,000 today). A sketch Smith drew of his apartment was found in his briefcase at the time of his death in 1991. It shows the walls of his 355 sq. ft. apartment lined with books, including under the bed, in front of the radiator, and even in the kitchen cabinets above the stove. See also the photos of Smith's apartment in chapter 10 of this book.
13. Letter 63 (August 7, 1959).
14. Letter 64 (October 25, 1959).
15. This language is taken from Smith's 1960 SBL presentation.

16. Smith, "Manuscript Material from the Monastery of Mar Saba, discovered, transcribed and translated by Morton Smith." Jewish Theological Seminary archives, box 13, folder 10.
17. Smith, *Secret Gospel*, 22–23.
18. Smith, *Secret Gospel*, 23.
19. Smith, *Secret Gospel*, 24. The quotation is a paraphrase of Goodenough by Smith. Italics are Smith's.
20. See, e.g., Arthur Langguth, "Murder in the Cathedral," *Harvard Crimson*, October 15, 1953, https://www.thecrimson.com/article/1953/10/15/murder-in-the-cathedral-pthe-new/.
21. Smith, *Secret Gospel*, 24.
22. Smith, *Secret Gospel*, 25.
23. Smith, *Secret Gospel*, 29.
24. Smith, *Secret Gospel*, 26.
25. Smith, *Secret Gospel*, 26.
26. "The History of the *TLG*," *Thesaurus Linguae Graecae*, http://stephanus.tlg.uci.edu/history.php.
27. Stählin, *Clemens Alexandrinus*, 4 vols.
28. Smith, *Secret Gospel*, 27.
29. Transcript of Smith's SBL presentation, p. 6, Biographical File (box 291, folder 21), University Archives, Rare Book & Manuscript Library, Columbia University Libraries.
30. Sanka Knox, "A New Gospel Ascribed to Mark," *New York Times*, December 30, 1960.
31. Letter from J. A. Sanders to Smith, January 19, 1961.
32. Sanka Knox, "Expert Disputes 'Secret Gospel,'" *New York Times*, December 31, 1960.
33. Knox, "Expert Disputes 'Secret Gospel.'"
34. Bruce Buckley, "Wrangle over 'Secret Gospel' Begins," *Morningsider*, January 6, 1961.
35. Letter 68.
36. Stroumsa, *Morton Smith and Gershom Scholem*, xvii n. 21.
37. Letter 40 (August 1, 1955).
38. Letter 42 (October 27, 1955).
39. Letter 45 (February 28, 1956).
40. Stroumsa, *Morton Smith and Gershom Scholem*, xvii n. 21. This letter can be found in Goodenough's papers (box 11) in the Yale University Archives.
41. Smith, "Aretology Used by Mark." See also Smith, "Authenticity," and Stroumsa, *Morton Smith and Gershom Scholem*, xvii n. 21.
42. Letter 72 (June 13, 1961).
43. Smith, *Clement of Alexandria*, 50. Also, at the November 4, 1977, meeting of the Columbia New Testament Seminar, the notes of which are in the

Jewish Theological Seminary archives, Smith was asked what he meant by "libertine," to which he replied, "Not under the law."

44. Unless otherwise indicated, Scripture quotations are from the New Revised Standard Version (NRSV).

45. For an accessible introduction to this complex set of issues, see Fredriksen, *Paul*, and her more recent book *When Christians Were Jews*.

46. Smith, *Secret Gospel*, 113–114.

47. Letter 76 (October 6, 1962).

48. Letter to Smith from Henry Chadwick, August 28, 1961.

49. In his letter of condolence following Smith's death in 1991, Helmut Koester remembers a formative conversation with Smith about his new discovery: "When I was spending a summer in Germany in 1963, teaching at the University of Heidelberg, Morton came for a visit of several days in order to discuss his manuscript on the 'Secret Gospel of Mark.' This initiated an important period in my own career. I became convinced that it was a genuine document, learned much from Morton Smith's hypotheses, tried—not without success, I think—to persuade him to drop some of his more outrageous conclusions, and incorporated Morton Smith's findings in my own assessment of the development of Mark's Gospel." Box 15, folder 1, of Smith's papers at the Jewish Theological Seminary archives.

Chapter Four. The Skeptic

1. In his November 21, 1973, reply to Quentin Quesnell, Smith explains why he did not raise the question of scientific tests on the manuscript with the head of the monastery or the Jerusalem Patriarchate: "I knew of no specialist in this field in Arab Jerusalem (as it was at that time); there was no equipment for such study at Mar Saba; and I was fairly sure that a suggestion that the manuscript be sent elsewhere for study would not be welcome."

2. Found on pp. 449, 451, and 453 of *Clement of Alexandria*. *The Secret Gospel*, on the other hand, has only one photograph of the manuscript (on p. 38), but it differs from the others because it shows the opening in the book where the first manuscript page immediately follows the final page of Voss's study.

3. Although he never explicitly defends his choice of black and white, Smith does express concern about the difficult circumstances under which he had to take pictures: "Photographing manuscripts is a tricky business, especially when the camera has to be held by hand, so I was anxious. By good luck all the shots turned out well (I had photographed half a dozen texts of the seventy-five I catalogued), and I was able to sit down and begin to study them." *Secret Gospel*, 14.

4. In his rejoinder to Quesnell's article, Smith blamed Harvard University Press for not reprinting his photographs correctly: "The photographs: I specified that they should be printed actual size and that the margins of the

pages should be shown; my text in *CA* [*Clement of Alexandria*] was based on the expectation that these directions would be followed. That they were not was the fault of the Harvard University Press." Smith, "Authenticity," 196.

5. From the letter dated November 9, 1973. See Pantuck and Brown, "Morton Smith as M. Madiotes," 112–116, for further evidence of mistakes in the modern Greek translation of Smith's manuscript catalogue that he was never given the opportunity to correct.

6. Smith's letter to Quesnell, dated November 21, 1973.

7. Smith's letter to Quesnell, dated November 21, 1973.

8. Quesnell, "Mar Saba Clementine," 50.

9. Quesnell, "Mar Saba Clementine," 49.

10. Quesnell, "Mar Saba Clementine," 53–54.

11. Surprisingly, there seems to be no trace of the English version of Smith's Mar Saba catalogue among his papers in the Jewish Theological Seminary of America archives, aside from a couple of index cards that contain notes on individual manuscripts. It is possible that his only copy of the English version was sent to the patriarchate to be translated into Greek, but this seems unlikely for someone whose papers were organized as assiduously as Smith's were.

12. Goodspeed writes, "It is the practice of scholars when any new discovery in ancient literature is brought to their attention to inquire as to the form in which it was found—the tablet, inscription, or manuscript from which it has been deciphered by its discoverer. What the scholar really desires is to see the very document itself, but failing that a photograph of it will usually answer the purposes of his investigation." *Strange New Gospels*, 3.

13. Quesnell, "Mar Saba Clementine," 48.

14. These matters are raised in "Mar Saba Clementine," 52–53. Quesnell does indeed quote from Smith's letter at two points in his article: at note 4 on p. 49 regarding procedures for admission to the tower library and the status of the manuscript since his 1958 visit, and at note 10 on p. 53 about the paleographers Smith consulted not observing anything suspicious in the manuscript, which might have led Smith to request a more detailed investigation from the patriarchate.

15. See the report of these events in Stroumsa, "Comments," 147–148. See also Stroumsa, *Morton Smith and Gershom Scholem*, xx–xxi.

16. Smith, "Authenticity," 197.

17. Quesnell, "Reply to Morton Smith."

18. Quesnell, "Reply to Morton Smith," 200.

19. Brown, *Mark's Other Gospel*, 35. This quotation does not have a note after it, but note 40 (on p. 246) states that Quesnell's personal recollections are quoted from two letters that he wrote to Brown.

20. Thomas Derr, email correspondence, July 28, 2020.

21. This was Smith's characterization of possible arguments for the manuscript being a modern forgery; see *Clement of Alexandria*, 287.

22. Brown, *Mark's Other Gospel*, 34.
23. As one example, see the praise of Quesnell's article by Edward Hobbs in the proceedings of the colloquy at the Graduate Theological Union in Berkeley, CA. Wuellner, "Minutes of the Colloquy," 60.
24. Quesnell's remarks about the Voss volume read as follows: "If this scribe had been studying Voss' *Ignatius* and not merely using it for copy paper, one would expect him to have attempted what Voss attempted: to distinguish genuine ancient epistles from fraudulent imitations. Voss would not copy an older manuscript without indicating what manuscript he was copying, where he had found it, and where he was leaving it." Quesnell, "Mar Saba Clementine," 51.
25. See his hypothesizing of an accomplice at Quesnell, "Mar Saba Clementine," 54 n. 12.
26. Quesnell, "Mar Saba Clementine," 55–56.
27. Quesnell raises the issue of Smith's dedications as the fifth and final of his "Further Questions for Smith" section, just before a brief conclusion (66); therefore, it rhetorically occupies a position of prominence in his article.
28. The quotation from Nock's letter to Smith appears in *Clement of Alexandria*, 88 n. 1; Quesnell invokes it in "Mar Saba Clementine," 54. See the fuller discussion of the dedication to Nock in the next chapter.
29. Quesnell, "Mar Saba Clementine," 49. Note that the direct quotation at the end of this passage is from Goodspeed, *Strange New Gospels*, 4, not from Smith's works.
30. Quesnell, "Mar Saba Clementine," 57. The passage to which Quesnell refers occurs in *Secret Gospel*, 23–25.
31. Smith, *Secret Gospel*, 25.
32. Quesnell, "Mar Saba Clementine," 58.
33. Smith, "Authenticity," 196.
34. Smith, "Authenticity," 201.
35. Thomas Derr, email correspondence, September 20, 2020.
36. Quentin Quesnell, "'Secret Gospel': Improbable Puzzle," *National Catholic Reporter*, November 30, 1973, 12.
37. Quesnell, "'Secret Gospel,'" 12.
38. Musurillo, "Morton Smith's Secret Gospel."
39. Murgia, "Secret Mark: Real or Fake?"
40. See Murgia's comments in Wuellner, "Minutes of the Colloquy," 60.
41. Neusner, "Who Needs 'The Historical Jesus'?," 115.
42. Neusner, "Who Needs 'The Historical Jesus'?," 116.

Chapter Five. The Popularizer

1. As one small but perhaps telling indication of Metzger's alignment with conservative Christianity, consider the dedication to his wife in his memoirs, *Reminiscences of an Octogenarian*: he praises his wife, Isobel, for her

"consistent Christian life." Although this may not appear to be a marker of any religious persuasion more specific than Christianity in general, the prominent and frequent use of the descriptor "Christian" is actually a distinctive practice of evangelical Christians that is not used as regularly in other branches of the Christian tradition. For a recent treatment of this term in American religious discourse, see Bowman, *Christian*.

2. James Sanders, email correspondence, February 19, 2020.

3. See, e.g., the reports of Robert Kraft and Helmut Koester that we discuss in chapter 1.

4. Metzger, *Reminiscences*, 129.

5. For the former, see Smith, *Secret Gospel*, 80–81, or his response to Fuller's paper from the Graduate Theological Union colloquy; Smith, "Response," 13–14. For the latter, see the infamous passage about manipulation with the hands/physical union in *Secret Gospel*, 113–114 (including n. 12 on 113).

6. On several occasions in his publications Smith includes a similar quip: "Holy man arrested . . . naked youth escapes"; see Smith, "Clement of Alexandria and Secret Mark," 458 n. 19; Smith, "Under the Sheet," *New York Review of Books*, February 8, 1979, https://www.nybooks.com/articles/1979/02/08/under-the-sheet/. However, the longer form quoted above is known only from William M. Calder III, a close friend of Smith's, who shared it with Scott Brown. See Brown, "Question of Motive," 360 n. 33.

7. Metzger, *Reminiscences*, 128.

8. Metzger, *Reminiscences*, 129.

9. Metzger, *Reminiscences*, 129–130.

10. Metzger, *Reminiscences*, 131.

11. Metzger, *Reminiscences*, 132.

12. Ehrman, *Lost Christianities*, 83.

13. Hedrick, "Secret Gospel of Mark."

14. Clark and Burns, "Editors' Note," 131.

15. Stroumsa, "Comments," 147–153. Stroumsa would go on to publish the correspondence between Morton Smith and Gershom Scholem several years later; see *Morton Smith and Gershom Scholem*, esp. xx–xxi, where Stroumsa again recounts his rediscovery of the manuscript.

16. Ehrman, "Response."

17. Ehrman, "Response," 155.

18. Ehrman's denial that he is accusing Smith reads as follows: "Let me state as clearly as I can: I am *not* saying that I think Smith forged the letter. I think that the jury is still out" ("Response," 159). We understand his "jury is still out" remark to mean that he is unsure whether Smith forged the manuscript, and is thus willing to seriously consider this as a possible explanation for the existence of the Mar Saba Clementine. He immediately follows this clarification with his three "hard" categories.

19. Ehrman, "Response," 159.

20. Ehrman, "Response," 160.
21. Both of these discrepancies were highlighted by Eric Osborn, one of the leading experts in the study of Clement of Alexandria's texts and thought; see his "Clement of Alexandria." Note, however, that although Osborn denies Clementine authorship in favor of a "pious forger," there is absolutely nothing in Osborn's discussion to suggest he believes it to be a modern forgery. Smith himself already recognized that these discrepancies were difficult to reconcile with authorship by Clement and attempted to downplay their significance; see Smith, *Clement of Alexandria*, 84–85.
22. Ehrman, "Response," 161. The earlier study to which Ehrman refers is Criddle, "Mar Saba Letter."
23. Letter from Morton Smith to Wilhelm Wuellner, dated August 5, 1976.
24. Smith, "The Letter of Clement and Secret Mark: Evidence and Arguments," unpublished essay for *Aufstieg und Niedergang der römischen Welt* (ANRW), page 6 of notes, note 33. Box 10, folder 1, of Smith's papers at the Jewish Theological Seminary archives.
25. See Smith's only published responses to the forgery hypotheses of Murgia and Musurillo, which are quite brief, in his "Clement of Alexandria and Secret Mark," 451.
26. For a detailed discussion of Smith's facility with Greek, see Pantuck, "Question of Ability."
27. Ehrman, "Response," 162.
28. Nag Hammadi codices (NHC) II 63.33–37. Reconstruction and translation by Geoffrey Smith. See Smith, *Valentinian Christianity*, 270–271.
29. Ehrman, "Response," 162. Cf. the comments in Quesnell, "Mar Saba Clementine," 66: "CA is said to be written 'for Arthur Darby Nock,' who, Smith tells in the book, refused till the day he died to admit the authenticity of the letter, suggesting instead that it was 'mystification for the sake of mystification.'"
30. This is best seen in Smith's recollection of Nock's initial impressions of the text; see his *Secret Gospel*, 24–25, and our discussion of this passage in chapter 3.
31. Taken from Nock's last substantial letter to Smith, dated September 20, 1962, of which Smith quotes a sizable excerpt in *Clement of Alexandria*, 88 n. 1.
32. The manuscript to which Nock refers is a papyrus fragment of Julius Africanus's *Kestoi*, designated Papyrus Oxyrhynchus II.412 (P.Oxy. 412). See the edition of this fragment in Grenfell and Hunt, *Oxyrhynchus Papyri*, vol. 2.
33. Quesnell, "Mar Saba Clementine," 66.
34. This is one of the interpretations of the pair of dedications that Peter Jeffery sees as possible; see his comments in *Secret Gospel of Mark Unveiled*, 242.
35. Ehrman, "Response," 162.

36. See Metzger's discussion of the "Amusing Agraphon" forgery by Paul Coleman-Norton in his *Reminiscences*, 136–139.
37. Bianchi, *Origins of Gnosticism*; Smith, review of *The Origins of Gnosticism*.
38. For more recent discussions of the category of Gnosticism, see, e.g., Williams, *Rethinking "Gnosticism,"* and King, *What Is Gnosticism?*
39. Smith, review of *The Origins of Gnosticism*, 83.
40. For a discussion of the importance of self-definition in the study of Gnosticism, see Geoffrey Smith, *Guilt by Association*, esp. 146–162.
41. Smith, "History of the Term Gnostikos."
42. Ehrman, *Lost Christianities*, 87.
43. Ehrman, *Lost Christianities*, 87.
44. Ehrman, *Lost Christianities*, 87.
45. Ehrman, *Lost Christianities*, 87.
46. Ehrman, *Lost Christianities*, 89.

Chapter Six. The Conspiracy

1. The most prominent of these other advocates of the forgery hypothesis include Jenkins, *Hidden Gospels*; Watson, "Beyond Suspicion"; Evans, "Morton Smith"; and Piovanelli, "Halfway."
2. His findings were published on the official website of the Society of Biblical Literature; see Stephen C. Carlson, "'Archaic Mark' (MS 2427) and the Finding of a Manuscript Fake," *SBL Forum*, August 2006, http://sbl-site.org/Article.aspx?ArticleID=577.
3. See Talley, "Le temps liturgique."
4. See Quesnell's comments in "Mar Saba Clementine," 52.
5. Paananen, "From Stalemate to Deadlock," 95–96, has an especially helpful and succinct discussion of the reactions to Carlson's book.
6. Hurtado, foreword to *The Gospel Hoax*, x.
7. Brown, "Reply to Stephen Carlson," 145 n. 4. In this note, he quotes from "Document Examination from a Photocopy," *FBI Law Enforcement Bulletin* 36 (1967): 23–24. Viklund and Paananen, "Distortion of the Scribal Hand," 238 n. 14, point out that Brown "asked the right question though [he] decided not to pursue the matter at that time."
8. For a more technical discussion of the "continuous tone"/"halftone" problem, see Viklund and Paananen, "Distortion of the Scribal Hand," 238–242. Especially valuable for its analysis is the essay by Melissa M. Teras, "Artefacts and Errors."
9. Viklund and Paananen, "Distortion of the Scribal Hand," 241.
10. In addition to images in their article, see those Roger Viklund presents on his website: "Tremors, or Just an Optical Illusion?," December 12, 2009, http://www.jesusgranskad.se/theodore2.htm. Note especially the following recurring differences between the images: (a) what appear to be ink

blobs in the black and white are revealed as fluid strokes in the color; and (b) the black and white especially distorts diagonal letter-strokes to appear choppy, whereas the color shows much more elegant formation of the letters.

11. Timo Paananen, though very appreciative of Brown's efforts, does fault him along these lines. See his "From Stalemate to Deadlock," 110.

12. Carlson, *Gospel Hoax*, 60.

13. Carlson, *Gospel Hoax*, 61–62.

14. Brown, "Factualizing the Folklore," 309. Italics in the original.

15. Brown, "Factualizing the Folklore," 308. Italics and bracketed glosses in the original.

16. Brown, "Factualizing the Folklore," 309–310.

17. The photograph in which this manuscript appears is on p. 37 (unnumbered) of *Secret Gospel*.

18. Carlson, *Gospel Hoax*, 42–43.

19. Carlson, *Gospel Hoax*, 43.

20. Pantuck and Brown, "Morton Smith as M. Madiotes," 115.

21. See Pantuck and Brown, "Morton Smith as M. Madiotes," 115 n. 27, and Chilton, review of *The Gospel Hoax*, 124.

22. See the full analysis of this uncropped photograph in Pantuck and Brown, "Morton Smith as M. Madiotes," 116–123.

23. Carlson, *Gospel Hoax*, 43.

24. This lexical information was obtained from *Langenscheidt's Standard Greek Dictionary*, ed. George A. Magazis (Berlin: Langenscheidt, 1996), 43 and 663, and from *The Oxford New Greek Dictionary*, ed. Niki Watts (New York: Berkley, 2008), 120 and 244.

25. Kruger, review of *The Gospel Hoax*, 424.

26. Chilton, review of *The Gospel Hoax*, 123.

27. Chilton, review of *The Gospel Hoax*, 124.

28. Paananen, "From Stalemate to Deadlock," 98.

29. Jeffery has expressed doubts on several occasions that testing the manuscript would resolve anything; see especially his online FAQ about his book (cited hereafter as "FAQ"), under the question "Why not just have the manuscript scientifically tested? The jury will be out until that happens" (http://music2.princeton.edu/jeffery/smithfaq.html).

30. See, for instance, Smith's remarks in *Secret Gospel*, 10: "Electricity had been introduced, and not even the magic of the Byzantine liturgy can survive direct illumination. Perhaps that was just as well; it enabled me to blame the lighting for my own failure to respond at forty-three as I had at twenty-six."

31. Jeffery, *Secret Gospel of Mark Unveiled*, 9.

32. Jeffery, *Secret Gospel of Mark Unveiled*, 10–11.

33. For instance, Francis Watson finds Jeffery's study to have "rather too much of such [psychological] speculating," despite Watson's belief that

Smith forged the Mar Saba Clementine; see his "Beyond Suspicion," 131 n. 10.

34. Jeffery, "FAQ," under the question "Your book is full of innuendos and suggestions that Morton Smith was mentally ill. Aren't you simply resorting to *ad hominem* attacks that are inappropriate in a scholarly publication?"

35. Jeffery, "FAQ," under the question "But your book consistently denigrates Smith for not believing as you do, beginning from the acknowledgements: 'I pray for the late Morton Smith—may God rest his anguished soul.' You seem to write throughout from a position of contemptuous superiority."

36. This should not be construed, however, as a declaration that Smith did not suffer from any mental health conditions, but only as our impression that if he did, he managed to conceal such conditions from those with whom he was closest—bearing in mind also that Smith was quite guarded about his private life.

37. Jeffery, "FAQ," under the same question cited in note 35. The 1949 article to which Jeffery parenthetically refers is Smith's "Psychiatric Practice and Christian Dogma."

38. The quotation appears in Smith, *Secret Gospel*, 6; see Jeffery's analysis of it in *Secret Gospel of Mark Unveiled*, 128–131.

39. Jeffery, *Secret Gospel of Mark Unveiled*, 92.

40. Jeffery, *Secret Gospel of Mark Unveiled*, 93; and we see what you did there.

41. Jeffery, *Secret Gospel of Mark Unveiled*, 93.

42. Jeffery, *Secret Gospel of Mark Unveiled*, 93.

43. Carlson, *Gospel Hoax*, 78.

44. Jeffery, *Secret Gospel of Mark Unveiled*, 242.

45. Jeffery, *Secret Gospel of Mark Unveiled*, 243.

46. Jeffery, *Secret Gospel of Mark Unveiled*, 35.

47. Jeffery, "FAQ," under the question "Your book is full of innuendos and suggestions that Morton Smith was mentally ill. . . ."

48. Jeffery, *Secret Gospel of Mark Unveiled*, 215.

49. See Foster, "Wilde, Oscar F.O.W. (1856–1900)."

50. Josephus, *Jewish Antiquities* 18.5.4.

51. Smith, *Secret Gospel*, 70, including note 8.

52. Jeffery, *Secret Gospel of Mark Unveiled*, 236.

53. Jeffery, *Secret Gospel of Mark Unveiled*, 238. On page 325 n. 58, he cites the study of ancient Greek obscenities by Euios Lēnaios (Charitōn Charalampous Charitōnidēs) that bears the title *Aporrēta* (Thessaloniki: Mich. Triantaphullos, 1935), which is the same word used in this passage from the letter of Clement. But Jeffery does not provide any specific instances from ancient Greek authors who use the word to refer to obscenities rather than secret teachings, so it is uncertain how common this alternative usage was.

54. Jeffery, *Secret Gospel of Mark Unveiled*, 238–239.
55. See the helpful discussion of veil imagery in Clement by Brown, *Mark's Other Gospel*, 130–132.
56. For the most extensive discussion of *The Mystery of Mar Saba*, see Watson, "Beyond Suspicion."
57. Schoenbaum, *Internal Evidence*, 197. This quote is highly appropriate to the debate over the authenticity of the Secret Gospel, but we cannot take credit for first applying it to this situation. Instead, it appears in the outstanding recent dissertation by Timo Paananen, "Study in Authenticity," 81 n. 278. An especially valuable contribution of Paananen's dissertation is his presentation, over several pages, of what he calls the "alternative narrative"—that is, a description of when, how, and why Morton Smith executed his forgery of the Mar Saba Clementine if the arguments for the forgery hypothesis are correct; see Paananen, 21–31. The scenario he presents, with extensive footnotes documenting where each claim appears, is devastatingly far-fetched.

Chapter Seven. The Handwriting

1. Bovon, "Apocryphal Acts," 16.
2. Bovon, "Apocryphal Acts," 18.
3. Stroumsa, *Morton Smith and Gershom Scholem*, xx–xxi.
4. Box 1, folder 8, Quentin Quesnell papers, Smith College Archives, CA-MS-00379, Smith College Special Collections, Northampton, Massachusetts. Note that Flusser's description of the Voss volume lying in a pile on the floor does not square at all with the implication from Stroumsa's report that the book was located on a shelf; it may be worth bearing in mind that Flusser was a strong advocate of the hypothesis that Smith forged the document.
5. Quentin Quesnell papers, box 1, folder 8.
6. Quentin Quesnell papers, box 1, folder 8.
7. The document was found by Agamemnon Tselikas and has been made available by *Biblical Archaeological Review*. See https://www.biblicalarchaeology .org/wp-content/uploads/agamemnon-anexe-1-the-ignatios-edititon.pdf (accessed February 9, 2021).
8. Hedrick and Olympiou, "Secret Mark."
9. Kallistos Dourvas reported this information to Nikolaos Olympiou, professor of Old Testament at the University of Athens, who then relayed it to Charles Hedrick, professor at Southwestern Missouri State University. See Hedrick and Olympiou, "Secret Mark."
10. See Talley, "Le temps liturgique," esp. 52.
11. "In the early 1980s, Quesnell was allowed to look at the two folios of the manuscript. He also obtained permission from the Patriarchate to have

color photographs made of the folios by a firm in Jerusalem." Collins, *Mark*, 491.

12. Hüller and Gullotta, "Quentin Quesnell's Secret Mark Secret."

13. The following quotations come from box 1, folder 8, Quentin Quesnell papers, Smith College Archives, CA-MS-00379, Smith College Special Collections, Northampton, Massachusetts.

14. Dragas's report was shared with us by Stephan Hüller, who interviewed Dragas over the phone.

15. Smith, "Autobiographical Sketch," 3. Box 1, folder 7, in Smith's papers at the Jewish Theological Seminary archives.

16. We know of two additional attempts to locate the manuscript since 1983, one by Nikolaos Olympiou in 1998 and another by Agamemnon Tselikas in 2015.

17. For a brief overview of the manuscript tradition of the Letter to Diognetus, see Ehrman, *Apostolic Fathers*, 2:128.

18. Bovon, "Apocryphal Acts," 23.

19. See the autograph of the ecumenical patriarch Callinicus III in Smith, *Clement of Alexandria*, 454.

20. Email correspondence, September 1, 2020.

21. For an image of this manuscript, see Chatzopoulou, Κατάλογος ἑλληνικῶν χειρογράφων, pl. 2.

22. For an image of this manuscript, see Chatzopoulou, Κατάλογος ἑλληνικῶν χειρογράφων, pl. 25.

23. For an image of this manuscript, see Litsas, Σύντομη εισαγωγή, pl. 62.

24. In his words, a "tendency to use the conservative *Brillenbeta* of older scripts, but a rather modern form of the theta."

25. Email correspondence, September 30, 2019.

26. Email correspondence, September 27, 2019.

27. The special issue is available online, and Dr. Tselikas's findings are available at "Agamemnon Tselikas' Handwriting Analysis Report," Biblical Archaeology Society, October 14, 2009, https://www.biblicalarchaeology .org/daily/biblical-topics/bible-interpretation/agamemnon-tselikas -handwriting-analysis-report/.

28. Email correspondence on September 13, 2020.

29. Metzger, *Textual Commentary*, 114.

30. Several native Greek speakers confirmed these usages for us.

Chapter Eight. The Author

1. Transcript of Smith's SBL presentation, Biographical File (box 291, folder 21), University Archives, Rare Book & Manuscript Library, Columbia University Libraries.

2. Eusebius, *Ecclesiastical History* 4.7.10.

3. Irenaeus, *Against Heresies* 1.25.3.

4. Eusebius, *Ecclesiastical History* 4.7.10.

5. Adapted portions of Clement's largely lost *Outlines* survive in a sixth-century Latin text known as the *Adumbrationes*. While this text does confirm the connection between Peter and Mark, it makes no mention of Mark's subsequent journey to Alexandria. See Smith, *Clement of Alexandria*, 20.

6. Sellew, "Eusebius and the Gospels," 117.

7. Rorem, *John of Scythopolis*, 58. See also Stevens, "Evangelists in Clement's *Hypotyposes*," 359.

8. Eusebius himself does this with his sources. See some examples discussed in chapter 8 ("The Use of Literature in the Conflict") of Bauer, *Orthodoxy and Heresy*.

9. Smith, *Secret Gospel*, 25.

10. The most thorough study of the Longer Ending is Kelhoffer, *Miracle and Mission*.

11. The two most recent studies of the Freer Logion are Frey, "Zu Text und Sinn des Freer-Logion," and Shepherd, "Narrative Analysis."

12. See the discussion of this passage in Metzger, *Textual Commentary*, 101–102. See also the very recent study of the strange manuscript in which this addition to Mark occurs by Larsen, "Real-and-Imagined Biography."

13. The New Revised Standard Version (NRSV), generally regarded as the most scholarly of English translations, still retains the "moved by compassion" reading; the New International Version (NIV) has recently changed to the "became angry" reading, despite the reputation of this translation for being more conservative and evangelical.

14. See, e.g., Koester, *Ancient Christian Gospels*.

15. See the cataloguing of explanations for this passage in Collins, *Mark*, 693–695.

16. See the discussion of these passages in Jennings, *Man Jesus Loved*.

17. Our translations. The NRSV downplays the homoeroticism by translating both phrases as "reclining."

18. See Halperin, *How to Do the History of Homosexuality*, for an influential attempt to understand the history of same-sex attraction as including both social construction and continuities across times and cultures.

19. For an excellent collection of essays on this complex topic, as well as examples of more recent scholarly attempts to think about gender and sexuality in the Greco-Roman world, see Dunning, *New Testament, Gender, and Sexuality*.

20. Readers might rightly wonder what we mean by a love that is erotic but not sexual. We are here making use of the notion of an ascetic *ars erotica* as defined by Virginia Burrus (and others): "Saintly love begins with resistance to the temptations of 'worldly' eroticism—resistance not merely to the transient pleasures of physical intercourse (opening onto a broader realm of tempting sensory delights) but also to perduring familial and po-

litical hierarchies, institutionalized relations of domination and submission that both structure, and are structured by, relations of sex and gender. Yet such resistance to cultural norms, aptly coded in contemporary terms as 'queer,' does not take an anti-erotic turn, proffering the sterile safety of a desexualized 'agape' in exchange for the firm repression of sexual desire. Rather, it gives rise to an exuberant art of eroticism in which the negativity harbored within resistance is eclipsed by the radical affirmation of desire also conveyed in resistance" (*Sex Lives of Saints*, 14). We will see concrete textual examples of this ascetic eroticism in the following chapter.

Chapter Nine. The Monastery

1. Tzaferis, "Early Monks," 45–47.
2. Smith himself makes this point, though he does not dig very deeply into the history of Palestinian monasticism: "Perhaps the strongest reason for thinking this one remained at Mar Saba is (after the fact that it was found there) the absence of any known reference to its content. This suggests that it did not circulate, but lay neglected in some corner of a single library." Smith, *Clement of Alexandria*, 288–289.
3. Stählin, *Clemens Alexandrinus*, 3:223–224. Mentioned by Smith, *Clement of Alexandria*, 6 and 285. Smith also reports that "Ishodad of Merv reportedly refers to a writing, possibly a letter, against heretics who rejected marriage, and such were the Carpocratians; but Stählin, III.lxff, thinks the reference merely an inference based on Eusebius, HE [*Ecclesiastical History*] III.30, where the passages cited come from the Stromateis" (6).
4. Eusebius, *Ecclesiastical History* 6.20. See also Hoek, "'Catechetical' School," 83, and Gamble, *Books and Readers*, 154.
5. Eusebius, *Ecclesiastical History* 6.13.3
6. Eusebius, *Ecclesiastical History* 6.11.6.
7. For references, see Zeddies, "Did Origen Write the *Letter to Theodore?*," 61. See also Broek, "Christian 'School' of Alexandria," and Scholten, "Die alexandrinische Katechetenschule."
8. Smith, *Clement of Alexandria*, 286.
9. For an accessible study of Pamphilus, Eusebius, and the library of Caesarea, see Grafton and Williams, *Christianity and the Transformation of the Book*.
10. See Schott, "Afterword: Receptions."
11. Smith, *Clement of Alexandria*, 286.
12. Smith, *Secret Gospel*, 18–19. See discussion in chapter 3.
13. The third is Cyril of Jerusalem. See Smith, *Clement of Alexandria*, 342, 350.
14. *Coptic Sayings of Macarius*. See also Brooks Hedstrom, *Monastic Landscape*, 92–93.

15. John Moschos, *Spiritual Meadow* 3. See also Ihssen, *John Moschos' Spiritual Meadow*, 1–4. All translations of John Moschos are our own, unless otherwise noted.
16. For an excellent study of St. Antony and his legacy in the church, see chapter 4 in Brakke, *Athanasius and Asceticism*.
17. The definitive study of Pachomius and Pachomian monasticism remains Rousseau, *Pachomius*.
18. For a fuller discussion of this form of monasticism, see Rapp, *Brother-Making*, 93–95.
19. John Cassian, *Conferences* 18.4, trans. *NPNF*. Quoted in Rapp, *Brother-Making*, 94.
20. John Cassian, *Conferences* 18.7.2, trans. *NPNF*. Quoted in Rapp, *Brother-Making*, 94.
21. See, e.g., passages in Jerome and the *Rule of Benedict* discussed in Rapp, *Brother-Making*, 94–95.
22. Cyril of Scythopolis, *Life of Sabas* 113. See also 171.11.
23. See Krueger, "Between Monks"; Rapp, *Brother-Making*; Schroeder, "Queer Eye for the Ascetic Guy?"
24. Cyril of Scythopolis, *Life of Sabas* 50.4; 91.8.
25. Cyril of Scythopolis, *Life of Sabas* 26.2. See also 224.23.
26. Cyril of Scythopolis, *Life of Sabas* 114.12 (*Lives of the Monks*, 123); and Patrich, *Sabas*, 14, 40, 263–264, 274.
27. Cyril of Scythopolis, *Life of Sabas* 91.8.
28. In private emails shared with us by Stephan Hüller, it is apparent that he too began to suspect that the ritual of *adelphopoiēsis* played some role in the Secret Gospel of Mark, though his suspicions largely concern the modern interest (and disinterest) in the manuscript rather than the monastic cultural context from which the *Letter to Theodore* and the Secret Gospel of Mark emerged.
29. Cyril of Scythopolis, *Life of Sabas* 14.
30. Most notably by Boswell, *Same-Sex Unions*.
31. Leontios of Neapolis, *Life of Symeon the Fool*, quoted in Krueger, "Between Monks," 31.
32. Horsesios, quoted in Wilfong, "Friendship and Physical Desire," 314.
33. Krueger, "Between Monks," 33.
34. John Moschos, *Spiritual Meadow*, preface (trans. Wortley).
35. Cyril of Scythopolis, *Life of Sabas* 47, 137–138. See also Patrich, *Sabas*, 267.
36. See appendix 1 in Rapp, *Brother-Making*.
37. Rapp, *Brother-Making*, 48.
38. Box 1, folder 8, Quentin Quesnell papers, Smith College Archives, CA-MS-00379, Smith College Special Collections, Northampton, Massachusetts.
39. Box 1, folder 8, Quentin Quesnell papers, Smith College Archives, CA-MS-00379, Smith College Special Collections, Northampton, Massachusetts.

40. Box 1, folder 8, Quentin Quesnell papers, Smith College Archives, CA-MS-00379, Smith College Special Collections, Northampton, Massachusetts.
41. We are grateful to Stephan Hüller for providing us with this and other valuable information about Dourvas.

Chapter Ten. The End

1. Smith to Goldin, July 29, 1990. Letter shared with us by Allan Pantuck.
2. Smith to Goldin, October 16, 1983. Letter shared with us by Allan Pantuck.
3. Smith to Goldin, November 2, 1983. Letter shared with us by Allan Pantuck.

Bibliography

Bauer, Walter. *Orthodoxy and Heresy in Earliest Christianity*. Philadelphia: Fortress, 1971.

Baumgarten, Albert I. *Elias Bickerman as a Historian of the Jews: A Twentieth-Century Tale*. Tübingen: Mohr Siebeck, 2010.

Bianchi, Ugo, ed. *The Origins of Gnosticism (Colloquium of Messina, 13–18 April 1966)*. Leiden: Brill, 1967.

Boswell, John. *Same-Sex Unions in Pre-modern Europe*. New York: Vintage Books, 1995.

Bovon, François. "Editing the Apocryphal Acts of the Apostles." In *The Apocryphal Acts of the Apostles*, edited by François Bovon, Ann Graham Brock, and Christopher R. Matthews, 1–35. Cambridge, MA: Harvard University Press, 1999.

Bowman, Matthew. *Christian: The Politics of a Word in America*. Cambridge, MA: Harvard University Press, 2018.

Brakke, David. *Athanasius and Asceticism*. Baltimore: Johns Hopkins University Press, 1998.

Broek, Roelof van den. "The Christian 'School' of Alexandria in the Second and Third Centuries." In *Centers of Learning: Learning and Location in Premodern Europe and the Near East*, edited by Jan Willem Drijvers and Alasdair A. MacDonald, 39–47. Leiden: Brill, 1995.

Brooks Hedstrom, Darlene L. *The Monastic Landscape of Late Antique Egypt: An Archaeological Reconstruction*. Cambridge: Cambridge University Press, 2017.

Brown, Peter. "Rise and Function of the Holy Man in Late Antiquity." *Journal of Roman Studies* 61 (1971): 80–101.

Brown, Scott G. "Factualizing the Folklore: Stephen Carlson's Case against Morton Smith." *Harvard Theological Review* 99, no. 3 (2006): 291–327.

———. *Mark's Other Gospel: Rethinking Morton Smith's Controversial Discovery*. Waterloo, ON: Wilfrid Laurier University Press, 2005.

———. "The Question of Motive in the Case against Morton Smith." *Journal of Biblical Literature* 125, no. 2 (2006): 351–383.

———. "Reply to Stephen Carlson." *Expository Times* 117, no. 4 (2006): 144–149.

Burke, Tony, ed. *Ancient Gospel or Modern Forgery? The Secret Gospel of Mark in Debate: Proceedings from the 2011 York University Christian Apocrypha Symposium.* Eugene, OR: Cascade Books, 2013.

Burrus, Virginia. *The Sex Lives of Saints: An Erotics of Ancient Hagiography.* Philadelphia: University of Pennsylvania Press, 2004.

Carlson, Stephen C. *The Gospel Hoax: Morton Smith's Invention of Secret Mark.* Waco, TX: Baylor University Press, 2005.

Chatzopoulou, Benetia. Κατάλογος ἑλληνικῶν χειρογράφων τοῦ Μουσείου Μπενάκη (16ος–17ος αιώνας). Athens: Benaki Museum, 2017.

Chilton, Bruce. Review of *The Gospel Hoax: Morton Smith's Invention of Secret Mark,* by Stephen Carlson. *Review of Rabbinic Judaism* 10, no. 1 (2007): 122–128.

Clark, Elizabeth A., and J. Patout Burns. "Editors' Note." *Journal of Early Christian Studies* 11, no. 2 (2003): 131.

Collins, Adela Yarbro. *Mark: A Commentary.* Hermeneia. Minneapolis: Fortress, 2007.

Criddle, Andrew H. "On the Mar Saba Letter Attributed to Clement of Alexandria." *Journal of Early Christian Studies* 3, no. 2 (1995): 215–220.

Cyril of Scythopolis. *Lives of the Monks of Palestine.* Translated by R. M. Price, with an introduction and notes by John Binns. Kalamazoo, MI: Cistercian Publications, 1991.

Dunning, Ben, ed. *The Oxford Handbook of New Testament, Gender, and Sexuality.* New York: Oxford University Press, 2019.

Ehrman, Bart D. *The Apostolic Fathers.* Vol. 2. Cambridge, MA: Harvard University Press, 2003.

———. *Jesus, Interrupted: Revealing the Hidden Contradictions in the Bible (and Why We Don't Know about Them).* New York: HarperCollins, 2009.

———. *Lost Christianities: The Battles for Scripture and the Faiths We Never Knew.* New York: Oxford University Press, 2003.

———. *Misquoting Jesus: The Story behind Who Changed the Bible and Why.* New York: HarperCollins, 2005.

———. *The Orthodox Corruption of Scripture: The Effect of Early Christological Controversies on the Text of the New Testament.* New York: Oxford University Press, 1993.

———. "Response to Charles Hedrick's Stalemate." *Journal of Early Christian Studies* 11, no. 2 (2003): 155–163.

Evans, Craig A. "Morton Smith and the *Secret Gospel of Mark*: Exploring the Grounds for Doubt." In Burke, *Ancient Gospel or Modern Forgery?,* 75–100.

Foster, Stephen Wayne. "Wilde, Oscar F.O.W. (1856–1900)." In *Encyclopedia of Homosexuality*, edited by Wayne R. Dynes et al., 2:1389–1391. New York: Garland, 1990.

Fredriksen, Paula. *Paul: The Pagans' Apostle*. New Haven: Yale University Press, 2017.

———. *When Christians Were Jews: The First Generation*. New Haven: Yale University Press, 2018.

Frey, Jörg. "Zu Text und Sinn des Freer-Logion." *Zeitschrift für die Neutestamentliche Wissenschaft und Kunde der Älteren Kirche* 93 (2002): 13–34.

Gamble, Harry. *Books and Readers in the Early Church: A History of Early Christian Texts*. New Haven: Yale University Press, 1995.

Goodspeed, Edgar Johnson. *Strange New Gospels*. Chicago: University of Chicago Press, 1931. Reprinted as *Famous Biblical Hoaxes*. Grand Rapids, MI: Baker, 1956.

Grafton, Anthony, and Megan Williams. *Christianity and the Transformation of the Book: Origen, Eusebius, and the Library of Caesarea*. Cambridge, MA: Harvard University Press, 2006.

Grenfell, B. P., and A. S. Hunt. *The Oxyrhynchus Papyri*. Vol. 2. London: Egypt Exploration Fund, 1898.

Halperin, David M. *How to Do the History of Homosexuality*. Chicago: University of Chicago Press, 2002.

Hamilton, Charles. *The Hitler Diaries*. Lexington: University Press of Kentucky, 1991.

Hedrick, Charles W. "The Secret Gospel of Mark: Stalemate in the Academy." *Journal of Early Christian Studies* 11, no. 2 (2003): 133–145.

Hedrick, Charles W., and Nikolaos Olympiou. "Secret Mark: New Photographs, New Witnesses." *The Fourth R* 13, no. 5 (September/October 2000): 3–16.

Hoek, Annewies van den. "The 'Catechetical' School of Early Christian Alexandria and Its Philonic Heritage." *Harvard Theological Review* 90, no. 1 (1997): 59–87.

Hüller, Stephen, and Daniel Gullotta. "Quentin Quesnell's *Secret Mark* Secret: A Report on Quentin Quesnell's 1983 Trip to Jerusalem and His Inspection of the Mar Saba Document." *Vigiliae Christianae* 71, no. 4 (2017): 353–378.

Hurtado, Larry W. Foreword to *The Gospel Hoax: Morton Smith's Invention of Secret Mark*, by Stephen C. Carlson, ix–xiii. Waco, TX: Baylor University Press, 2005

Ihssen, Brenda Llewellyn. *John Moschos' Spiritual Meadow: Authority and Autonomy at the End of the Antique World*. Farnham, UK: Ashgate, 2014.

Jeffery, Peter. *The Secret Gospel of Mark Unveiled: Imagined Rituals of Sex, Death, and Madness in a Biblical Forgery*. New Haven: Yale University Press, 2007.

Jenkins, Philip. *Hidden Gospels: How the Search for Jesus Lost Its Way*. New York: Oxford University Press, 2001.

Jennings, Theodore W., Jr. *The Man Jesus Loved: Homoerotic Narratives from the New Testament*. Cleveland: Pilgrim Press, 2003.

Kelhoffer, James. *Miracle and Mission: The Authentication of Missionaries and Their Message in the Longer Ending of Mark*. Tübingen: Mohr Siebeck, 2000.

King, Karen. *What Is Gnosticism?* Cambridge, MA: Harvard University Press, 2003.

Koester, Helmut. *Ancient Christian Gospels: Their History and Development*. London: SCM; Philadelphia: Trinity Press International, 1990.

Krueger, Derek. "Between Monks: Tales of Monastic Companionship in Early Byzantium." *Journal of the History of Sexuality* 20, no. 1 (January 2011): 28–61.

Kruger, Michael. Review of *The Gospel Hoax: Morton Smith's Invention of Secret Mark*, by Stephen C. Carlson. *Journal of the Evangelical Theological Society* 49, no. 2 (2006): 422–424.

Larsen, Matthew. "The Real-and-Imagined Biography of a Gospel Manuscript." *Early Christianity* 12, no. 1 (2021): 103–131.

Litsas, Euthymios K. Σύντομη εισαγωγή στην ελληνική παλαιογραφία και κωδικολογία. Τεύχος 2, Πίνακες με επιλαγμένα δείγματα γραφών και σχόλια. Thessaloniki: University Studio Press, 2001.

Metzger, Bruce. *Reminiscences of an Octogenarian*. Grand Rapids, MI: Baker, 1995.

———. *A Textual Commentary on the Greek New Testament*. 2nd ed. Stuttgart: German Bible Society, 1994.

Moschos, John. *The Spiritual Meadow*. Introduction, translation, and notes by John Wortley. Kalamazoo, MI: Cistercian Publications, 1982.

Murgia, Charles E. "Secret Mark: Real or Fake?" In *Longer Mark: Forgery, Interpolation, or Old Tradition? Protocol of the Eighteenth Colloquy: 7 December 1975*, edited by Wilhelm H. Wuellner, 35–40. Berkeley: Center for Hermeneutical Studies, 1976.

Musurillo, Herbert. "Morton Smith's Secret Gospel." *Thought* 48, no. 3 (1973): 327–331.

Neusner, Jacob. "Who Needs 'The Historical Jesus'? An Essay-Review." *Bulletin for Biblical Research* 4 (1994): 113–126.

Osborn, Eric F. "Clement of Alexandria: A Review of Research, 1958–1982." *Second Century* 3, no. 4 (1983): 219–244.

Paananen, Timo S. "From Stalemate to Deadlock: Clement's Letter to Theodore in Recent Scholarship." *Currents in Biblical Research* 11, no. 1 (2012): 87–125.

———. "A Study in Authenticity: Admissible Concealed Indicators of Authority and Other Features of Forgeries—A Case Study on Clement of Alexandria, Letter to Theodore, and the Longer Gospel of Mark." PhD diss., University of Helsinki, 2019.

Pantuck, Allan J. "A Question of Ability: What Did He Know and When Did He Know It? Further Excavations from the Morton Smith Archives." In Burke, *Ancient Gospel or Modern Forgery?*, 184–211.

Pantuck, Allan J., and Scott G. Brown. "Morton Smith as M. Madiotes: Stephen Carlson's Attribution of Secret Mark to a Bald Swindler." *Journal for the Study of the Historical Jesus* 6, no. 1 (2008): 106–125.

Papadopoulos-Kerameus, Athanasios. Ιεροσολυμιτικη Βιβλιοθηκη: ητοι, Καταλογος των εν ταις Βιβλιοθηκαις του Αγιωτατου Αποστολοκου τε και Καθολικου Ορθοδοξου Θρονου των Ιεροσολυμων και πασης Παλαιστινης αποκειμενων Ελληνικων κωδικων, συνταχθεισα μεν και φωτοτυπικοις κοσμηθεισα πιναξιν. 1894. Reprint, Brussels: Culture et civilization, 1963.

Patrich, Joseph. *Sabas, Leader of Palestinian Monasticism: A Comparative Study in Eastern Monasticism, Fourth to Seventh Centuries.* Washington, DC: Dumbarton Oaks, 1995.

Piovanelli, Pierluigi. "Halfway between Sabbatai Tzevi and Aleister Crowley: Morton Smith's 'Own Concept of What Jesus "Must" Have Been' and, Once Again, the Questions of Evidence and Motive." In Burke, *Ancient Gospel or Modern Forgery?*, 157–183.

Potter, Roland. "Spirituality of the Judaean Desert—II: Mar Saba and St John Damascene." *Life of the Spirit (1946–1964)* 13, no. 154 (April 1959): 435–442.

Quesnell, Quentin. "The Mar Saba Clementine: A Question of Evidence." *Catholic Biblical Quarterly* 37, no. 1 (1975): 48–67.

———. "A Reply to Morton Smith." *Catholic Biblical Quarterly* 38, no. 2 (1976): 200–203.

Rapp, Claudia. *Brother-Making in Late Antiquity and Byzantium: Monks, Laymen, and Christian Ritual.* New York: Oxford University Press, 2016.

Rorem, Paul. *John of Scythopolis and the Dionysian Corpus.* Oxford: Clarendon, 1998.

Rousseau, Philip. *Pachomius: The Making of a Community in Fourth-Century Egypt.* Berkeley: University of California Press, 1999.

Sabar, Ariel. *Veritas: A Harvard Professor, a Con Man, and the Gospel of Jesus's Wife.* New York: Doubleday, 2020.

Schoenbaum, Samuel. *Internal Evidence and Elizabethan Dramatic Authorship: An Essay in Literary History and Method.* Evanston, IL: Northwestern University Press, 1966.

Scholten, Clemens. "Die alexandrinische Katechetenschule." *Jahrbuch für Antike und Christentum* 38 (1995): 16–37.

Schott, Jeremy. "Afterword: Receptions." In *Eusebius of Caesarea: Tradition and Innovations*, edited by Aaron Johnson and Jeremy Schott. Washington, DC: Center for Hellenic Studies, 2013. https://archive.chs.harvard.edu/CHS/article/display/5866.afterword-receptions-jeremy-m-schott.

Schroeder, Caroline. "Queer Eye for the Ascetic Guy? Homoeroticism, Children, and the Making of Monks in Late Antique Egypt." *Journal of the American Academy of Religion* 77, no. 2 (2009): 333–347.

Sellew, Philip. "Eusebius and the Gospels." In *Eusebius, Christianity, and Ju-daism*, edited by Harold W. Attridge and Gohei Hata, 110–138. Leiden: Brill, 1992.

Shepherd, Thomas R. "Narrative Analysis as a Text Critical Tool: Mark 16 in Codex W as a Test Case." *Journal for the Study of the New Testament* 32, no. 1 (2009): 77–98.

Smith, Geoffrey S. *Guilt by Association: Heresy Catalogues in Early Christianity*. New York: Oxford University Press, 2015.

———. *Valentinian Christianity: Texts and Translations*. Oakland: University of California Press, 2020.

Smith, Morton. *The Ancient Greeks*. Ithaca, NY: Cornell University Press, 1960.

———. "The Aretology Used by Mark." In *The Aretology Used by Mark: Proto-col of the Sixth Colloquy of the Center for Hermeneutical Studies in Hellenistic and Modern Culture, 12 April 1973*, edited by Wilhelm H. Wuellner, 1–25. Berkeley: Center for Hermeneutical Studies, 1975.

———. "On the Authenticity of the Mar Saba Letter of Clement." *Catholic Biblical Quarterly* 38, no. 2 (1976): 196–199.

———. *Clement of Alexandria and a Secret Gospel of Mark*. Cambridge, MA: Harvard University Press, 1973.

———. "Clement of Alexandria and Secret Mark: The Score at the End of the First Decade." *Harvard Theological Review* 75, no. 4 (1982): 449–461.

———. "Ἑλληνικὰ χειρόγραφα ἐν τῇ Μονῇ τοῦ ἁγίου Σάββα." Translated by Archimandrite Constantine Michaelides. NEA ΣΙΟΝ 52 (1960): 110–125, 245–256.

———. "The History of the Term Gnostikos." In *Sethian Gnosticism*, edited by Bentley Layton, 796–807. Vol. 2 of *The Rediscovery of Gnosticism: Proceed-ings of the Conference on Gnosticism at Yale, New Haven, Connecticut, March 28–31, 1978*. Leiden: Brill, 1981.

———. *Jesus the Magician*. San Francisco: Harper & Row, 1978.

———. "Monasteries and Their Manuscripts." *Archaeology* 13, no. 3 (1960): 172–177.

———. *Palestinian Parties and Politics That Shaped the Old Testament*. New York: Columbia University Press, 1971.

———. "Psychiatric Practice and Christian Dogma." *Journal of Pastoral Care* 3 (1949): 12–20.

———. Review of *Aufstieg und Niedergang der römischen Welt*, by Wolfgang Haase. *Journal of the American Oriental Society* 102, no. 3 (1982): 544–546.

———. Review of *Beiträge zur Siedlungs-und Territorialgeschichte des nördlichen Ostjordanlandes*, by Siegfried Mittmann. *Journal of Biblical Literature* 91, no. 4 (1972): 548–550.

———. Review of *The Origins of Gnosticism*, by Ugo Bianchi. *Journal of Biblical Literature* 89, no. 1 (1970): 82–84.

———. *The Secret Gospel: The Discovery and Interpretation of the Secret Gospel according to Mark*. New York: Harper & Row, 1973. Reprint, Clearlake, CA: Dawn Horse, 1982.

Stählin, Otto. *Clemens Alexandrinus*. 4 vols. Leipzig: Hinrichs, 1905–1936.

Stevens, Luke J. "The Evangelists in Clement's *Hypotyposes*." *Journal of Early Christian Studies* 26, no. 3 (2018): 353–379.

Stroumsa, Guy G. "Comments on Charles Hedrick's Article: A Testimony." *Journal of Early Christian Studies* 11, no. 2 (2003): 147–153.

———, ed. *Morton Smith and Gershom Scholem, Correspondence 1945–1982*. Jerusalem Studies in Religion and Culture 9. Leiden: Brill, 2008.

Talley, Thomas. "Le temps liturgique dans l'Église ancienne. État de la recherché." *La Maison-Dieu* 147 (1981): 29–60.

Teras, Melissa M. "Artefacts and Errors: Acknowledging Issues of Representation in the Digital Imaging of Ancient Texts." In *Kodikologie und Paläographie im digitalen Zeitalter 2 / Codicology and Palaeography in the Digital Age 2*, edited by Franz Fischer, Christiane Fritze, and Georg Vogeler, 43–61. Norderstedt: Books on Demand, 2009.

Tzaferis, Vassilios. "Early Monks and Monasteries in the Holyland." Δελτίον της Χριστιανικής Αρχαιολογικής Εταιρείας 15 (1991): 43–66.

Viklund, Roger, and Timo S. Paananen. "Distortion of the Scribal Hand in the Images of Clement's Letter to Theodore." *Vigiliae Christianae* 67, no. 3 (2013): 235–247.

Watson, Francis. "Beyond Suspicion: On the Authorship of the Mar Saba Letter and the Secret Gospel of Mark." *Journal of Theological Studies* 61, no. 1 (2010): 128–170.

Wilfong, Terry. "Friendship and Physical Desire: The Discourse of Female Homoeroticism in Fifth Century C.E. Egypt." In *Among Women: From the Homosocial to the Homoerotic in the Ancient World*, edited by Nancy Sorkin Rabinowitz and Lisa Auanger, 304–330. Austin: University of Texas Press, 2002.

Williams, Michael. *Rethinking "Gnosticism": An Argument for Dismantling a Dubious Category*. Princeton: Princeton University Press, 1999.

Wuellner, Wilhelm H. "Minutes of the Colloquy of 7 December 1975." In *Longer Mark: Forgery, Interpolation, or Old Tradition? Protocol of the Eighteenth Colloquy: 7 December 1975*, edited by Wilhelm H. Wuellner, 55–71. Berkeley: Center for Hermeneutical Studies, 1976.

Zeddies, Michael T. "Did Origen Write the *Letter to Theodore*?" *Journal of Early Christian Studies* 25, no. 1 (2017): 55–87.

Index

Note: Page numbers in italics refer to figures.